-0. OCT. 1982

0251025 KIERNAN T.

B/POL

5 JUL 1981

(The Roman
Polanski story)
Repulsion. The
life & times of
Roman Polanski

D1461405

REPULSION

REPULSION

The Life and Times of Roman Polanski

Thomas Kiernan

NEW ENGLISH LIBRARY

TIMES MIRROR

Typeset by Fleet Graphics, Middlesex.

Printed and bound in Great Britain by Biddles Ltd., Guildford and King's Lynn

ISBN 450 04837 3

INTRODUCTION

'ROMAN POLANSKI?'

It was eight o'clock in the evening of Friday, 11 March 1977. The notorious Polish director was crossing the lobby of the luxurious Beverly Wilshire Hotel in Beverly Hills when he was stopped by two plainclothes detectives.

'Yes?' Polanski was, as usual, in a hurry. Another glorious California weekend was about to start. There were amusing people to see, beautiful girls to meet and seduce with his legendary sexual charm. Pleasures of every description awaited him among the fast-living members of the international film colony.

'You are under arrest!' Sergeant Peter Vanatter of the Los Angeles Police Department thrust an official warrant at him.

Polanski frowned in annoyance. Since the brutal Manson murders of his wife, Sharon Tate, and friends eight years before, he was no stranger to the Los Angeles Police. What was this, some kind of police joke? A set-up for *Candid Camera?* What had he done, spat on the sidewalk?

Ignoring his protests and the stares of those watching, the detectives shoved their diminutive quarry into a corner and frisked him like a common criminal.

It was no joke.

Could it be what was in his pocket, Polanski suddenly thought? A flip of his wrist and the white tablet fell to the floor, a move instantly noted by his captors. Police lab analysis later proved the tablet to be a large dose of methaquaalone or Quaalude, the powerful illegal tranquilizer that is banned in the United States as a dangerous drug.

'Let's go!'

Upstairs in his suite, the detectives confiscated several vials of pills, among them more Quaaludes, and a pile of color transparencies of several extremely young girls in various stages of nudity.

'What is this? I demand to know what's going on! You can't do this.'

They not only could, they did. 'Put out your wrists!'

In another few moments, one of the world's most famous and controversial film-makers was in handcuffs and being marched, still protesting loudly, through the posh hotel lobby to a waiting car and the ride to a West Los Angeles Police Station.

At the station, the reason for the rough treatment became clear. He was unceremoniously booked on the following charges:

(1) Furnishing Quaaludes to a minor
(2) Child molesting
(3) Unlawful sexual intercourse
(4) Rape by use of drugs
(5) Oral copulation
(6) Sodomy

All were classified as felonies under various statutes of the California Penal Code.

Before Polanski could fully absorb the enormity of what was happening, he was hustled into a side room, fingerprinted and forced to pose for mug shots. At last, he was allowed to make a phone call. The problem was it was Friday night at the height of the social season. His lawyer was nowhere to be found. Finally, frantic, he reached a friend who promised to send a lawyer as soon as possible.

6

Next he was handed over to the custody of jailers. They clearly regarded him as scum as they shoved him into a holding cell. The wait was interminable. But for the first time, Polanski had a chance to think. They had told him he was in deep trouble. Now, he began to understand why.

The girl!

He still could not believe it.

At last the lawyer, a stranger to Polanski, arrived. He and the prisoner were allowed to confer briefly. Shortly after midnight, exhausted and confused, Roman Polanski stood ashen-faced before a Municipal Court judge for a preliminary hearing on charges that he had drugged and then raped a thirteen-year-old girl from a nearby San Fernando Valley suburb.

Thus began yet another chaotic episode in the strange and tumultuous life of Roman Polanski. It was a life of baffling extremes and harrowing twists of fate and fame that caused some people to hail him as a genius, others to recoil from him as a creature of evil. He'd been called everything from the Devil Incarnate to a pathetic victim of Hitler's holocaust and Charles Manson's executioners.

The evil and violence of such Polanski films as *Rosemary's Baby, Macbeth* and *Chinatown* ran parallel to the terrors of his own life, which included being a fugitive Jewish child on the run in Nazi-occupied Poland and the brutal cult murders of his wife and unborn child by the Manson Family. His tastes for sexual deviance had long been a matter of speculation, much of it joking, until this March night in 1977 when his victim was, unforgivably in the eyes of many, a thirteen-year-old child.

I had first met Roman Polanski ten years before, in 1967, at a chic private party in London's Eaton Square. He was with the incredibly beautiful Sharon Tate. A few weeks later, I was among the guests who attended their wedding. Gradually, through the years, I have grown to know various members of the Polanski circle – producers, agents, performers and writers, as well as members of his tight-knit group of Polish expatriates, including the brilliant novelist, Jerzy Kosinski.

7

This biography is based in large part on what I have learned from them. It is meant neither as a hatchet job nor an apologia for Roman Polanski. Rather, I have tried to make it an unsparing exploration of the man, his childhood and the brutal facts of life in Nazi Poland, his cunning as a manipulator of people and situations, his bizarre sexual and drug experiments, his equally bizarre cinema experiments, his unscrupulous business dealings and betrayals of trust, his role in the Manson murders – and finally, the child rape that repelled even those adoring friends who have always found excuses for his behavior.

My early impressions of him were of a charming *poseur* with a self-centered contempt for the world, a man who Jerzy Kosinski later described as an emotional fascist. As time went on, I grew increasingly fascinated. I had seen *Knife In The Water, Repulsion* and *Cul de Sac* and felt the power and frenzy of his unique cinematic vision. I observed his development as a film-maker and jet-setter. Along with many, I wondered how any man could endure the gruesome murder of his wife in circumstances of such horror – a death he narrowly escaped sharing only because of a last-minute switch in plans.

In 1973, four years after the murder, I approached Polanski about doing a book about his life. He declined. 'At the moment,' he told me, 'I feel very strongly against it. This may change, of course, with time. If,' he added ominously, 'I live long enough.'

In 1975, I raised the question again when I encountered him at a trendy London night club. Once more he declined. Then came his arrest in Los Angeles in 1977 and the subsequent legal drama that eventually led to his jumping bail, fleeing the United States and becoming a fugitive from American justice.

During this time, Polanski bitterly complained to friends that his side of the story was being suppressed by the courts and the press. Once more, I offered him an opportunity to tell his story through a book. Once more, he declined – this time with the explanation that he intended to write the book himself and had received a publishing contract.

Fair enough, I thought, and dropped the subject. But then

word came that the book Polanski was going to write had been canceled by the publisher because of his legal status as a fugitive. I thereupon decided to proceed with this book – known in the trade as an 'unauthorized biography' – without further attempts to enlist Polanski's cooperation.

In putting together my research for this project, I have spoken with many close friends and acquaintances of Polanski, some of whom, as I have indicated, are friends and acquaintances of mine. From them, I have received a wealth of knowledgeable and intimate insights into the man. However, few of these sources desired to be identified by name. I have honored their wishes.

Even the closest friends of Polanski with whom I talked conceded that however intimate their knowledge about him, it was only about part of him since he allowed them to know him only in part. (As one said, 'Remember, Roman started out as an actor. He has never stopped being an actor.') Like me, they wonder today how and why a man possessing so much in the way of opportunity, talent, money and recognition has managed to visit so much in the way of personal tragedy and professional grief upon himself and others.

It is my hope that this book will answer that question.

Thomas Kiernan
New York
November, 1979

PROLOGUE

THE THIRTEEN-year-old's head was spinning and her breath snagged on what she imagined to be a fish hook in her throat. Lying down on the bed had not helped. The combined effect of the champagne and methaquaalone had overcome her will to fight the nausea and dizziness that washed over her. The idea that she might die flashed across her mind just before she lost consciousness. The last terrified image she had was that of Jack Nicholson, the movie star, gazing at her with stern disapproval from a blown-up photo she had seen earlier in one of the rooms of his house.

It was 10 March 1977. Just out of her seventh grade classroom, she had been brought to the house high on Mulholland Drive with the promise that she would meet movie star Jack Nicholson. Indeed, the house, she was told, was where Nicholson lived. She had agreed to come in the expectation of being able to boast to her friends back in the Valley about what Jack Nicholson was really like.

The man who had taken her to the house was Roman Polanski. Thirteen-year-old girls tended to be entranced by movie stars, not movie directors. Besides, the forty-four-year-old Polanski seemed to this thirteen-year-old – well, a bit 'icky'. He was small and ferret-faced, a foreigner with an accent and style of talking that were alien to the ears of a California girl barely into her teens. As diligently as he had tried to charm her, his efforts had been, to her, comical. And yet earlier in the afternoon, while posing for his still camera, she had felt confused and even threatened by his remarks and questions. Was she still a virgin? he had wanted to know. Had she ever – what was the word? – masturbated? Would she like him to show her what masturbation was? Questions like that. She had not known what to make of them, nor how to answer. She had made a few self-conscious attempts to toss off worldly replies, but had been betrayed by her blushes. It was only when he had asked her if she would like to go to Jack Nicholson's house and have some photos taken with the movie star that she gained some enthusiasm for Polanski.

Aside from his often gory films, Roman Polanski's chief notoriety centered on the fact that he had been married to the actress Sharon Tate when, eight years before, she and several of their friends had been brutally murdered in Los Angeles by members of the Manson gang. In 1969, the girl who was now thirteen was five. The Manson-Tate-Polanski affair, despite several years of unremitting media exposure, had floated beyond the reach of her juvenile awareness. Growing up in a series of Los Angeles suburbs during the 1970s, her pre-puberty passions had focused on several movie and rock-music celebrities of the day, among them Jack Nicholson. Nicholson, who rose to stardom in the early seventies, was American to the core with his flat, nasal New Jersey accent and his smartass garage mechanic's face. His movie magnetism derived from his universal identifiability – he was the ordinary guy who was not afraid to fight or scheme against the establishment to get his piece of the pie. And he did it with a smoldering unpredictability that kept everyone on their toes. He was at once sensitive and violent, cool and explosive, capable of being heatedly involved and wryly disengaged in whatever screen world he found himself. Projecting an underlying vulnerability, he was every guy's best friend and every girl's rough lover and every mother's troublesome but redeemable son. People responded to Nicholson, both to his screen persona and to the real-life myth constructed by his press agents in the fan magazines and gossip columns. And no one responded with more enthusiasm than the pretty thirteen-year-old blond girl who lay passed out, nude, on the bed in his house.

She was nude because after arriving at the house with Polanski and learning from a neighbor that Nicholson was not at home, she had agreed to stay and pose for more pictures before the late afternoon's light gave way. The photographs were ostensibly for a commission Polanski had been given by the French magazine *Vogue Homme* to produce a pictorial feature on the beautiful young girls of America. Polanski had learned of the girl the year before when he had picked up her mother, a divorced, hard-living, would-be actress, at a bar in Hollywood. The girl, although mentally her twelve years, was physically mature for her age. After a brief affair with her mother, Polanski returned to his home in London. When he came back to Hollywood a year later with his *Vogue Homme* commission, he looked up the mother and persuaded her to let him photograph her thirteen-year-old daughter for the feature. He also persuaded her to leave the girl alone with him, using the photographer's traditional rationale, that the girl was likely to be self-conscious with her mother around during the photo sessions. Without the older woman there, Polanski explained, spontaneity would be easier to achieve.

At first the picture-taking had been innocent enough, except for Polanski's sexual insinuations. The initial session had been done a few weeks earlier on the slopes behind the girl's home in Woodland Hills – just Polanski and the girl posing in various outfits selected by her mother. Today's was the second session. Polanski had brought the girl to the rented house of a friend, for indoor photos before proceeding to the Nicholson house. Throughout the afternoon his sexual comments had become more blatant and personal.

Although he wasn't there when they arrived at his hilltop aerie with its panoramic views of Los Angeles and the San Fernando Valley, Jack Nicholson's presence pervaded the house. The girl was immediately impressed by the familiar ease with which Polanski moved through the rooms. The afternoon light was fading and Polanski suggested they do some final wrap-up shots while waiting for Nicholson to arrive. What he neglected to tell her was that Nicholson was on a skiing vacation in Colorado and would not be arriving that day.

Before getting out his cameras, Polanski broke open a bottle of champagne from Nicholson's refrigerator and offered a glass to the girl to celebrate the wrap-up of their photographic sessions. He rhapsodized on the delights of the Dom Perignon and pressed another glass on the girl. She hesitated, telling him that the last time she had drunk champagne, it had made her violently ill. She was asthmatic, she said, and the bubbly had brought on an asthma attack.

It must have been bad champagne, Polanski countered, probably one of those God-awful American varieties. 'Come on, darling, have another. This is the pure stuff, straight from France. It could never hurt you.'

She took another glass to please him. But as she sipped it, she began to feel a familiar discomfort creep up on her. 'God,' she said, 'I'd die of shame if I got sick here.' She felt her lungs beginning to constrict. 'When will Jack Nicholson be here?'

Polanski skipped over her question, but was all sympathy. He remarked that there was a combination hot-tub and Jacuzzi at the other end of the house. 'Come,' he said, slipping his hand into hers. 'You jump in the hot tub. It will make you feel better. And I can take some shots of you.'

'But my bathing suit,' said the girl. 'I need my bathing suit.'

'Nobody around here goes into a hot tub with a bathing suit,' said Polanski.

The girl's head was beginning to swim. 'How do they go in?'

'No clothes,' said Polanski, urging her toward the hot tub.

The girl resisted. 'No, I have to wear my bikini.'

'You don't have to be modest in front of me,' Polanski said.

'Still,' replied the girl, 'my mother . . . '

Polanski sighed. 'So where is it?'

'It's in my bag, in your car.'

Polanski went out to his car and returned a few moments

later with the girl's bag. He found her lying on the sofa.

'I really don't feel good,' she said. 'I knew I shouldn't't've had that champagne.'

'Okay, love, no more champagne. Get your bikini on, quickly, and get into the tub. I promise the Jacuzzi makes you better in no time.'

He led her to the other end of the house. She changed in a guest bathroom, and when she emerged a minute or so later in a brief white bikini, Polanski's eyes glinted in appreciation. 'You are beautiful,' he said.

And she was, after a fashion. Dusky blond hair tumbled to her bare shoulders, setting off a face that was distinguished by high cheekbones and a full, shapely mouth. Only her nose, thick and slightly flattened, marred the otherwise pleasant balance of her features. Her body had already begun to take on the hint of a grown woman's. She was tall, taller than Polanski, and lean, with sinuous legs and breasts that seemed well on their way to maturity.

The girl was not feeling beautiful though. She complained again about her dizziness and shortness of breath. Polanski approached her with a vial of pills. He told her he had found them in Nicholson's bathroom while she had been changing. Jack also suffered from asthma, he said, and these were the pills he took for it. He gave her a tablet and told her to take it, assuring her it would counter the effects of the champagne.

The girl dutifully swallowed the tablet. Then she slipped into the hot tub. Polanski also neglected to tell her that the tablet was not an anti-asthma pill from Jack Nicholson's medicine cabinet but a high-potency Quaalude from his own pocket.

Polanski began to snap pictures as the girl posed uncertainly at the edge of the tub, her complexion ashen. 'Take off your top,' he casually instructed after a few shots.

Increasingly giddy and disoriented, the girl started to unsnap her bikini top. Then, suddenly, she stopped, her eyes blinking in confusion.

'Go ahead,' said Polanski.

'No,' she said, her voice whiny.

'Why?'

14

'My mother.' The girl was having trouble breathing as she spoke. 'My mother said . . . no . . . '

'It's alright,' Polanski whispered. 'I talked to her. She said it is okay.'

'When?'

'You don't believe me?'

The girl shrugged weakly. 'Maybe I better call her.'

Polanski offered to make the call and hurried into another room. When he got the girl's mother on the phone, he explained that it would help his photo layout to have a few topless shots of the girl. He conceded that in America there were still taboos about being photographed topless. But in Europe, it was routine. These pictures would not be seen in America. 'So,' he said to the mother, 'is it alright with you if I just take a few?'

The woman asked to speak to her daughter. 'Are you alright,' she inquired when the girl staggered in to take the phone from Polanski.

The pill Polanski had given the girl didn't seem to be working. Her speech was thick and faltering, she knew, but she was determined to hide it. Her mother would kill her if she knew she had been drinking champagne. 'I'm fine,' she said, struggling to articulate.

'You don't sound fine,' replied her mother in a rising voice.

'I just had a little too much sun before.'

'What are you wearing?'

'My bathing suit.'

'Do you want me to come and get you?'

'No,' replied the girl. 'Jack Nicholson's going to be here soon. Really, mother, I'm fine.'

'Okay,' said her mother, 'put Roman back on.'

The girl wandered back to the hot tub while Polanski spoke for another minute or so with her mother. The woman finally agreed to a few topless shots – reluctantly, she would later claim. She extracted a promise from Polanski, though, that he would show her the prints and let her make the final decision on whether he could use any after she saw them.

Polanski hung up and headed back to the tub. The girl was in the water again, her eyes glazed. The Quaalude was taking effect.

'It's alright, darling. Your mother said. You can take your top off.' *

---

* The re-creation of this and other real-life scenes in this book are based on grand jury testimony, police reports and interviews with various people who have personal knowledge of the events in the criminal case that was eventually brought against Roman Polanski.

CHAPTER 1

It COULD be said that Roman Polanski was preordained for grief and trouble from the time he was born. By all rights his life should have ended before it had a chance to really begin. Only a benevolent uncle and a fortunate quirk of fate stood between him and early annihilation. Even today it is often a wonder to him that he survived when so many of his childhood Jewish contemporaries vanished in the gas chambers and ovens of Nazi Europe.

Polanski had one good break at the beginning, however. He was born – on 18 August 1933 – in Paris, thus making him eligible for French citizenship when he needed it. Although it did not help him as a youth, it was this circumstance that would protect him from the wrath of American justice forty-five years later.

Polanski's father, a Polish Jew with artistic pretensions, had traveled from his home in Cracow a few years before Roman's birth to test the libertine waters of Paris. By all accounts, Riszard Polanski was a competent painter but lacked the language and cunning to impress the sophisticated *salonistes* of the French capital. While unsuccessfully struggling to establish

17

himself in the art world, he met a woman slightly older than himself. Her name was Bula Katz, and she was also a Jew but of Russian birth. In 1932 Riszard Polanski and Bula Katz were married. With her young daughter from a previous marriage, the two moved into a tiny flat in the Bastille section of Paris.

At the time, Paris was filled with thousands of wealthy White Russian exiles from the Bolshevik Revolution, as well as numerous expatriate members of Polish royalty, bogus and otherwise. Riszard and Bula Polanski found no acceptance in the monied Polish and Russian communities. Although not outwardly religious, they were still Jews and therefore unworthy of the attention of their innately anti-Semitic countrymen. Their attempts to develop a market for Riszard's art work in these communities failed. By the time Roman Raimund Polanski was born in the summer of 1933, his father was reduced to working in a small recording factory.

Shortly thereafter, Adolf Hitler began to make threatening pronouncements about the fate of Europe. Hitler and his nascent regime were beginning to appeal to many on the Continent. Particularly appealing were the German leader's diatribes against the Jews of the world, which reinvigorated the deepseated tradition of anti-Semitism in most of Europe's countries, including France.

In 1936, Riszard Polanski lost his factory job because of his French employer's newly discovered distaste for Jews. He spent the new year working catch-as-catch-can as a free-lance artisan and carpenter. By mid-1937, however, unable to find even part-time work in Paris, Riszard moved his family back to Cracow. This despite the fact that by then Hitler was talking about forcibly annexing Poland and, among other things, ridding it of its large Jewish population.

Cracow was a medieval city of south-central Poland, set on the banks of the Vistula River and in the shadow of the Carpathian Mountains, which formed Poland's southern border with Czechoslovakia. Roman Polanski's first conscious memories are those of when he was four years old, during the summer of the year after he was brought to Cracow; he has no recollection of his earlier childhood in Paris. From his early days in Cracow he recalls playmates in a park near the modest flat into which his family settled in the city's ancient Jewish quarter, and long hours spent with his mother learning to draw and read.

Roman's father continued to have difficulty making a living. Those who knew him say that Riszard Polanski, then well into his thirties, was a man whose continuing artistic and intellectual frustrations turned him into a husband and father given to fits of petulance and surly rage. With both wife and son he frequently used a brutal hand to enforce his wishes at home. To the outside world he exhibited an increasingly noxious charm in his attempts to ingratiate himself with prospective employers and establish himself as a citizen of importance among his friends. The outside world was on the whole unimpressed, and Riszard was unable to find the kind of work he thought was worthy of his talents and intellect. Finally, late in 1938, he accepted an offer from his brother Raimund to join him in the operation of a small Cracow merchandising concern.

Riszard's career as a businessman was shortlived. In the fall of 1939 Germany set off World War Two by invading and occupying Czechoslovakia and much of Poland. Thereafter the Nazis imposed restrictive regulations on the country's Jewish population. Cracow, located near Czechoslovakia, was among the first of the major Polish cities to feel the effects of these measures. The Jewish district was rapidly encircled by barbed wire fencing and all the city's and nearby countryside's Jews were herded into it.

Roman Polanski, not yet seven years old, had barely completed his first week in school when Cracow's Jewish quarter was turned into an internment compound by the Germans. He would not see the inside of a school again for another six years.

Roman was a naturally shy child made the more so by his despotic father and shrill, protective mother. His timidity was reinforced by his appearance. He was small and almost girlish-looking in his facial features, which were sharply pointed in the fashion of his mother. A long nose, closely set eyes and pursed lips set against a broad but angular Slavic face lent him a slightly furtive, wounded look that early on provoked sympathy in the women of his mother's circle and derision in the men of his father's.

Roman's basic boyhood character was forged out of his experience in the Jewish ghetto of Cracow. He would soon learn to suppress his timidity in favor of assertiveness, but he would never lose his furtive aspect. For a while the German and Polish authorities left the Jewish population alone, merely isolating it and forcing it to become dependent on itself. Poland was an historical hotbed of anti-Semitism, however, and the Nazis soon learned that they would encounter little Polish resistance if they scheduled a more rigorous fate for the country's Jews than mere ghettoization. In mid-1940 they started to construct concentration camps at various sites in Poland. Concurrently they increased the restrictive regulations in all of Poland's city-ghettos.

Stories of the concentration camps reached the Cracow ghetto early in 1941. Quickly the ghetto became stricken by ugly anxiety as families jockeyed against one another to find ways out. Bribery and informing represented the two chief hopes of escape. There would be little escape, however. No matter how much a family had to offer the authorities in the way of money and information on others, they were inevitably stalled and eventually double-crossed by the ghetto administrators.

Roman Polanski, although his family was not wealthy enough to try to buy its way out of the Cracow ghetto, was a youthful witness to much of the subterfuge and spying. As certain more privileged families sought to gain favor with the authorities, he heard his mother and her friends speak bitterly of Jews setting themselves against other Jews in order to get special treatment. Roman began to form the impression that to be a Jew in the world was not a very favorable thing. His impression was sharpened by the events on the streets of the ghetto.

In anticipation of shipping Jews off to the concentration camps, the Nazi authorities and their Polish counterparts had begun to crack down on petty violators of ghetto rules with public beatings and on-the-spot executions. No longer, for instance, were curfew breakers let off with simple reprimands; they were mercilessly beaten by squads of Polish goons hired by the Nazis to patrol the ghetto's streets.

Young children were not as closely supervised as adults, however. With most of the Polanski family's money gone, and with food growing scarcer, Roman's father sent him into the streets on scrounging missions. Roman learned to sneak into cellars and comb through rubbish bins looking for scraps of food and clothing. Soon he joined two or three other neighborhood boys who had found a sewer tunnel that led them under the ghetto's wire fence and into Cracow proper. Thereafter he traveled almost daily into the main city to steal food from Cracow's shops.

One day a shopkeeper spied Roman and another boy stuffing their pockets with potatoes. Shouting in fury, he chased them. Several other citizens joined the pursuit. The quick and agile Roman managed to escape through a series of alleys. But his companion, a chubby eight-year-old who could not run fast enough, was caught after several blocks and turned over to the police. Roman, panting with exhaustion and fear, eventually made his way home through the sewers.

A few hours later, a squad of German soldiers marched his bloodied companion back into the ghetto and brought the boy to his parents' house, which was across the street from Roman's. Roman, frightened, watched from behind closed curtains as the squad leader knocked on the boy's front door. The knock was answered by an elderly woman, the boy's grandmother. At first the German squad leader seemed polite and deferential, letting the boy go and explaining why he and his soldiers were there. Other members of the boy's family gathered at the door, and a few passersby paused to watch. Although Roman could not hear what was being said, he could see that the German was smiling effusively as he talked to the fat boy's grandmother. Even the old woman broke into a smile as she turned to say something to her family. Then, with a suddenness that would be forever etched into Roman's memory, the squad leader, still smiling, raised his weapon. He shot the woman in the head, freezing the smile on her face.

21

The incident had immediate and lasting repercussions for the Polanski family. At first Roman had been enormously relieved, believing the boy from across the street had not informed the Germans that Roman had been with him on their shoplifting expedition. The next day, however, the Germans began a selective round-up of Cracow's Jews for shipment to concentration camps. Roman had once again ventured into the city that morning in search of food, this time on his own. He returned a few hours later to find the round-up in progress.

As he approached his house he saw a group of wailing women milling about in the street, guarded by a squad of German soldiers. Men and children, shouting and crying, were trying to reach the enclosed circle of women, only to be pummeled away by the soldiers. Roman was twenty-five yards away when the door of his own house flew open and a woman was dragged out by four Germans. The woman was Roman's mother.

The Germans tussled the protesting Bula Polanski to the street and sent her sprawling into the circle of other women. Roman cried out and started to run to her. When she saw him coming she shook her head furiously – No!

Roman stopped a few yards away from the soldiers. His mother signaled to him with her eyes, motioning him into the house.

Roman began to back away. Other women were being added to the group. Then he heard his mother shout, 'Go!'

Roman, only seven years old, was paralyzed by confusion and conflicting impulses. A German soldier looked up at him menacingly. His mother cried out again, 'Go, Roman! Hide!'

He ran to an alley and made his way around to the back of his house. When he got inside he rushed to a window. By then a dozen more neighborhood women, and a few elderly men, had been added to the group. Suddenly the German commander barked an order. Prodding the group with the butts of their weapons, the German soldiers herded their captives down the street toward the gates of the ghetto. Roman caught one last glimpse of the back of his mother's head before the throng disappeared around a corner.

Roman sat by the window for well over an hour, weeping,

while the street outside fell silent and empty. Then, from another room in the flat, his father appeared. Riszard Polanski, in a fury at Roman, gave him a brutal beating. He blamed Roman for the fact that Bula Polanski had been taken away. Between blows, Roman learned from his enraged father that the boy from across the street had implicated Roman to the Germans after all. When the Germans had knocked on the Polanski door, Bula Polanski had answered it. Riszard, in another room when the Germans came, had dived into a closet hiding-place when he heard the commotion at the door. Bula had been seized and forced into the street with the other Jews selected for deportation. A quick search of the flat by two of the German soldiers had failed to reveal Riszard Polanski's hiding-place, and his wife had remained silent as to his whereabouts before being dragged from the house. Riszard had remained in the closet until he was sure that the danger to himself had passed.

Only the intervention of Roman's uncle Raimund saved the boy from serious injury at the hands of his father. Raimund showed up to find Riszard Polanski beating his son and the boy trying to explain through his tears that it was only because Riszard had ordered him to go out and steal food that he had almost been caught. Raimund shouted at Riszard, 'They were taking only women today, you fool. It has nothing to do with Roman.'

Roman's father refused to believe it. While they argued, Roman escaped to another room and collapsed in pain and grief. Eventually the argument in the next room between his father and uncle abated, and the two turned to formulating a plan to escape the ghetto before the next round-up. Roman only half-listened to it. He grew more despondent about his mother as the reality of what had happened to her began to dawn on him. Yet the reality did not prevent him from anticipating her return – that night, the next day, sometime. He had no idea that he would never see her again.

A few days passed. Bula Polanski did not return, and Riszard Polanski's irrational disgust with his son failed to abate. Roman could not understand his father's fury. What he did gradually understand was that for his own self-preservation, he had to steer clear of his father. Two weeks after his mother's disappearance, he fled the family flat and found sanctuary at his uncle's.

The boundaries of the Cracow ghetto grew proportionately smaller as the population was further depleted by daily round-ups. In anticipation of the final round-up, Roman's uncle had collected his few remaining funds and offered them to a Catholic family in a Cracow suburb in exchange for their taking in his two children, Zbigniew and Josef, and protecting them from harm. Now, unknown to the family, Roman was added to the transaction. The name of the family was Koslewski. *

On the eve of the Nazi's evacuation of the remaining ghetto populace to concentration camps, Raimund Polanski gave Roman directions to the home of the Koslewski family and instructed him to lead his two younger cousins there by way of the sewer route out of the ghetto.

Roman safely guided the two boys to the Koslewski home, carrying with him a satchel of money from his uncle. The family had not expected Roman, however, and they ordered him back to the ghetto. Only if he brought money from his own father, he was told, would he be welcome.

Frightened, alone, missing his mother, Roman made his way back to the ghetto three days later to find his father. When he arrived, the streets and houses were empty. Everyone, including his father and uncle, was gone.

The next few years – the formative years of Roman Polanski's life – were spent alternately shuttling between non-Jewish Polish

* It was an irony of Roman Polanski's life that the Koslewskis were related to another Catholic family in Cracow named Wojtyla. Among the Wojtyla family in 1941 was an eighteen-year-old youth who had given up his theatrical ambitions to study for the priesthood at a Cracow seminary. His name was Karol Wojtyla, and over the next thirty-eight years he would rise to become a Cardinal of the Church and Archbishop of Cracow before, in the fall of 1978, being elected Pope. In 1977, a year before his ascension to the Papal Throne as Pope John Paul II, Cardinal Wojtyla would receive a plea for help from Polanski, then languishing in a California prison.

families that temporarily would have him and existing by his own wits on the run.

Having found the ghetto empty and his family gone, Roman returned to the Koslewski family and pleaded for sanctuary. Instead of taking him in, the Koslewskis passed him off to another family on the outskirts of Cracow named Tomasialowicz, providing some money from his cousins' funds as an inducement to give him a roof over his head.

Mrs Tomasialowicz, the matriarch of the family, was an alcoholic. According to a story Polanski tells, she not only quickly squandered the money she had been given for his protection on drink, she also talked too much. One day she boasted to a neighbor that she was hiding a Jewish boy. The next day a German patrol arrived at the house. By then Roman, who had just turned eight, knew what the sight of German uniforms meant. He was playing in the backyard with the Tomasialowicz children when the troops arrived. He fled in panic over a wall and spent the night hiding in terror in the basement of a nearby granary.

The next morning, Roman found his way back to the house where his cousins were being kept. They had been integrated into the family and had even taken on the Koslewski name. There was still no room for Roman, but his doleful look was too much for Mrs Koslewski. The woman of the house prevailed upon her husband to take him in until other arrangements could be made.

With Cracow's ghetto emptied, the German administration of the city set about to restore normality. Motion picture theaters were once again allowed to operate, although only German-made propaganda films were permitted to be shown. Polanski later told friends that he clearly remembered nights in the ghetto in 1940 during the summer before he fled. The Germans had taken to projecting crude propaganda movies at night against the walls of buildings just outside the ghetto in order to indoctrinate the non-Jewish citizens of Cracow. By taking a perch on the roof of a building at the edge of the ghetto and craning his neck, Roman was able to watch the films. He had been fascinated by the flickering images and stentorious sounds and had wanted to see more of them close up.

One evening in the fall of 1941, with nothing to do, Roman wandered from the Koslewski house and found himself in a neighborhood on the outskirts of Cracow. There he came upon a recently re-opened cinema, before which stood a long line of people waiting to get in. He talked himself into the line and managed to get into the theater. His fascination with motion pictures intensified as he watched a heroic film about German industrial progress and cultural superiority. 'It was my first time in a film theater,' he later said. 'After it was over, I couldn't wait to go again.'

Roman was allowed to stay at the Koslewski home only on the condition that he begin to make a financial contribution to his upkeep and stay out of trouble. He was given an assumed name – the name of a distant relative of the family who had been killed during the Nazi invasion of 1939 – and sent out to do the work of many of Cracow's young boys: selling newspapers and cleaning streets. Roman was assigned to a street corner in Cracow's business district, next to the Gestapo headquarters, and given a stack of newspapers to hawk each day. Out of each day's proceeds he was paid a fraction, which he was then expected to hand over to his surrogate family for food and household expenses.

On an evening in early 1942, Roman was caught sneaking into a movie theater. The manager turned him over to the local police, who delivered him to his surrogate family with a stern warning. The family threatened to turn him out if he ever got into trouble again, since further police attention was the last thing they could afford. The chastened Roman solemnly promised to stay out of any more trouble.

But his fascination with movies had by then become an obsession. Within the population of Cracow, an underground resistance to the German occupation had grown. Although feeble, it was vocal. Among other things, it tried to mount a boycott against the German-made movies that were the only fare offered by Cracow's cinemas. Poles who patronized the movie houses were accused through wall graffiti and other means as being collaborators and traitors. Local 'partisans'

26

would follow people emerging from movie houses to their homes, there to verbally harass them, paint damning messages on the walls of their houses, and throw rocks through their windows.

Roman understood little and cared less about the contents of the movies he saw. His fascination was with the story-telling power of film, the way in which time and space were manipulated through moving photographic images to impart a concentrated, larger-than-life experience. Grainy and coarse though the films he watched were, they were also for him a compelling escape from his loneliness and longing for his mother, and from the tedium of daily life in Cracow with its German-imposed curfews and other restrictions on children.

Roman began to withold money he got from selling newspapers so that he could pay his way into local movie houses. One afternoon in the winter of early 1942, he was accosted by a group of older boys as he emerged from a cinema. He was beaten up and warned never to be seen again patronizing a German movie. Although bruised and frightened, his movie-going compulsion overpowered his fear. He thereupon began to devise ways to attend films without being detected by the partisans. As he once remarked in later years, 'Going to see films in Cracow during the war was the most sublime sensual experience. Except for watching films, there was absolutely nothing else to provide any sort of pleasure to an eight- or nine-year-old boy. The visual and mental vistas that were opened up to me by those terrible German movies almost made being in Cracow worth it. Had there been no Germans, had there been no war or occupation, I probably would have ended up a merchant. And hated every minute of my life.'

By the summer of 1942 he was contributing less and less of his meagre newspaper earnings to his surrogate family and spending more and more on movies. The family did not know that Roman had secretly continued his movie-going until they began to question his reduced contributions to the household. It was one of his cousins who finally informed on him. Once again he was threatened with expulsion from the house. For a while thereafter, a member of the family was assigned to stand with Roman at his street corner and confiscate his money each day after the last newspaper was sold.

Now desperate for money to continue his movie-going habit, Roman soon became involved with a gang of older boys who looted garment warehouses and sold their booty in Cracow's back-alley black market. At first he did not realize it, he later said but he had taken up a dangerous game – particularly for a Jewish boy masquerading as an ordinary Pole. The Cracow police had sent undercover operatives into the streets to combat black marketeers. A number of youths had already been arrested, several of them young Jews who had also escaped the ghetto and were living in packs in the city's abandoned cellars. Any arrested youth who 'looked' Jewish was made to strip, and his genitals observed for circumcision. Although not all non-Jewish male Poles were uncircumcized, all Jewish males *were* circumcized. An arrested youth found to be circumcized, unless he could prove he belonged to a local non-Jewish family, was summarily turned over to the Germans. If he survived the torture designed to elicit from him the identities of other underground Jews in Cracow, he would then be shipped to a concentration camp, probably never to be heard from again.

The nine-year-old Roman Polanski did not have the look of most of Eastern Europe's Jews. One day he was picked up by police with several other members of his group. Trembling with fear, he watched while two of his Jewish compatriots were stripped. Betrayed by their circumcisions, they were tortured and in turn betrayed the identities of several other Jewish boys hiding in Cracow. For some reason he could not account for later on, they failed to mention Roman to the police. They were turned over to the Germans and, that night, he was released. Afraid that the two boys might still betray him to the German authorities, he took refuge for several days in the cellar of an abandoned building rather than return to his surrogate family. All he had for light was a candle. Fiddling with it one night, letting its melted wax drip onto his finger, he was suddenly struck with an idea that was undoubtedly his first venture into

28

theatrical artifice. Necessity never proved more the mother of invention than at this time.

Roman's idea, inspired by the melted candle wax dripping onto his finger and then hardening there, was to fashion an artificial foreskin for himself out of candle wax so that, unless his penis was inspected closely, he would appear to be uncircumcized. After spending several days perfecting a method of applying soft, hot candle wax to his penis and shaping it into a foreskin, he tentatively displayed the results to some of the other Jewish gang members who had survived the arrest of the two boys. His waxen foreskin was adjudged a better disguise than nothing at all and Roman was hailed as a genius by his cohorts. In no time at all, word of his invention spread through Cracow's underground. Fugitive Jewish men began to adopt it, as did non-Jews who had been circumcized at birth.

It is difficult to determine whether there is any truth to this story. Or if true, whether the idea of a waxen foreskin had originated with the nine-year-old Polanski or had been invented by someone else and appropriated by him. My sources insist that it is true, and that Roman developed quite a trade of grafting similar foreskins onto the penises of his friends. One source claims that it is not only true, but that the device came to be known, in the slang of the time, as the 'Polanski Prick'. Polanski has remained mum on the subject.

Nor is it known if the novel idea actually helped to save any lives. But several survivors of that time later joked that it marked the beginning of Roman Polanski's preoccupation with the male sexual organ – particularly his own.

According to one witness, the crafting of fake foreskins led directly to a fascination within Polanski's group for the handling and fondling of each other's sex organs. Out of that grew a heightened awareness of the rewards of sexual sensation. This soon produced sessions of mutual masturbation among the boys.

As the putative inventor of the foreskin, Roman, although a year or more younger than the other boys, quickly emerged as the brains of the group and one of its leaders. When he saw how the other boys deferred to him, he quickly lost his timidity and became assertive and talkative. He also became one of the chief orchestrators of the group's sexual sessions.

'Perhaps his sexual jadedness as an adult has something to do with his first experiences with sex,' says the witness to that time. 'Those boys learned about sex solely as a source of physical pleasure. There were no emotions connected with it, no tenderness, no romance. It was purely mechanical, like relieving one's bowels.'

The Polanski gang managed to make it into early 1943 before being decimated and finally broken up by arrests. Roman himself was again nabbed, on Christmas Eve of 1942 while selling a black-market sweater to an undercover policeman posing as a yule shopper. Skinny, small and waiflike, he was taken to the local police station and thrust into a cell with a dozen other boys. As he waited to be questioned, his heart pounded with terror. He was not wearing his foreskin!

Luck was with him though. It was the end of the day and the police shift was changing. He was overlooked in the shuffle and not forced to strip. When he claimed membership in the Cracow family that had originally given him sanctuary, one of its adult members showed up and claimed responsibility for him. Roman was released after the family paid a small fine.

But the sternly Catholic family had had enough of Roman. In the spring of 1943 they shipped him off to distant relatives – tenant farmers who scratched a subsistence living from a few acres of land in Central Poland, almost a hundred miles from Cracow.

Roman's new surrogate family, the Borocowskas, were simple-minded peasants and strictly orthodox Catholics who were unaware that Roman was a Jew. They thought he was a bona fide member of the Cracow branch of the family, the son of a Polish soldier who had been killed during the Nazi invasion. Roman had been warned to maintain the fiction at all costs. He was given the name Raimund Borocowska.

Assigned sleeping quarters in the straw loft of a barn a few yards away from the ramshackle Borocowska farmhouse, Roman was immediately pressed into a daily dawn-to-dusk round of farmwork. He was also incorporated into the family's harsh religious routine, which consisted of prayer sessions three times a day, weekly trips to the local church, and attendance three evenings a week at the religious school.

The summer of 1943 was a particularly cruel one for the people of Poland, with drought and increased Nazi oppression bending the spirit of the adult population. It was no less a trial for Roman. Now close to ten years old, the smart, agile street-kid from Cracow found the routine of religion-oriented farm life an unprecedented form of tedium. Only the ready availability of food made his existence tolerable. Otherwise he was miserable, much preferring the perils and material deprivation of Cracow to the relative material abundance but sensual starvation of rural Poland. He could in no way relate to his new family, which made his longing for his real family, especially his mother and stepsister, all the more painful. He had no way of knowing, of course, that tens of thousands of Jews in the concentration camps not too far away would gladly trade their plight for his.

Life in the Polish countryside only sharpened the young Polanski's propensity to get into trouble. The area in which he lived was comparatively free of a physical German presence, but representatives of the Church – priests and nuns – were everywhere. In Roman's mind, they soon became the Germans of his life. And with their built-in antipathy for anything Jewish, they could be almost as dangerous.

He made few friends, viewing himself as stuck in an alien environment and refusing to mix with the unsophisticated children of the local peasant families. Yet as a boy recently arrived from the city, he was besieged by local youths with questions about life there. He indulged his questioners, often embellishing his responses with gross exaggerations of what life in Cracow was really like. Particularly graphic were his tales of the films he had seen – films being totally foreign to the experience of the local peasantry. Once or twice, he accidentally came close to revealing his real identity and ethnic background. Luckily, the unschooled peasants failed to understand his slips of the tongue when he referred to his origins.

The local Church authorities quickly took a dim view of

Roman. He resisted or seemed indifferent to their religious instruction, and they began to regard him as a malevolent influence on their herd of faithful and obedient youngsters. They cautioned the local youth to stay away from him until he was thoroughly bowed to their authority.

One girl, however – a thirteen-year-old named Eva – would not be denied access to Roman's sagas of Cracow. Buxom, physically precocious and rebellious, she had vexed her teachers and parents long before Roman's arrival on the scene. She was enthralled by the young outsider, captivated by his tales of life in the city, of movie-going and black-marketeering, of his veiled hints at dancing and sexual liaisons. Once, Eva confided to Roman, a few years before, a troupe of actors had appeared in the local town to perform an Easter version of *The Passion Play,* a virulently anti-Semitic interpretation of Jesus Christ's final days in Jerusalem. Ever since seeing that, she had secretly nurtured an ambition to be an actress. She planned to run away to Warsaw when she was old enough.

Eva, to use the phrase of today, became the ten-year-old Roman Polanski's first groupie, furtively following him about and showing up at his barn loft in the early evenings to listen to him spin exaggerated tales of his life in Cracow. A Catholic, she had been raised like everyone else in the neighborhood to despise Jews. Polanski, although he had been repeatedly warned to hide his true stripe, finally could not resist boasting to her of his foreskin invention of the year before. When the curious Eva asked for a demonstration one afternoon, Roman took her into a neighboring farmer's barn with a candle and some matches and swore her to secrecy about himself.

As one thing led to another, Roman found himself being seduced by the older girl as he demonstrated his candle trick on his penis. At first he was embarrassed and awkward, his only prior sexual experience having been with boys. But with the girl's help he soon got the hang of what he was supposed to do. As he followed her instructions about how to position himself, he dreamily decided that girls were much more rewarding than boys as providers of sexual pleasure.

Afterward, they lay nude together on a blanket. They played

with each other's genitals for a while and soon Roman was ready to go again. Now he took the initiative, twisting around to mount Eva while she coyly resisted and tried to shove him away. As they struggled, half-playfully and half in earnest, neither noticed that Roman's foot had knocked the lighted candle into the hay mow below.

Roman finally subdued the girl and she lay back, panting from her exertions but ready to receive him again. Roman was in a frenzy of newly discovered sexual passion. He was oblivious to everything but the swollen aching of his groin, oblivious to the thickening acrid smoke that had begun to waft up from the hay mow.

It was the girl who was first aware of it. She gave a muffled scream and pushed Roman off her. She scampered to the edge of the loft and looked down to see flames licking at the sides of the barn. When she looked back at Roman she could barely see him through the smoke.

By this time he realized what was happening. He threw Eva's clothes at her and started to dress himself. But the rapidly spreading smoke and heat from below made him aware that if they didn't get out immediately they would be trapped.

Indeed, Roman and Eva barely escaped with their lives. Still naked, carrying their clothes and choked by smoke, they scrambled blindly out of the flaming barn to be met by several field workers who had spotted the smoke and were rushing up to fight the blaze.

When confronted by the owner of the barn, Roman denied any knowledge of how the fire started. The next day, however, talk of the two emerging naked from the inferno was all over the neighborhood. Word soon reached Eva's father, a pious elder of the local Catholic parish. He cornered her in her room and gave her a furious beating. Despite Roman's warnings that she must never reveal the truth about him, she confessed to the business about the candle.

And what were they doing with a lighted candle in a hay barn, her father demanded to know?

'Papa,' blurted the cowering Eva, 'he is a Jew.'

INTERLOG 1

THIRTY-FIVE years later, Roman Polanski would again get into trouble because of a thirteen-year-old girl.

'You can take your top off now,' he had said to the nubile thirteen-year-old in Jack Nicholson's hot tub.

The girl was now in a deep champagne-Quaalude daze, according to what she later told the police. She tried to comply with Polanski's instructions but her fumbling fingers could not manage to unhook the straps of her bikini top. She giggled to herself, then groaned in a combination of discomfort and frustration. She stared into the swirling water of the Jacuzzi and saw it as an immobile block of ice. Then she looked up at Polanski and saw dozens of him, all swirling and spinning and grinning crazily. The room beyond had become a kaleidoscope of blurs.

Within seconds Polanski was out of his clothes and into the tub. As he unfastened the girl's bikini bra her head fell back against his powerfully muscled shoulder, then sagged forward into the water. After he got her top off he fondled her breasts, then reached under the water and began to work her bikini briefs down her legs. The girl, who had been slipping into unconsciousness, suddenly revived. She stiffened and resisted Polanski's efforts, jack-knifing her knees and pressing her heels into her buttocks. 'Don't do that,' she managed to say as clarity momentarily returned.

'It's only for pictures, darling,' Polanski whispered. 'Your mother said is okay.'

'My mother?' the girl murmured disbelievingly. But then she relaxed and allowed Polanski to complete the operation.

With the girl naked, Polanski instructed her to brace her arms on the curving side of the tub and let her body float on the water's surface. When she achieved a semblance of the position he wanted, he grabbed his camera, positioned himself between her spreadeagled legs, and began snapping pictures of her flattened breasts as the water washed over them. His lens roved further about her body while Polanski kept encouraging her with 'That's great, that's super, my darling.' Finally it stopped at her crotch, where the silky wisps of her first pubic hairs floated like tiny eels in the roiling water.

Polanski reached out to fondle the girl. At his touch she recoiled. He said something to her in a foreign language and snapped a few more pictures. Then he tossed his camera onto the rug beside the Jacuzzi and gripped her by the ankles. He moved toward her between her legs. She suddenly felt a finger or thumb probing her backside and recoiled again. She managed to kick Polanski away, stand up in the tub, and drag herself half-awake onto the carpet at its side.

She was shivering and ashen and weeping as she coiled into a fetal position on the carpet. 'I'm sick,' she mumbled drunkenly. 'I want to go home . . . my father . . . ' She tried to haul herself to her feet but collapsed back into a naked heap next to Polanski's camera, gasping for breath in shrill, raspy heaves. Mucus spilled from her nostrils.

Concern suddenly filled Polanski's face. It was not so much for the girl as for himself. His life had been tainted by all sorts of scandal. It would be unspeakable for him to be involved in the death of a naked American teenager. Death came to his mind because he had seen so much of it. He realized that the child-woman he was staring at appeared to be in the throes of a potentially fatal seizure. She was now shaking violently and urinating in tiny, pulsating jets on the tubside rug.

He quickly pulled himself from the Jacuzzi. Collecting a pile of bath towels, he covered the girl with them. He touched her forehead with his hand and felt a dangerous heat. He wondered whether he should call an ambulance or the police. He decided to wait, more out of his own drug-induced panic than considered judgment.

Within minutes the girl's trembling subsided. Her desperate high-pitched gasps lapsed into hoarse, hollow breathing. One water-wrinkled hand jutted out from the towels he had piled on her. For the first time Polanski noticed that she had a fingernail-biting habit – an odd imperfection in such an otherwise perfect creature.

Then she was talking to him. She had regained consciousness, had twisted her head around and was looking up at him through fogged eyes. 'Feeling . . . better,' she said thickly. 'Can I . . . go home now?'

Polanski had no desire to deliver the girl to her mother in such a condition. He shook his head. 'Better to rest a while,' he said. 'Can you walk?'

'I think so,' she breathed.

'There is a bedroom down the hall,' Polanski said. 'You have a sleep.' He stood up and leaned over her. 'Come on, I help you.'

With his aid the girl struggled to her feet, trying to gather towels about her. As she stood wobbling, Polanski looked at her in wonder and thought, 'How can this bird only be thirteen?' She had the perfect body of a twenty-five-year-old, a body that rivaled that of his murdered wife.

'Oooh, I'm woozy,' she said.

Polanski supported her and led her in faltering steps to the nearby guest bedroom. She alternately gasped and giggled as he settled her onto the bed and ran his hands over her nakedness. She pushed his hands away and half-covered herself with the bed's spread. 'I feel so hot,' she muttered.

'You sleep,' Polanski said soothingly. 'I come back later and take you home, okay?'

36

'Mmmmm.' The girl's eyes fluttered as she watched Polanski recede from her vision. Lying on her back, her breathing grew again more difficult. She wanted to turn over but couldn't muster the energy. The ceiling of the room was spinning. She fought mentally to stop it but failed. Then came the spinning image of Jack Nicholson, his face set in a disapproving scowl, as she lapsed once more into unconsciousness.

The girl had no idea how long she'd been out. But it could not have been more than half an hour, as she later reconstructed it to a grand jury. * There had been moments when she thought she had drifted back to some sort of wakefulness to see a blurred naked male figure standing over her, watching her. She could not swear to that, though. Her first tangible memory was of being nudged into semi-consciousness by some strange activity going on between her legs. At the beginning it was merely a series of unfamiliar sensations – the unaccustomed feel of hair tickling the insides of her thighs, then of heat and dampness filling her pubic area, then of an object, moist and coarse, penetrating her vagina.

As she came awake and looked down through her breasts, she could see that her knees were arched and her legs were spread and that the head of the naked Roman Polanski was buried in some curious way in her crotch. Fascination was at first her only reaction. It was as though what she was seeing was happening to someone else, not her. But then, as she realized that it *was* happening to her, her body stiffened and she tightened her thighs against Polanski's ears. Polanski looked up from his labours and his drugged eyes met hers. She tried to wriggle from the grasp of his mouth and tongue but had no strength. Polanski muttered something in what sounded like French, tightened the grip of his hands on her hips, and

---

* During the criminal proceedings that followed the encounter at the Nicholson house between Roman Polanski and the thirteen-year-old girl, her identity, along with that of her family, was shielded by the courts and the media. Their identity will remain concealed in this book.

returned to his task. She momentarily fell back into unconsciousness.

Moments later she was half-awake again, prodded into a vague form of alertness by the feel of Polanski's swollen penis being forced into her mouth. With her breathing still impaired by the effects of the Quaalude and champagne, she immediately gagged and retched. She tried to scream but could not produce a sound. But she was wider awake now, her eyes staring in terror at Polanski.

He finally withdrew himself from her mouth. 'You don't like?' he said.

She shook her head violently, shutting her eyes to avoid looking at Polanski's erect, glistening penis.

'Then we fuck instead,' he declared. 'You let me fuck you, yes?'

The girl froze.

'Come on,' Polanski mumbled. 'You been fucked before, no?' When the girl didn't answer he became more insistent. 'You tell me the truth, you been fucked before, I know.'

The girl's cheeks were now wet with silent tears. After a moment she nodded, turning her eyes away from Polanski's.

'You want no more in mouth?' he said with a hint of threat in his voice.

The girl shook her head.

'Then you let me fuck you.'

She nodded imperceptibly.

'Yes?' Polanski said.

She nodded again.

'No trouble,' he said. 'You don't tell anyone, eh?'

Still silent, she agreed with another shake of her head.

Polanski quickly lubricated himself from a jar by the side of the bed. As he entered the girl, he asked her when she had had sexual intercourse before.

'Last month,' she replied hazily. 'With my boy friend. We only did it once.'

'You like?' Polanski asked.

'I don't know.'

'Well,' he said, beginning to thrust slowly inside her. 'I will

38

teach you to like, eh?'

'Couldn't I just go home?' the girl said after a moment.

'After,' said Polanski. Then, completing a few more slow thrusts, 'How does that feel, darling?'

The girl felt strange being called 'darling' by this man she hardly knew. 'Answer,' Polanski insisted. 'Tell me how it feels.'

'It feels alright,' the girl said without enthusiasm. 'I mean, it doesn't hurt or anything. Can we stop now?'

Polanski released a gutteral laugh. 'Why to stop, I can go like this for a long time.' There was a boasting intensity in his voice that meant nothing to the girl except for the defenselessness it generated in her. She remained dizzy and weak, her breathing still constricted. As the moments passed she was surprised to find that the older man's movements inside her and the feel of his hands as they teased her nipples distracted her from her discomfort. Yet her arms and legs remained taut and stiff. They were beginning to ache, and she felt a cramp growing in her calf.

'You are too tense,' Polanski said with impatience in his voice. 'Relax and enjoy. Tell me you enjoy. I feel like I'm fucking a corpse. Wrap your legs around me . . . '

'I can't,' said the girl, beginning to writhe. 'I have a cramp in my legs. Please get off me . . . please!'

'Shit!' muttered Polanski as he withdrew from her.

The girl rolled off the bed and started shaking out her cramped leg. But her head started to spin again, forcing her back onto the bed. She deliberately lay face down this time, thinking that this would foil any designs Polanski might have of continuing. It was a naïve notion.

Polanski roughly grasped her hips from behind and elevated her backside. 'Don't be afraid,' he barked at her. 'We try something different now. I bet you never have this before. I teach you everything about how to make love good.'

With that the girl felt his fingers coating her rectum with lubricant. Then he started to penetrate her anally. She cried out and tried to wriggle free, but she was no match for Polanski's strong grasp of her hips. 'Stop!' she shrieked. 'It hurts.'

'Shut up!' Polanski said. 'Otherwise I give it to you in the mouth again. You want that?'

'No, but what you're doing hurts me.'

Polanski was halfway inside her rectum. 'Stop twisting about so much,' he ordered. 'It won't hurt if you keep still.'

The girl now burst into tears. 'But it's so dirty!' she wailed.

Polanski snickered. 'Nah – it's the best way to fuck.' His hands tightened on her trembling flank. 'It's so good,' he moaned, forcing himself further into her.

His ecstasy was abruptly interrupted by a knocking at the bedroom door. The girl heard a shouted exchange between Polanski and whoever was on the other side of the door. At first her thought was of Jack Nicholson and she was mortified at the idea that Polanski might tell him to come in. Then she realized that the voice on the other side of the door was that of a woman.

Polanski roughly withdrew from the girl and tumbled off the bed. She heard the door open and a brief, heated conversation between Polanski and the woman who belonged to the voice. The girl slid beneath the bedcovers in shame.

Moments later the door closed and Polanski was again on the bed. He yanked back the bedcovers and ordered the girl to turn over. Threatened by the harsh urgency in his voice, she did so, dreading another assault on her mouth. But Polanski was all business now, quick and perfunctory. He forced open her legs and mounted her. She closed her eyes and felt him penetrate her once more. He started to pump himself in and out at an increasingly rapid pace, muttering to himself in French and staring into her half-opened eyes with a look that was at once dazed and dripping with contempt. Then he climaxed with a series of animal grunts. She felt it deep in her insides as a quick flash of heat.

Polanski collapsed on top of the girl and whispered something harsh in her ear in what was yet another language foreign to her. After a few moments she began to struggle for breath as his weight crushed her chest. Polanski quickly pulled himself up and rolled to the other side of the bed. 'Do you know what to do?' he asked without looking at her.

'What do you mean?' the girl said. Her head, though still

a swim, was clearer than before. There was a foul taste in her mouth.

'Get up,' Polanski ordered. 'Get into the bathroom and take a bath. Make it fast. Be sure to clean yourself good.'

Relief flooded through the girl. At last it was over and she was going home. So grateful was she that she almost felt a fondness for Polanski.

As she weaved toward the bathroom, Polanski's voice stopped her. 'Remember,' he commanded, 'you tell no one of this. Ever . . . eh?'

She nodded obediently, still fighting her residual dizziness and grasping the doorjamb to keep herself upright.

But she knew she would never obey the order. She could not wait to get home and tell her boyfriend what had happened to her at Jack Nicholson's house.

CHAPTER 2

'YOU ARE harboring a Jew!'

It was the night after the barn fire. The irate voice belonged to the girl Eva's father. Having beaten the truth about Polanski out of his daughter, the man stood pounding and bellowing at the door of the Borocowska farmhouse.

Roman, in his sleeping loft in the nearby barn, sat up in alarm. Through a crack in the rough siding he saw the man's silhouette.

'Open up, Borocowska!' the man demanded as he continued to pound on the door.

Roman saw the door swing open. Standing in a faint pool of lantern-light was Zigmund Borocowska, the father of the family, in his underwear.

'The boy!' said Eva's father. 'He is a Jew!'

'What boy?' replied Borocowska.

'The boy from Cracow. The boy you tell everyone is your cousin's son.'

'Raimund?'

'He is a Jew, I tell you.'

Zigmund Borocowska, still half-asleep, was befuddled, 'You

are crazy.'

'I will prove it,' said Eva's father. 'Where is he?'

Borocowska motioned toward the barn.

When Roman saw Eva's father stride toward the barn, he cringed in fear. The man found him in the loft and dragged him back to the house, thrusting him through the door. He grabbed the lantern from Borocowska and ordered Roman to remove his pants.

Roman looked at Borocowska. 'Why should I?' he said.

Eva's father clapped him across the head with his hand. 'Take them off!' he commanded.

The blow stung and Roman started to cry. Eva's father forced him to the earthen floor. Holding the lantern high with one hand, he ripped off the boy's stained and threadbare pants with the other. Roman was again caught without his disguise.

Eva's father lowered the lantern close to Roman's crotch. 'There,' he said to Zigmund Borocowska, 'you see? I am right. He is a Jew.'

To the peasant Borocowska, the sight of Roman's circumcized penis was mystifying. He didn't know what to make of it, never having heard of circumcision.

'It is the sign of a Jew,' Eva's father explained. 'All Jews must have their male childrens' fixed like that. It is part of their religion.'

After some harsh grilling by the suddenly angry Zigmund Borocowska, Roman confessed his true origins.

'Is it any wonder he has been so disobedient to the priest and the nuns?' said Eva's father.

Awakened by the clamor, the rest of the Borocowska family had congregated in the chilly room. Eva's father was pleased with his vindication but still brimming with outrage. He announced that he would take Roman to the nearest German garrison and turn him over.

Zigmund Borocowska thought about that for a moment. Then he said, 'No.'

'What do you mean, no,' said Eva's father.

Borocowska said that he feared the Germans would punish him. Besides, with his sons taken by the war, cheap farm labor was impossible to find. He wanted to keep Roman, despite the fact he was a Jew.

'But my daughter,' exclaimed Eva's father. 'Do you know what he did to her?'

'I will make it up to you,' said Borocowska. He offered the man a litter of recently born piglets in exchange for his silence. After further wrangling, Eva's father finally agreed. He would not mention to anyone that Roman was a Jew. But the boy must never come near his daughter again.

That was not the only condition Roman had to meet to remain safe. After Eva's father left, Borocowska warned him that he would only be able to stay with the family if he renounced his religion, agreed to undergo an immediate Roman Catholic baptism, and obediently accepted the Roman Catholic teachings he had up to then been thumbing his nose at.

Roman had scant consciousness of Judaism as a religion, understanding it only as an ethnic heritage. What did it matter? He meekly agreed to Borocowska's conditions.

Thus he was baptized a few days later, only the local priest sharing in the knowledge of his real background. The matter of his having been born a Jew was discreetly put aside. For a while, at least.

If baptism was a simple matter for him to accept, the subsequent pressures imposed on him by the Borocowska family to absorb and accept without question the never-ending parade of orthodox Catholic children's teachings were not. He stubbornly remained an alien to the tradition he was being immersed in. Moreover, he grew exasperated by the dullness of the Borocowskas themselves, the stoic, humorless adults and their dimwitted children. Finally, he could stand it no longer. On an early spring day in 1944, a sweet scent in the air tempting him, he decided to run away.

Roman set out by foot toward the south-west, which he had heard was the direction to Cracow. He had gone about eight miles when he came to a busy road intersection. Weary from his hike, he tried to hitch a ride. His hair was cut short and his appearance was still gaunt. Despite this, none of the trucks that passed on their way from the central Polish city of Lodz to

Cracow would stop for him.

Soon a German patrol car rolled up to the intersection. Two soldiers got out and set up a roadblock, stopping trucks and checking their drivers' papers. Roman darted to the line of halted trucks and began to beg a ride. One of the soldiers watched as he was rebuffed time and time again. Finally, taking pity on him, the soldier beckoned Roman to one of the trucks. 'Where are you going?' he asked in Polish.

Roman mumbled that he was trying to get to Cracow.

The soldier had a brief conversation with the driver of the truck, then turned back to Roman with a smile. 'This one will take you part of the way.'

Roman smiled back shyly.

'But first,' said the soldier. 'let me see your identity card.'

Roman had no identity card. He shrugged, the expression on his face turning hapless.

The soldier's expression suddenly became menacing. 'Identity!' he barked.

Roman was mute, his heart beginning to pound. He looked around, then began to back away from the soldier.

'Halt!' the soldier ordered, removing his pistol from its holster.

Roman panicked when he saw the weapon. Another truck had pulled to a stop nearby. He dove beneath its body and scrambled to the other side. On his feet again, he raced across the road and plunged into the woods that adjoined it. He heard the soldier shout at him, then call out to the other soldier in German. In a second the two Germans were after him. He could hear them crashing into the woods behind him, cursing and ordering him to stop.

His face and arms whipped by branches, Roman raced blindly on. The chasing soldiers pegged several shots at the sounds he was making. The bullets whizzed past him, ricocheting off tree limbs. Roman sprinted another hundred yards deeper into the forest, his heart now in his throat, before the noises behind him began to recede. Once he was sure the soldiers had given up the chase he slowed down. But he continued to move deeper into the forest, changing direction several times. Finally, starved and exhausted, he came upon a large uprooted tree and hid himself in its lee as rain began to fall. He spent the night there, frozen-wet and frightened of the forest's eerie night sounds. He imagined all sorts of horrors descending upon him. The night left an imprint on his mind that would never be erased.

There had been a sharp increase in German military movements across central Poland that spring as the Nazis sought to shore up their eastern front against Russia after a disastrous winter. And throughout Poland itself the Germans were tightening the screws on the population in their efforts to destroy the burgeoning resistance movement. During the night in the forest near Lodz, Roman realized that he would be in continuing peril as a lone boy without identity papers. When morning came – a bitterly cold and rainy morning – he cautiously made his way back to the Borocowska homestead. He arrived that night, drenched and sick.

'Where have you been?' the senior Borocowska thundered, oblivious to the boy's condition.

'I went for a walk,' Roman lied. 'I got lost in the forest.'

'You have missed two days of work. You will pay.' Borocowska pounded Roman with his fists, knocking him to the floor. Roman, trembling with fever, burst into tears. His tears were not from the pain or humiliation of the beating, though. They came from his relief at being safe again after his harrowing experience of the day and night before.

Roman remained with the Borocowskas for another five months, pretending to accept the family's primitive Catholicism once he realized that it was the only way to get along and avoid further beatings. Within himself, however, he continued secretly to resist the imposition of religious dogma on his Jewish soul. Not that he felt any Jewish religious stirrings. Indeed, as he would later say, he had learned at his early age to view all religious training as inane.

The fall months of 1944 were the most dreadful of the war in Poland. During the summer, following the Allied invasion of France in June, the German front in Russia began to collapse under the weight of the furious Soviet counteroffensive. By

October, the decimated German armies were retreating westward through Poland in the face of the Soviet onslaught. Death and devastation among the civilian population of eastern and central Poland multiplied as both Germans and Russians indiscriminately ravaged the land with artillery barrages and bombings. The carnage continued with the coming of the early winter snows in November, staining the landscape in blood.

The Borocowska farmstead was commandeered by a German garrison in late October, 1944. Members of the family fled to other farms in the region while Roman, now eleven, was left to fend for himself. He took refuge in another barn nearby, but after a few days was driven out into the cold by lice and rats.

As the snows of early November began to fall, Roman wandered south-westward on foot with a group of refugees in an attempt to stay ahead of the battles being waged between the retreating Germans and the pursuing Red Army. After several days they reached the Warta River, but he was unable to go on. The fever he had caught five months earlier, had never totally disappeared. Now, fed by undernourishment, the cold and the infectious lice bites he had suffered the week before, it had returned to completely debilitate him.

Left behind by the refugees, he barely managed to drag himself into a recently deserted ox barn near the river. There he burrowed himself into a large pile of manure, which provided some warmth. With his strength quickly ebbing and his fever turning him delirious, he failed to notice the worms and maggots that crawled out of the steamy manure to attach themselves to his skin. Soon he was unconscious. Once again he was close to an encounter with death.

Roman was jarred back to consciousness the next morning by the feel of hands roughly pulling him out of the manure pile. He had no memory of where he was. He opened his eyes to see several men and teenaged boys standing over him. One of them bent down and started picking maggots out of his hair, while another threw a heavy overcoat over his wasted, trembling body. Then he passed out again.

The men were members of a Polish communist resistance group operating behind German lines. The stable was their command post, from which they mounted nightly sabotage missions to hinder the German retreat. All were from Cracow, and one of the group. Casmierz Musial, was a former medical student. He carried the unconscious Roman to a nearby village and got him into a bed in the home of a partisan family. Musial looked in on the boy daily during the next three weeks. With the few medicines he was able to obtain, he nursed Roman back to health.

Roman was back on his feet just before Christmas, 1944. By then, the Germans had halted their retreat and were counter-attacking the Russians. Early in January 1945, word reached the members of the resistance group that the Soviets were poised on the outskirts of Cracow, a hundred miles to the south, and that the Germans had dug in to defend it to the last man. They decided to head for Cracow so that they could take part in the fighting to liberate their home city. Since Roman was also from Cracow, and was well enough to travel, they brought him with them.

During their trek they indoctrinated the boy in communist ideology and gave him an ancient gun to use in the coming battle. By the time they reached Cracow a week later, however, the Germans were gone and the liberated but battered city was under Russian occupation. Roman was overwhelmed by the destruction he saw, and by the sorry sight of thousands of bewildered Poles streaming back into the city from the havens they had fled to in the neighboring mountains.

The citizenry's joy over the liberation from Nazi oppression was brief. The city was largely in rubble. Moreover, the Soviet military administration was hardly more benevolent than the German. The Russians were intent on bringing the populace quickly into line in order to expedite the transformation of Poland into a full-blown communist satellite of the Soviet Union. New partisan groups sprang up – these anti-communist factions whose design was to sabotage Soviet intentions. Communist groups such as the one Roman had traveled with were given special privileges in order to eliminate the anti-communist elements. Soon Roman found himself with special papers that gave him free rein to roam the city as a messenger for a local liaison unit of Polish communists.

As soon as he acquired his papers, Roman made his way back to the ghetto to see if he could learn of his family's fate. He returned to the flat the family had last occupied and found the building severely damaged and deserted. As he rummaged around in the ruins, he pushed some rubble through a hole in the floor. Buried in the rubble was an unexploded artillery shell. When it hit the floor below, it went off. The blast sent Roman hurtling into a wall and knocked him unconscious with a concussion. He was found a few hours later and taken to a hospital. After being treated and released, he suffered from severe headaches for weeks.

This was the first in a series of traumatic head injuries that would plague the young Polanski. In the view of many who knew him later in life, these injuries contributed significantly to his often contradictory behavior as an adult. 'Roman can be altogether sweet and appealing one minute, a horrible intolerant ogre the next,' says one close friend of his today. 'I'm sure the terrible blows he suffered to his brain when he was young have something to do with it.'

The end of the war in the late spring of 1945 brought little cheer to Cracow. During the summer the Russian occupation became more and more stern. The liaison group for which Roman had been running errands was absorbed into the Soviet administration, and Roman was left with little to do but search for his mother and father. When he failed to find any sign of them, he took to roaming the streets again and with three other young survivors formed a gang of scavengers. One day they broke into an abandoned warehouse and found a cache of ten brand-new German army bicycles. The bicycles gave them mobility, enabling them to travel around the city at will. Each keeping a bike for himself, they sold the remaining six at exorbitant prices to citizens hungry for means of transportation. For the first time in his life, Roman found himself with a substantial sum of money in his pocket.

In July, the soon-to-be twelve-year-old was bicycling along a street near the old ghetto when a man shouted to him, 'Roman!'

49

Roman turned to see the short, gaunt, bedraggled figure of his uncle Raimund. He stared at the emaciated man for a moment, then leaped off his bike and ran toward him in tears. His uncle embraced him and Roman recoiled at the smell of him. It was as if, he later recalled, his uncle's innards were leaking through the parchment that was his skin. Raimund Polanski had just returned to the city after being liberated from the Mautthausen concentration camp, where tens of thousands had died.

'Where is my mother?' Roman asked.

His uncle was silent for a moment. Then he said, 'Your father is here.'

'I have been looking all over for them.'

'He came back with me,' said Raimund Polanski.

'What about my mother? Where is she?'

'Come,' said Raimund, 'I will take you to your father.'

When Roman was reunited with his father an hour later, he was more stunned than when he had seen his uncle. Riszard Polanski had also survived four years at Mautthausen. He was in even worse condition than Raimund, but he had lost none of his anger at Roman. Harshly he told the boy that his mother was long dead, consumed in the ovens of Auschwitz. He made it clear to Roman immediately that he still held him responsible.

Roman received the news of his mother's fate with stony silence. The pleasure he had experienced upon first seeing his father evaporated, and he felt his old fear and hatred return. He ran from his father, then collapsed in grief as the realization that he would never see his mother again sank in.

During the next few weeks, Roman's uncle reorganized what was left of the family. He found a barely habitable house and installed Roman and his father there, along with the remnants of his own family and several other Polanski relatives. In the fall, when Riszard and Raimund Polanski had regained some of their strength, they were conscripted by the authorities to work on the clean-up of Cracow. Citing his still-weakened condition, Riszard appropriated Roman's cherished bicycle. Roman's protests fell on deaf ears. His resentment against his father grew more bitter.

Roman still had some of the money he had acquired from the sale of the other bikes, however. He sought out the people who had bought them with an offer to buy one back. He had no takers, but word of his offer reached an older Cracow street-boy. The older boy let it be known that he had a bike for sale. One day, accompanied by a friend from his own gang, Roman tracked him down.

The older youth confirmed that he had a German bike stashed away. He was willing to sell it and offered to lead Roman and his friend to it: it was hidden in the basement of a nearby bombed-out building. Roman and his cohort followed the boy to the building after Roman showed the bike's seller his money. When they reached the building, the older boy forbade Roman's companion to proceed any further, expressing his fear that the two would gang up on him and take the bike without paying him. Roman would have to proceed alone, and the transaction would be completed solely between Roman and the older boy once Roman saw the machine.

Over his companion's protests, Roman agreed. The other boy was left to wait in the street while Roman, with his money, followed the bigger youth into the building's pitch black basement. The older boy, pointing a flashlight, urged him into the farthest reaches of the basement, assuring him that he would find the bike there. Having gone as far as he could go, Roman discovered that there was no bike. Before he could react, though, he was struck over the head with the flashlight by the older boy. His head was pummeled repeatedly, fracturing his skull, as Roman lay sprawled, unconscious, in a pool of his own blood. His assailant quickly relieved him of his money and fled the basement, leaving Roman for dead.

Roman's waiting companion saw the assailant, his clothes spattered with blood, run from the building. He gave chase. Roman, meanwhile, regained consciousness. As he tells it today, 'When I woke up, my money was gone. Blood was pouring over my face and into my eyes like water. To this day, when I get under a shower and the water starts, I can feel that blood. I staggered out of the building. A woman came up to help me. I pushed her away, leaving a bloody handprint on her coat, which I also still see.' Polanski would later use such real-life memories and images of blood to graphic effect in several of his films. Indeed, one of the most startling scenes in his quasi-horror movie *Cul-de-Sac* was one of a woman showering in blood.

The assailant was soon caught and jailed, but Roman never got his money back. His wounds were treated and he spent several weeks fighting frequent headaches and blackouts while convalescing.

It was during his recovery period that Roman first got an inkling of what he wanted to do with his future. It was the spring of 1946 and Stalinism had completely replaced Nazism in Poland. All the amenities of life, such as they were, had been organized into rigid state-run systems. One of the few escapes people had from the drabness and harshness of postwar existence in Poland was listening to the radio, which was devoted to programs of heroic Russian music and to dramas designed to further indoctrinate the populace in the glories of communism. The entire communications system was run by the state, and the new Soviet-controlled government-made radio sets, imported from Russia, readily and cheaply available to everyone. Roman's uncle had acquired a set, and during his convalescence Roman listened to it incessantly. He particularly enjoyed the dramas that were presented, not so much for their political content as for the opportunities they gave him to exercise his imagination. Radio was the first thing since his earlier preoccupation with movies to really capture his interest. As he listened to the programs, he found himself making up elaborate pictures and scenes in his mind to augment what he was hearing.

Because of his continuing alienation from his father, Roman came more and more under his uncle's influence as a twelve-year-old in 1946. His uncle arranged for him to receive special tutoring in elementary-school subjects to make up for the schooling he had missed during the war. In 1946, the Polish school system was reorganized under communist-state guidelines and all children were required to enter a technical or vocational school. Roman decided that he wanted to enroll in a school that specialized in communications so that he could take courses in radio and film-making.

His father would not hear of it, though. Riszard Polanski was growing increasingly jealous of the fact that his only child responded more readily to his brother than to him. He had met a woman and was preparing to re-marry in order to remove himself from the crowded conditions of his brother's house. He decided at the same time to re-assert his control over Roman. Upon Riszard's insistence, and after a series of violent arguments with his brother, Roman was forced to enroll in a Cracow technical school that specialized in training electrical and electronics engineers. It was not what Roman wanted, but at least it would eventually enable him to take part and put together radio sets.

Roman's technical education was to last for four years. He adjusted quickly to the daily discipline that had theretofore been foreign to him. Indeed, he responded positively and aggressively to his sudden immersion in education. Despite the fact that he was less than enthusiastic about being trained for a career in electrics, he found the theory behind the subject fascinating and became particularly interested in the technical drawing he was required to do. In fact, drawing soon became his primary passion. He quickly extended his facility for exact technical drawing into more imaginative free form areas.

Along with the re-birth of radio in postwar Poland came the revival of the cinema, this time under the same state-controlled auspices. The Russians were proponents of film-making, since Lenin had decreed that among all the arts, cinema was the most important in advancing communist ideology among the masses. Russian-made films replaced German propaganda movies in Cracow's film houses, and now it was alright for the citizenry to patronize them. Roman Polanski became a habitual movie-goer again.

At the beginning his motives were the same as they had been during the war – to provide himself with an hour or two of escape from his unhappiness. His father had remarried early in

1947 and Riszard Polanski insisted that his son live with him and his new wife. Curiously, having taken a new wife, Riszard's contemptuous attitude toward Roman softened. Conversely, although Roman was relieved by the change in his father, he himself grew increasingly contemptuous of Riszard for what he viewed as his betrayal of his vanished mother and he took much of his contempt out on his new stepmother. 'I hated her,' Roman said years later.

Upon his remarriage, Riszard Polanski secured a modest house for himself and his new wife near Cracow's old Jewish ghetto. Thereafter he went to work trying to revive a small plastics business that had been started before the war by his new wife's family. Roman lived in the house for a little more than a year before his behavior became so disruptive that Riszard sent him back to his uncle's. Although his uncle was the only man in the family he could relate to, Roman had grown to despise his uncle's children, among whom were the two cousins who had imperiled his safety during the war. Consequently, Roman's behavior failed to improve upon his return to his uncle's still-crowded house. Besides, the uncle's house was a considerable distance from Roman's school.

Finally, late in 1947 after Roman turned fourteen, he was sent by his father to board with a family that lived near the school. He would never live with his father again, and over the next few years would see him only periodically. On those occasions his father would have little to say except to viciously berate him for not doing better at school.

That Roman did not do better in school was not a matter of intelligence but of attitude. Despite his interest in drawing and things technical, the school's curriculum, as well as its teachers, bored him. As he grew, his intelligence sharpened and expressed itself with increasing acuity, according to a former schoolmate. His curiosity was insatiable, and in regaining his independence from his father his personality became more assertive and authoritative. He would not hesitate to argue communist dogma with his teachers and would often loudly reject party-line pieties, offering his own carefully thought-out alternatives. The only good thing about communism, he would often say, was that it promised to rid the world of its enslavement to religion. Ironically, he renounced religious beliefs with a ferocity that made him appear the perfect communist in the eyes of many of his contemporaries.

Roman used his assertiveness at fourteen to finally begin doing something he enjoyed. Still a regular listener to nightly radio programs that would be discussed in school the next day, he became a frequent critic of the acting ability of the performers who appeared in the dramatic programs. One day, a program director appeared at the school to give a lecture on the technical aspects of broadcasting. During the question-and-answer period that followed, Roman piped up with a few derogatory remarks on the talents of several radio actors. No matter how technically proficient the programs were, he said, their effects were destroyed by the stiffness and artificiality of the actors' voices as they read their dialogue.

His audacity shocked his teachers. They ordered him to be quiet, while a few of his fellow students hooted at him derisively.

The director was amused, though. 'Do you think you could do better?' he asked.

Roman, blushing, waited for the laughter to die down. Then he said, 'Yes.'

INTERLOG 2

ANJELICA HUSTON was the daughter of famed actor-director John Huston and the girlfriend of Jack Nicholson. She had met Nicholson when her father co-starred with him in the 1973 movie *Chinatown,* which had been directed by Roman Polanski. Polanski and Nicholson had become close friends in the years following the movie. A dark, willowy woman in her late twenties who had modeled in England and Europe before arriving in Hollywood to try to become a film star herself, Anjelica had alternated her affections between Warren Beatty and Nicholson before finally settling down with Nicholson. Despite her connections, Hollywood had showed little interest in her as an actress. Whatever fame she had collected came as a result of her stormy relationship with Nicholson.

Anjelica was not fond of Roman Polanski. She viewed him as an overgrown child and despised the way he treated women as chattels. She was particularly resentful of the influence Polanski seemed to have on Jack Nicholson. When they were together, Nicholson assumed a boisterous and phony-macho personality. They had had arguments about Polanski. Although their spats had made her feel no better about the Polish director, she had learned to grit her teeth and tolerate him. But this was too much.

That afternoon, Anjelica had returned from a late lunch and a shopping expedition in Beverly Hills. The Nicholson house was one of three homes in a compound set on a bluff off Mulholland Drive, near Coldwater Canyon. Across the way was the house of Marlon Brando, who lately was spending most of his time on his island near Tahiti. At the end of the drive was a smaller house occupied by Helena Kallianiotes, a tough-talking character actress who had made a name for herself a few years before when she appeared opposite Nicholson as a kooky hitchhiker in the movie *Five Easy Pieces*. She looked after the Nicholson and Brando homes in her spare time.

When Anjelica arrived at Nicholson's house late that Thursday afternoon, she recognized Roman Polanski's rented Mercedes in the drive. With Nicholson away in Colorado, she was in no mood for a visit from Polanski. Anjelica marched down to Helena Kallianiotes' cottage, intending to chew her out for allowing Polanski into the house. Kallianiotes was indifferent to Anjelica's ire. She told Nicholson's girlfriend that Polanski had arrived with a young girl and had asked to use the house to take some pictures. Nicholson 'wouldn't've minded,' she said, so she couldn't see why Anjelica was 'bitchin' about it.'

Resignedly, Anjelica traipsed back to the house, now enshrouded in the gathering dusk. When she entered she saw no sign of Polanski or the girl Helena Kallianiotes had said he had with him. But then she heard sounds from one of the bedrooms. Jesus, she thought, her indignation rising, Polanski is in there getting himself laid! 'The nerve,' she murmured to herself. She pounded on the bedroom door.

A few seconds later the door opened and Polanski peeked his head around it. Anjelica took in the scene. Polanski was obviously naked. Beyond, in the bed, she saw movement under a pile of covers.

Anjelica expressed her dismay at finding Polanski there, at his using the house for a sex fling when no one was around. They argued for a few moments. Then Polanski grew contrite and promised to leave. Satisfied, Anjelica turned away and the door closed.

Twenty minutes later Polanski emerged, dressed, from the bedroom. Behind him trailed a dazed-looking girl. Polanski introduced them. Anjelica Huston later said. 'She was breathing high in the throat, wheezing, you might say . . . She seemed sullen to me, which I thought was a little rude.'

The thirteen-year-old would later insist that she felt embarrassed meeting Jack Nicholson's well-known girlfriend in such a way. She was still feeling woozy and was trying to hide it. Moreover, she had the feeling that Anjelica Huston was looking at her with contempt. What Anjelica described as sullenness was really shame, according to the girl.

Polanski drove the girl back to her home in Woodland Hills, inquiring along the way as to whether she took birth control pills. When she said she didn't, he cursed under his breath.

When they reached her house, the girl studiously avoided her mother. Polanski talked with the woman for a few minutes, showing her some test Polaroids he had taken of her earlier in the day and reassuring her about the topless photos. He promised to bring her the prints the following week. He made no mention of what had happened at the Nicholson house except to say that the girl seemed to have had a slight attack of asthma.

Polanski left the house without having an opportunity to speak again to the girl or say goodbye – she had taken refuge in her bedroom. When he left, however, he was confident that she would keep their secret. He had begun to dislike her bossy and officious mother and could see that the girl was afraid of her. The girl, he was sure, would be scared to let her mother know what had happened. He only worried about the possibility that he might have gotten her pregnant. As he drove back to the Beverly Wilshire, he weighed the odds. Then he dismissed the likelihood. Nevertheless, he told himself, he would have to keep his fingers crossed for a few weeks.

While Polanski was still en route along the San Diego

Freeway to Beverly Hills, the girl's sixteen-year-old boyfriend arrived at her house. She took him into her room and, after getting him to promise never to repeat it to her mother, told him what had happened at the Nicholson house. The boy reacted with adolescent indignation, and soon the two were in a high-pitched argument. The girl's older sister, passing the bedroom, stopped to eavesdrop. In short order she learned what the two teenagers were arguing about. Indignant herself, she returned to the family living room and repeated what she had heard to her mother, who was watching television with her own live-in male friend.

The mother later testified that she was dumbfounded at the news brought to her by her older daughter. She immediately strode to her younger daughter's room, followed by her companion. The argument was still going on, her daughter's boyfriend heatedly vowing to wreak revenge on Polanski for having raped her, while she sought to calm him.

When the mother had heard enough, she burst into her daughter's room. The girl, ordinarily gregarious with others, had long been at odds with her mother and had fallen into a habit of sullen incommunication that chronically infuriated the woman. This time, the mother vowed, she would get her daughter to talk even if she had to beat her.

The mother sent the girl's boyfriend packing and even ordered her own boyfriend out of the room. Then she confronted her daughter. The girl cowered in fear. 'I want to know everything!' said her mother, her voice heavy with intimidation.

At first the girl, unaware that her sister had overheard most of the details and not knowing what her mother knew, feigned ignorance. 'I don't know what you're talking about,' she said.

'You most certainly do,' hissed her mother. 'Polanski. I want you to tell me exactly what he did to you.'

'He didn't do anything,' the girl whispered. Avoiding her mother's eyes, she began to tremble as she fought to hold in her tears.

Her mother suddenly felt her anger at the girl dissolve, replaced by a rush of love and compassion. She moved toward her and embraced her. 'Honey,' she said, 'it's me. Do you remember? I'm your mama, and I love you more than anything. Let's not fight. Something terrible has happened – I know. We've already heard part of it. You can talk to me . . . you can tell me . . . '

The girl gave in to her tears, breaking into an agonized weeping and suddenly returning her mother's embrace, gripping so hard that the older woman had to pry her daughter away after a moment. She let the girl sob for a while, holding her loosely, then looked into her tear-blurred eyes. The girl returned her look with a pleading expression.

'Can you talk now?' her mother asked, dabbing the girl's cheeks with a tissue.

Her daughter nodded and held her mother's gaze.

'Alright. I want you to start from the beginning and tell me everything that happened, everything he did to you.'

When the girl finished her story, her mother embraced her for a moment and then stood up. She was overpowered once more by anger, most of which stemmed from the guilt she felt at having permitted the girl to go with Polanski. She knew her daughter was not an innocent, that she had probably already had experiences with local boys in sex and drugs. And she knew that many of the girl's behavioral hi-jinks in the past were motivated by her resentment of her mother. Life was easy in Southern California and kids grew up much faster than most parents wished. Raised in an atmosphere in which her pretty but aging mother had done little to shield her children from her own proclivity for casual sexual liaisons, this thirteen-year-old had grown even faster than most – not just physically but in her superficial outlook on life. Yet she was still thirteen. No matter how mature she sometimes seemed, her basic emotions and reactions remained those of a child. The mother silently berated herself for exposing her daughter to the shame and degradation she imagined her having suffered at Polanski's hands. Since she had had her own sexual experience with the Polish director, she was easily able to visualize what her daughter had been through. The thought reviled her. Even if the girl, in relating the story, had bent the truth a bit to make herself seem more of a victim than she actually had been, even if the girl had in some naïve way led the man on, Polanski had brutally violated the mother's trust. Even if he *had* been encouraged by the girl, he had no business . . .

The focus of the woman's anger quickly shifted to Polanski. The man had made promises the year before about helping the woman to advance her acting career. He had failed to act on them. Now he had violated her daughter – an unforgivable slap in the face.

'What are you going to do, said the thirteen-year-old as she watched the expression on her mother's face harden.

The woman looked at her coldly. 'Do you promise that everything you've told me is the truth?' she said. 'The absolute truth?'

'Yes,' the girl cried, her complaint at being doubted implicit in her voice.

'There was nothing you did that could possibly be interpreted as having led him on?'

'I already told you – NO! That's why I telephoned you. He was trying to get me to take my top off and I said I needed your permission.'

'But why didn't you tell me then that you were drugged? Why did you tell me you were alright? I would have come and gotten you.'

'I was embarrassed,' the girl explained. 'I didn't know it was going to get worse. And I was afraid of what you'd say if you knew I had champagne.'

The woman regarded her daughter. 'I don't know what I'm going to do. I better talk to Al' – meaning her own boyfriend, who by then had returned to the television set in the living room with another can of beer.

'Are you going to punish me?'

'That depends on whether you're telling the truth or not.'

'But I am telling the truth,' the girl insisted.

'You've lied to me before in order to avoid being punished for something.'

'Okay,' the girl conceded. 'But I'm not lying now. If you don't believe me, why don't you ask him. Go ahead, call him

61

up and ask *him* if I'm lying.'

'Roman?' the mother said.

'Yes,' shot back the girl. 'Him.'

The woman smiled. 'Honey, I believe you.'

She consulted with Al. He took a cavalier attitude on the matter, hinting that he believed the girl had invented most of her story. This angered the woman even more, for she was now convinced her daughter had told the truth. By doubting her daughter, the man was doubting her.

'How dare you think she'd lie about a thing like this,' she said.

Her boyfriend shrugged. 'What difference does it make?' he said. 'Even if it happened like she says, who's gonna do anything about it?'

'I will!' the woman cried. 'I'm not going to let that stinking little Polack get away with it.'

'How? How're you gonna do anything?'

'Call the police or something,' the woman said. .

'Hah!' exclaimed her boyfriend. 'It's her word against his.'

'Your're a big help.'

'You don't believe me? Okay – call a lawyer and ask him. Ask him who the police'd believe.'

As the girl's mother later testified before a grand jury, she did not have a lawyer, so, 'I called my accountant to suggest a lawyer – I called the lawyer, but he wasn't home. So then I called the police because the accountant said, "You have to call the police right away." '

The die was cast. Polanski was by then back in his suite at the Beverly Wilshire. Perusing a film script that had been left at the hotel desk for him, he had no idea of what was happening in Woodland Hills. The script had been sent over from the office of Italian producer Dino de Laurentiis. Attached to it was a note: 'Roman, let's talk about this – Dino.' The script had a South Seas setting. De Laurentiis wanted to talk to him about directing it. An image of dark-skinned, bare-breasted Tahitian girls began to form in Polanski's mind. He had completely forgotten about the thirteen-year-old.

CHAPTER 3

ROMAN AT fourteen, suddenly found himself with a job as a radio actor in Cracow.

The school lecturer to whom he had voiced his criticisms had taken him up on his challenge and invited him to the radio station the next day for an audition. He went and had a voice test. Then he was told to read several boys' parts from different scripts. His voice impressed the director of a long-running dramatic serial that was broadcast late each afternoon. As it happened, the regular young actor who played the part of one of the youths in the serial was sick. The director asked Roman if he thought he could play the part for a few afternoons. Again, Roman had no hesitation in saying yes.

The sick actor never got his job back. Roman was so effective in the first few programs that he was given the part permanently. The serial was an adventure of youthful communist derring-do. Aimed at Cracow's young people, it was heard all over the city. The derisive hoots of Roman's schoolmates quickly turned to envy.

Getting into radio work was to sharply change Roman's life and outlook. No longer was he simply a bored, restless technical-school student being trained for a drab career as a communist-state technocrat. His exposure to the mercurial and temperamental older actors working at the radio station lit a flame in his imagination. Indeed, as he continued to act in other radio dramas, learning to use his voice to project a variety of emotions, his imagination became the central focus of his life. As did the personal styles of some of the more flamboyant actors he worked with. The older actors became objects of Roman's hero-worship, and he began to emulate them.

Many radio actors in Poland doubled as stage and film performers in the country's burgeoning propaganda-entertainment industry. Most of Cracow's actors were notorious as being 'different' from the city's run-of-the-mill citizens. Because they were considered valuable functionaries in the state-controlled propaganda network, they were often forgiven certain sins by the communist authorities that ordinary citizens would not be – for instance, failure to show up at the weekly neighborhood party seminars that were compulsory for most of the population. Finally, they were given freedoms that most ordinary citizens were denied. The more celebrated actors were allowed to have cars and given liberal gasoline rations in order to travel to theatrical appearances in distant cities or make movie appearances at the newly founded state-run film institute at Lodz. They were provided special priority in housing for themselves and their families at a time when ordinary working families were crowded into tiny apartments. They were able to circulate among Cracow's coffee houses and night spots, making loud wisecracks about the state of life in Poland and about the communist aspirations of the authorities, when ordinary citizens would dare only whisper such criticisms for fear of arrest and 'doctrinal rehabilitation'. All this appealed mightily to the youthful Polanski.

After appearing in several radio dramas in 1947, Roman began to exploit his eminence among his school friends. He took to parroting the sophisticated banter he heard among the older performers at the broadcast studio and began to set himself apart from his peers. Concurrently, he sought out the company of his fellow actors, especially the younger among them, and began to form ideas about performing and performers that were later to solidify into dogmatic artistic vision.

In the beginning, Roman found himself no more adept at speaking dialogue into a microphone than the actors he had so precociously criticized. He soon came to realize that it was not so much the actors' faults as those of the scripts from which they read. Most if not all of the scripts were produced by a committee of writers in the Cracow branch of the Ministry of Internal Information. Before they reached the radio producers, they were subjected to several special readings by various ministry functionaries whose jobs were to furnish them with more potent communist morals and object-lessons. As these censors and embellishers did their work, the generally supple original scripts took on the stiffness – in plot and dialogue – of boards. Only the final approved versions could be broadcast, and any actor heard to alter a line did so at the risk of losing his job and being returned to the ranks of ordinary citizens.

Radio became the instrument of the most widespread communist propaganda and indoctrination in postwar Poland. With cheap radio sets available to most families, radio was the easiest and quickest way of reaching the populace. But because the large majority of the masses were untutored rural workers and mentally limited country peasants, the level of sophistication in radio broadcasts was kept at a minimum. Which accounted for the dramatic rigidity of the scripts Roman and his co-actors were required to read, and for the deliberate monotone of the dialogue. Emotional flourishes and vocal nuances by the actors were usually discouraged lest they confuse the audience. Whatever dramatic tension existed in the scripts, was only a vehicle to get the political message across. The authorities who ran the state radio system did not want the listeners to be diverted from the message by dramatic subtleties.

Such strictures were not enough to prevent the actors from practicing and perfecting their craft, however. 'For fun,' Polanski once recalled, 'we used to do our rehearsals with all the vocal bombast and inflection we could produce. We would get our desire to really act out of our systems, and then go on the air and do the programs the way we were supposed to, without emotion or verbal nuance.'

Despite the prestige his radio work brought him among his schoolmates, Polanski soon grew restless with its monotony. Because fewer Poles had access to the theater and cinema, and because the audience for these arts constituted the more educated and therefore sophisticated segment of the population, a greater realism and range of performing techniques was permitted in stage and film productions. Roman perceived this after seeing two or three local theatrical productions during the summer of 1948. Consequently he prevailed upon one of the older radio actors to get him an audition with a Cracow theater group. He displayed an uncommon naturalness when he read scenes from several Polish plays for the theater's director. His obvious talent overshadowed his diminutive size, and he was accepted.

The group was made up mostly of older actors devoted to the theatrical precepts of the legendary Russian director and teacher, Constantin Stanislavsky. Stanislavsky had recently become known in the United States as the spiritual inspiration behind the founding of New York's Group Theatre and, later, the Actors Studio. The Actors Studio, under the guidance of Lee Strasberg and Elia Kazan, would soon begin turning out young American performers steeped in the Stanislavsky 'method' of naturalistic acting. Marlon Brando and James Dean, early members of the Actors Studio, would become models for a whole new style of acting in American films and plays, a style that was alternately subdued and explosive. Their example and popularity would have a signal influence on the next generation of young acting stars in America – people like Jack Nicholson and Faye Dunaway. Ironically, Polanski would direct Nicholson and Dunaway in a major Hollywood motion picture twenty-five years later.

While the Stanislavsky-inspired Actors Studio was becoming established in New York in 1948, the fifteen-year-old Roman Polanski was immersing himself in the Stanislavsky acting method in Cracow. The naturalistic style lent itself well to postwar Polish dramatic production, in which somber realistic plays about worker oppression and military heroism, overlarded with communist dogma, were just about the only presentations the authorities would allow.

Roman appeared in his first stage play in the fall of 1948, cast as the son of a Polish soldier who went off to war never to return. His was a small role, but he acquitted himself competently. Even more valuable to the troupe, however, was his enthusiasm for the behind-the-scenes work of the theater. Roman, anxious for the approval of his acting and directing elders, slavishly toiled at the nitty-gritty details of backstage work. He flung himself into the construction and painting of sets, into the acquisition of props and costumes, into cleaning out dressing rooms and tidying up the small theater after performances.

He was rewarded with more roles of increasing visibility during the company's winter season in 1948-49. By then he was spending all of his spare time at the theater and much of his school time as well. The school authorities eventually complained to his father.

Roman's father had begun to make a success of his small plastic-goods business. In its postwar transformation into a communist state, Poland had discouraged the impulse toward private enterprise; yet it allowed private enterprise to exist in a limited way in order to boost employment and smooth the transition to a completely communist economy. Nevertheless, those relatively few entrepreneurs who were permitted to engage in profit-making ventures were viewed by the authorities as potentially dangerous corrupters of the communist ideal. They were watched closely, and if they caused the government any problems their businesses were summarily taken away from them. Riszard Polanski could not afford to be placed in the spotlight of government scrutiny because of complaints about his son. Although Roman no longer lived in his father's house and saw little of him, Riszard was still considered responsible for his actions. Thus he severely reprimanded his son. 'He told me that I could not continue with the theater group and threatened to put an end to my separate living arrangements unless I reapplied myself at school,' Polanski was later to say.

Then fifteen, Roman argued violently with his father. Years of pent-up resentment tumbled from his mouth. His curses were undeterred by the repeated slaps his father delivered to his face for his insolence. The confrontation took place at his uncle's house, and again it took the intervention of Raimund Polanski to prevent serious injury to both Roman and his father.

Raimund took Roman aside and explained the reasons for his father's concern. Somewhat chastened, Roman apoligized to his father. 'I would not obey his edict about quitting the theater. I promised to pay more attention to school, but only on the condition that I be allowed to continue with my acting.' Riszard Polanski, after bewailing Roman's interest in the theater as a useless pursuit, agreed to a probationary period. If there were no more complaints from the school, he could continue with his frivolous stage activities.

A scant few years before, Roman had had the equivalent of an illiterate peasant's formal education – which is to say almost no education at all. But during the first year after the war, with the special tutoring he received with the help of his uncle, he made up much of what he had lacked in the form of reading, writing, mental comprehension and historical information. Indeed, his native intelligence and learning aptitude had impressed his tutors as being superior to those of most children of his age.

At the technical school, the impression he gave his instructors was similar. Roman was a rapid learner, so quick that he was often ahead of his teachers as they tried to drum rote knowledge of various subjects into the heads of the other students. What marked his intelligence more than anything else was not its depth or its capacity for analytical progression, which are what are sought in technical students, but its intuition and imagination. When Roman grew bored, as he quickly did, with doping out mathematical formulas or executing mechanistic sketches, he would create his own bizarre formulas and draw macabre pictures to amuse his schoolmates. Many of his creations came from an imagination that seemed to feed on images of horror and terror. For instance, he would make up

68

chemical formulas for blood, and his drawings would depict macabre scenes such as a man being struck by lightning or a human being exploding like a bomb.

His teachers were more amused than troubled by Roman's personal expressions of himself. Generally he was well-behaved, although he had a tendency, nurtured by his rather devious adolescent personality, to quietly create a disruptive situation in the classroom and then watch with silent mirth and satisfaction as other students – his foils – took the punishment for it. 'There was a hard cynical bite to his character,' one of his teachers once said, 'and a lurking combativeness that was a combination of a hyperactive nature and his self-consciousness about his small stature. The boy had had a tough time during the war, but no tougher than many of the other students. The difference was that they were stoics, accepting it as their lot in life, whereas Roman, by virtue of his superior intelligence, had refused to accept it. He would never let the world dictate his life if he could help it. One could see that he was driven by some inner force to dictate his life despite what the world tried to make it.'

Says another who knew him in Cracow at the time, 'Roman was a chameleon. That quality in him was, I believe, fostered by his experiences in acting. He quickly became an actor in real life when he was about fifteen. He could be threatening, menacing, sullen, argumentative at one time, then turn around and be sweet, sympathetic, kind and gentle at another. It was his way of getting attention and surprising people off guard. It got to be that each day Roman came to school he would come as a different character. We would laugh at his posing a lot, because we knew he was hungry for attention, but we also envied his daring and ability to give his life such variety. Purely through his talent for striking a pose he held us all in a kind of awe. He could essentially get anything he wanted, could get out of trouble or get a free magazine from a book stall, by assuming a character. We all felt that Roman was vastly different from the rest of us, and that he could accomplish something terrific if he did not get caught out for what he really was – an actor who used his talent and intelligence to manipulate the environment.'

An example of Polanski's youthful manipulative talents was recently described to me by a man who was, with Roman, a young member of the Cracow theater group. During the summer of 1949, the troupe was invited to Warsaw to participate in a festival in which various regional stage groups were to perform plays for awards and prizes. The Cracow group chose as its vehicle a Russian revolutionary melodrama that demanded a large cast of young and elderly women. The Cracow company did not have enough actresses to fill all the roles, so arrangements were made to borrow student-actresses from a Warsaw acting school for the production.

Roman was given several parts to play. Most were of the supernumerary variety, but one was a key speaking role in which he had to carry out an eight- or ten-line dialogue with a girl. The girl's role was to be cast and rehearsed after the company arrived in Warsaw; in the meantime, Roman rehearsed his part in Cracow with a man reading the girl's lines from the script.

When the company arrived in Warsaw, a group of local actresses, young and old, appeared to audition for the various female roles that were waiting to be cast. By a quirk of coincidence, the young student-actress who was given the role of the girl who would play opposite Roman in the brief but crucial scene was none other than the farm-girl named Eva who had betrayed him five years before. By then nineteen, she had made good on her dream of going to Warsaw to become an actress.

Although she had made good on her dream, Eva was not a very good actress. She had the unfortunate habit of declaiming all her lines in breathless gasps. Moreover, she had learned to memorize her lines solely from the cues provided by the last words of the lines delivered to her by whomever she was playing against.

Roman was more than slightly astonished to see who had been given the part when the full cast gathered for its first run-through. Recalling the fright and humiliation he had suffered at the hands of her father after the barn-fire in 1944, he decided to exact his revenge. His decision was made easier by the fact that Eva was an embarrassing performer and that she did not recognize him. His name was different from the name she had known him by. Besides, she was so wrapped up in her role and herself that she barely glanced at him when they were introduced.

Polanski shared his intention with several of his fellow-Cracow actors. During the first rehearsal of his scene with the girl, he had immediately noticed her dependence on the proper word-cues to deliver her lines. At the final rehearsal, Roman deftly changed the last word on two of several of his lines, causing Eva to hesitate and then verbally stumble about in search of the right line to say. The other actors who were in the scene began to snicker. The play's director, who was not aware of what Polanski was doing, called a halt and chastised Eva for being unprepared. 'Start it again,' he ordered.

This time Roman garbled the ends of a few other lines and Eva again became lost. More snickers followed and she burst into tears.

The day's rehearsal was the last chance the company had to get the play right before that evening's presentation to the public and the festival judges. The harried director called a halt and allowed Eva a minute or two to compose herself. Then, warning her that they could not spend all day on the scene and that she would have to be replaced if she muffed her lines again, he called for one last try.

The result was the same. The director was not really listening to Roman's lines because he knew the play so well. Roman transposed two or three lines of the dialogue, Eva froze, and the scene lumbered to a halt amid the giggles of the other actors. Roman's face remained set in stone as the director hurled an epithet at Eva and she once again exploded in sobs. She was dismissed and another actress was brought in to replace her. After two quick run-throughs, the new actress had the scene down perfectly and the rehearsal continued to the end of the play without any further problems.

So far as anyone knows, Eva was never again seen on the stage. Just turned sixteen, Polanski had gained a sweet revenge. To some at the time, though, it seemed excessive. 'Roman boasted about what he had done to the girl for many years

71

after,' says a man who knew him. 'At first it seemed amusing, but we couldn't understand why he carried it through to the end. There was something demoniacal in the way he completely shattered the girl. We could see, you know, inflicting a little humiliation. But we couldn't understand how he could carry it all the way through. There was something excessively cruel and perverse about it.'

Whether Eva, even today, realizes that Roman Polanski was the instrument of her failure as an actress is not known. But as another one-time friend of Polanski, a Hollywood actress, remarked to me, 'I've heard the story about the Polish actress and it's typical of Roman. Revenge is a big thing with him, and he particularly enjoys humiliating women. It doesn't matter whether they're ordinary women or actresses, he goes out of his way to invent techniques to debase them. Who knows, maybe that was how he learned to do it. Having succeeded once, it became a great ego trip for him, and he's been doing it ever since.'

By all accounts, Roman was a competent but hardly riveting actor as a youth. By the time he was seventeen, however, he realized that acting was not what he really wanted to do in the theater. In the first place, he knew that his small stature was against him: the Polish theater preferred its actors to look tall and heroic. Second, he had been directed by a number of different men and had the opportunity to observe the backstage power a strong director exercised. He had also seen the adulation such a director often received from his actors.

Thus, he began to imagine his life in terms of being a director himself. When he asked a noted teacher in Warsaw what was required to become a top stage director, he was told that he must strive for admission to the national theater school and 'you must read, you must read every great play ever written until you know them as well as you know your hands and can direct them in your imagination.'

Roman was due to complete his final year in technical school in the spring of 1950. His father had blithely assumed that afterward he would go on to a postgraduate school for advanced electronics studies. The alternative was certain conscription into the army through Poland's military draft. But during the winter of 1949-1950, Roman made it clear to his father that he had no desire for a career in electrics or electronics and instead wanted to study formally for the theater.

His father would have none of that. Until Roman reached the age of twenty-one, he was Riszard Polanski's charge and would do what Riszard Polanski told him to do. Riszard Polanski wanted him to go to a school for advanced electronics, while Roman continued to press for theater school. Eventually, another compromise was struck with the help of Raimund Polanski.

Roman's facility at drawing, Raimund pointed out, was an aptitude that the boy could exploit when he reached adulthood. Architecture, design and construction engineering were short-handed professions in postwar Poland, which had lost a large segment of its builders in the war years and was nevertheless attempting to rebuild its war-ravaged cities. The country was providing special subsidies to parents of young men and women who pursued careers in architecture and design. Roman would be doing a service to himself and the country by developing his drawing talents, argued Raimund. Once he had his certificate to be an architectural draftsman, he could then test himself in a theatrical career. If he failed, he could always fall back on his architectural qualifications. And having such qualifications could not hurt him in the theater, since the theater depended for its stage sets on people who could design and build.

As he had on many occasions earlier, Roman yielded to his uncle's persuasions. However, when he applied to one and then another of Poland's state architectural and engineering schools during the summer of 1950, he was repeatedly rejected. He would learn later that his rejections derived partly from the poor attendance records he had compiled at his technical school and other behavioral problems he had caused there. But the rejections also had something to do with the fact that he was a Jew. The Polish state board that supervised the country's architectural and engineering lycees and passed on admissions was heavily weighted with men who had collaborated during the war with the Germans in the running of Poland's building and manufacturing industries. The very lowest levels of labor used in these industries during the early stages of the Nazi occupation were Jews plucked from Poland's concentration camps – before they became mass-extermination camps. These underfed and abused Jews – most of them formerly merchants and office workers – had proved to be unwilling and unproductive physical laborers in the eyes of the Germans and their Polish collaborators. After the war, when these same collaborators found themselves functionaries of the Russian-controlled communist government, their inherent Polish anti-Semitism was heightened by their experiences under the Germans. As far as they were concerned, what remained of Poland's native Jewish population was suited only for the Jews' traditional mercantile work. Jews should be excluded from the task of rebuilding Poland and its industry. They should therefore be excluded from the state schools that had been formed to train the people who would contribute to the rebuilding.

Roman Polanski, unable to get into a state-sponsored architectural or engineering school, had to settle for a local draftsmen's academy in Cracow. If he could not aspire to become a foremost architect or construction engineer, he could at least be formally trained as a draftsman and make his contribution to Poland working in the ranks of the country's building industry.

Roman was enrolled in the drafting school in the fall of 1950. Because his father was permitted to continue in his plastics business as a private entrepreneur, rather than devoting his labors to the state, he was required to pay for his son's continuing training at the school. Roman was by then earning a small amount of money from his acting assignments. His father cut off his donations to Roman's separate room-and-board and decreed that his son, if he insisted on continuing with his theatrical activities, would have to support himself through his earnings. Riszard would only pay Roman's school tuition, which he was required to do lest he endanger his own position as a private businessman.

Roman took to his new school with considerably more enthusiasm and determination than he had to the electronics school. For one thing, the new school specialized in a talent he had already developed, and his facility at drawing made it easy for him to gain notice among the teachers. Second, the student body at the school contained a liberal sprinkling of girls. At seventeen, Roman had begun to take an interest in the opposite sex. The only trouble was, the ordinarily quick-witted, sharp-tongued young man was ill at ease with girls. Since his brief encounter with Eva in the barn seven years earlier, it is unlikely that he had had a sexual experience.

A friend from that time claims today that Polanski had been sexually traumatized by his experience with Eva. Indulging in a bit of amateur psychology, the friend says that because of the trouble Roman got into as a result of Eva, he had learned to repress the sex drive and curiosity most normal young men manifest when they reach adolescence. Why? Because he associated sex with trouble, with getting caught at something, with being betrayed. Indeed, adds the friend, Roman was a late bloomer sexually.

'Which accounts for the fact that once he eventually rid himself of his sexual repression – and this did not happen until he was well into his twenties – he went overboard on sex. He realized how inexperienced he was, and how much catching up he had to do. When most of us were taking sex for granted, he was just beginning to learn of its delights. Until he was in his twenties, he was sexually retarded. He was tremendously shy and wary of girls in school. He would talk a lot about them, but when he was around them he would be timid, almost moronic.'

INTERLOG 3

It was late in the evening of Thursday, 10 March 1977, when the mother of the thirteen-year-old girl made her call to the police. At first she had called the Woodland Hills police department. But since the crimes she was alleging had taken place on Mulholland Drive in Los Angeles, they referred her to the West Los Angeles Division of the LAPD. When she reached the West Los Angeles Division, her call was transferred to Detective Sergeant Peter Vanatter.

Vanatter listened, detached, as the woman on the other end of the line indignantly poured out her story. A seasoned cop, he was accustomed to female indignation and the way it so often got in the way of the facts. As he absently took notes, he asked the woman to slow down. Only when he heard the name Roman Polanski did the bored expression in his eyes change. 'I'd better come out and see you,' he said to the woman.

Vanatter drove to Woodland Hills. After speaking with the woman and her boyfriend, he interviewed the girl. He immediately formed the impression that the youngster, although she looked a year-or-two older than her age, 'was not really knowledgeable.' He winced a bit as he listened to the girl recount in confused bits and pieces what had happened at the Nicholson house that afternoon. He had seen lots of girls her age – runaways – cruising the Sunset Strip and being picked up for prostitution and drug trafficking. Such girls, though immature, knew what they were about. This girl, unless she was putting on a terrific act, did not seem the type. Vanatter doubted that it was an act. Most kids her age, especially girls, tended to be intimidated by cops. When they lied, it quickly became apparent through their voices and gestures.

But Vanatter knew that he would need more than the girl's story to take the action her mother demanded. The first rule in such cases was to start compiling physical and eyewitness evidence. Vanatter had no way of knowing that when he arrested Polanski the next evening, the director would make it easier by conceding that he had had sex with the girl.

Following the standard procedure, the sergeant took the girl and her mother to Los Angeles's Parkwood Hospital, which had a rape-victim unit that was regularly used by police to secure physical evidence. There the girl, under questioning by a doctor, admitted to having had two prior sexual experiences – both of her own volition with her boyfriend and the last one a few weeks earlier.

Although the girl's mother expressed what Vanatter viewed as phony shock when she heard this, he was not surprised. The age at which Los Angeles kids began experimenting with sex was growing younger and younger. The girl was no different from thousands of others, except that she was more physically appealing than most. Which probably had made the pressures on her from boys to start engaging in sex even greater. Actually, if it was true that she had only had sex twice before, she was below the norm. He doubted that she would willingly have intercourse with a man in his forties.

After describing to the physician what had happened to her during her afternoon with Polanski, the girl was given a physical and gynecological examination. The exam revealed minor bruising at the girl's anus. Vaginal and anal slides were taken. These tested negative for the presence of semen, according to the later lab report. But an analysis of the panties the girl said she had worn after her encounter with Polanski showed strong traces of semen.

'There, you see?' the girl's mother triumphantly crowed when the news of the panties came down from the lab.

Vanatter nodded, but the finding troubled him. He knew that if it was used as evidence in a later legal proceeding, it could easily be attacked – especially since the girl had admitted to having had sexual intercourse a few weeks before. The girl had not been wearing the panties when he had first interviewed her in the living room at her home. He had asked her to get them for him so that he could take them to the hospital for analysis. She had disappeared into her bedroom and returned with them. Although she had insisted that they were the panties she wore that afternoon, there was no way of proving it. Others might claim that the last time she had worn them was after her previous sexual encounter. Or that they were not hers at all, but belonged to her older sister or to someone else who had recently had sex.

The presence of semen on the panties, then, was not enough evidence to support an arrest. Vanatter would have to determine by independent means that Polanski had been alone with the girl in the bedroom at the Nicholson house at the time of the alleged drugging and sexual violation. It would help in addition to be able to provide independent evidence that Polanski knew the girl's age.

The girl's mother had already insisted that the Polish director was aware of her daughter's age. She had told Vanatter that she had been surprised at Polanski's initial photographic interest in the girl when she had earlier been led to believe that his feature for *Vogue Homme* was to involve only girls of about ten. From their various discussions about age, she had said, she was one-hundred per cent sure that Polanski knew how old her daughter was.

When Vanatter had asked the girl about witnesses, she mentioned the episode with Anjelica Huston. She also recalled seeing a woman neighbor when she had first arrived at the Nicholson residence with Polanski. The woman had had keys to the house, and it was she who had let them in.

Vanatter returned the girl and her mother to their home after the hospital visit and told the mother that he would be in touch with her the next day. The following morning he made his way to the Mulholland Drive compound and encountered Helena Kallianiotes.

Without telling her specifically why he was there, Vanatter drew from Kallianiotes corroboration of the fact that she had been present when Polanski arrived with the girl at the Nicholson house the day before.

'And then what happened?'

'Well, he asked to be let in, so I let him in.'

'And the girl?'

'She went in too,' said Kallianiotes, looking at Vanatter as though his question was too dumb to warrant a response. The sergeant noticed for the first time that she had a tattoo on her left shoulder.

Kallianiotes described the girl. Then Vanatter asked if she had seen Polanski and the girl drinking champagne.

'I don't know about the girl,' she answered brusquely. 'But Mr Polanski had some.' She added that she had shown him where the champagne was, and had even had a sip herself before she left them alone in the house.

In his best Colombo style, Vanatter asked Mrs Kallianiotes to accompany him across the compound to the Nicholson house. There he met Anjelica Huston, the angular, dark-haired young woman who, in his eyes, was not compellingly attractive – certainly not the type he imagined Jack Nicholson to be involved with. He thought Nicholson would be more apt to hanker after buxom-blond types.

Vanatter saw, after his first two or three questions, that Anjelica Huston was not going to provide him with any more useful information than that Polanski had been there the day before. The way Huston kept nervously glancing at Mrs Kallianiotes told more than she was withholding, however. Which led Vanatter, when he reported the results of his investigation to the District Attorney's office later that morning, to request a search warrant for the Nicholson house as well as arrest and search warrants for Polanski. He was convinced that he now had a prosecutable case.

Based on the formal complaint of the thirteen-year-old girl's mother, an assistant district attorney dug into the California penal code and came up with six separate felony charges against Polanski, on the basis of which he went into court and asked for warrants. Later that afternoon the warrants were issued and handed to Vanatter and three other detectives to execute. While Vanatter and one of the detectives went to the Beverly Wilshire Hotel later Friday afternoon to track down Polanski, the other two headed for the Nicholson house on Mulholland Drive.

The two officers sent to Nicholson's confronted a stunned Anjelica Huston as she was about to leave the house. When they presented themselves to her in the driveway, she testily complained that she had already been questioned by a detective earlier in the day and saw no reason for the return visit. She was in a rush to get somewhere, she insisted, and had no time to answer further questions.

When the detective announced that they were there to talk about Roman Polanski, she responded that what Roman Polanski did was none of her business.

'Sorry,' said the other detective, 'but I'm afraid it is your business.' Patiently he explained that Polanski had been charged with a series of crimes that were alleged to have been committed inside the house. 'If they were in fact done in your house, then it very definitely is your business, M'am.'

'But this isn't my house,' Anjelica shot back with a hint of rebellious triumph in her voice. 'The house belongs to Jack Nicholson.'

'But you live here?' said the first detective.

Anjelica would only say that she was staying there – that most of the time she lived abroad.

'Isn't it a fact, though, that you were in the house yesterday afternoon when Roman Polanski was here?'

Anjelica started to say she had only arrived home the day

before to find Polanski there. She quickly swallowed her words, however, and haughtily insisted that she was under no obligation to answer questions.

'Is Mr Nicholson still in Colorado?' the other detective inquired.

'Yes,' Anjelica said. 'I just spoke with him on the phone.'

'And did you inform him that you had a visit earlier today from a police officer?'

'No,' she replied. 'I didn't think it was that important.' Actually she had complained on the phone to Nicholson about his friend Polanski using the house and had indicated that she thought Roman might be in trouble.

'Well, Miss Huston,' said the first detective as he withdrew a sheaf of documents from his pocket, 'we have a court-authorized search warrant here and we're going to have to ask you to step inside.'

Once in the house, Anjelica Huston hid her nervousness with defiance. 'Where do you want to start?' she challenged.

'Why don't we start with your handbag?' the first detective said, masking his smile.

'My bag?' exclaimed Huston. 'You mean you want to search me?'

'That's the idea,' the detective replied laconically. He waved the warrant in front of her. 'That's what it says here.'

Half an hour later, when the two officers had completed their sweep of the house and Anjelica Huston's belongings, they informed her that she was under arrest for the possession of illegal drugs. In her handbag they had found a small quantity of cocaine. In her bedroom dresser they had come upon a brick of hashish.

As far as cementing his case against Polanski was concerned, Sergeant Vanatter's hunch about Anjelica Huston had proved a fruitful one.

In the meantime, Vanatter and his partner had confronted Polanski in the lobby of the Beverly Wilshire and arrested him. Polanski was incredulous. 'What do you mean, I haven't done anything, what do you mean, this is a mistake, what do you mean . . . ' Polanski shouted, oblivious of passersby in the lobby. When Vanatter suggested they move to an unoccupied corner of the lobby for the obligatory frisk, Polanski became even more heated. Vanatter hushed him, warning him that he was drawing a crowd. The detective reminded him that 'anything he said could be used against him.' Polanski still refused to be quiet. 'So I fucked a chick,' he exclaimed. 'So what?'

Vanatter and his partner forcibly hustled Polanski to a corner of the lobby. While they frisked him, the Pole continued to protest. The girl had willingly gone to bed with him, he insisted. Why should he get into trouble for giving in to a girl.

On their way to the corner, Polanski had tried to get rid of the tablet in his pocket. Vanatter's partner had spotted it and picked it up. 'What's this,' he said to Polanski. The director spluttered, embarrassed at being caught.

Vanatter had done some tedious, unrewarding gumshoe work during the Sharon Tate murder case eight years before. He had never met Polanski, but had heard about him from veteran detectives who had worked on the Tate and Manson cases. He had arrived at the Beverly Wilshire prepared to dislike the Pole. But now, as he faced him in the hotel lobby, he felt an odd compassion for him. 'The guy was genuinely astonished. He started talking a blue streak. I tried to shut him up. I told him that anything he said I might have to testify to, if there was a hearing or trial. But he wouldn't listen. He had no idea of what being arrested in America meant.'

Polanski's protests immediately convinced Vanatter that the director knew why he was being arrested. 'He didn't agree with it, but he knew what it was all about. The more he talked, the more he admitted to the crimes he'd been charged with. I mean, he readily conceded that he had been with the girl, had screwed her, had known she was a minor. The only thing he refused to admit was giving her dope. I asked him about it, going back to the station house in the car. He was wary on the dope thing. But he had no hesitation talking about the sex. He just couldn't understand why screwing a kid should be of concern to anyone.

He'd screwed plenty of girls younger than this one, he said, and nobody gave a damn.'

When they got to the West Los Angeles police station, Polanski feverishly continued to proclaim his innocence. 'The more he talked, the more he dug himself into a hole. I kept warning him that I'd probably have to testify as to his statements. But he didn't get it. He thought he could talk me into letting him go. It was all a big mistake, he said. He kept insisting that the girl had been willing. For all I knew, that could have been true. At least, Polanski was very convincing about it. But the fact remained that she was thirteen. *That* was his problem. But he couldn't see it.'

Despite his momentary pity for Polanski, Vanatter felt secure in the knowledge that he was putting together a solid case against him. The district attorney's office was always complaining that police detectives were deficient in gathering sufficient hard evidence and witnesses to make successfully prosecutable cases. This time, Vanatter thought, there would be no cause for complaints.

While Polanski was being fingerprinted and photographed, Vanatter related what had happened at the Beverly Wilshire to the assistant district attorney who had been involved in obtaining the arrest and search warrants. The young assistant winked at him. 'This should be a fun case,' he said. 'We should all get some good ink out of it.'

'You seem pretty confident,' Vanatter said.

'Haven't you heard?'

'What?'

'My God, man, it was your idea. Your ploy worked. The boys just brought in the Huston girl. They caught her with coke and hash. She's on her way over to the court now with her lawyer. We're going to talk to them after she's arraigned. Do a little bargaining.'

After being 'printed', Polanski was allowed the traditional phone call to summon a lawyer. The director began to argue vehemently that he didn't need a lawyer because he hadn't done anything wrong. Another detective was called in who had worked on the Sharon Tate case eight years before and knew Polanski. He patiently listened to Polanski's protests for a few minutes, then cut him off, reminding him that he was under arrest.

'Complaining to the cops' was not going to do him any good, the detective later recalled telling Polanski. 'I had to explain to him several times that once arrested, he could not be 'un-arrested'. That no matter how much he claimed innocence, he was going to need a lawyer since his case would be going into the court system. And that if he didn't get his own lawyer, the court would appoint one. I asked him if he wanted to spend the night in jail, maybe the next few weeks. He said no. So I told him if he didn't, he'd better get a lawyer. Otherwise he might not be able to obtain a release on bail or recognizance when he was brought into court for the arraignment. My impression was that Polanski was embarrassed about having to call a lawyer. A couple of police reporters were at the station when he was brought in. They recognized him and were pestering us for information. He had heard the clamor. He was obviously worried about the publicity he was about to receive, because he kept saying to me, 'This is going to ruin me, this is going to ruin me'. I said, 'Hell, Roman, you're only charged, you're not convicted'. I told him if he wanted any chance at getting out of it, he would definitely have to have a good lawyer. So then he asked me to recommend a lawyer – again, I think he was embarrassed about having to call friends, tell them what happened, ask them to find him a lawyer. It was as though – well, if he didn't make the phone call, the whole thing would go no farther . . . as though everybody would realize eventually that it was all a big mistake and he'd be allowed to go home.'

It took an hour of further argument to finally persuade Polanski to start phoning for a lawyer. Six calls later he located a friend and told him what was happening. The friend promised to have a lawyer on hand as soon as possible.

The attorney who showed up half an hour later would prove to be only a temporary stopgap, as criminal law was not his speciality. He knew enough, though, to be appalled when he learned of what Polanski had already spontaneously conceded to the police. All he could do was counsel the frantic director to keep his mouth shut and argue with the assistant district attorney over the question of bail.

When Polanski was led into the West Los Angeles Municipal Court at around midnight for a preliminary hearing on the arrest charges, he was astonished to see Anjelica Huston leaving. She was in the company of several men, among whom were her lawyer and Sergeant Vanatter. Vanatter had a few words with the lawyer in the hallway, making arrangements for a meeting the following Monday to discuss the Polanski case. Then he returned to the courtroom.

Polanski, his eyes wide with alarm, shrilly stagewhispered. 'What is she here for?'

'I can tell you this,' Vanatter replied. 'She isn't here to make bail for you.'

Because of Polanski's celebrity, a high-level prosecutor from the district attorney's office – deputy D.A. Roger Gunson – had been summoned from his home to represent prosecution in the preliminary hearing. After hastily conferring with Vanatter, Gunson called him to the stand to describe his investigation of the charges lodged by the alleged victim's mother the day before and to repeat some of the statements Polanski had made upon his arrest. He then called Vanatter's partner, who corroborated Vanatter's testimony.

'Your honor,' said the prosecutor, addressing the magistrate after eliciting the statements of the policemen, 'it is the state's contention that defendant Polanski committed all of the crimes as charged. At the moment the state feels that it is advisable that defendant be held only on the count of rape, or unlawful sexual intercourse. There is a thirteen-year-old involved here, and the state believes that her life and state-of-mind could be irreparably harmed by exposure to an open hearing such as this. We have the arresting officers' testimony that defendant was in fact in the bedroom with the victim, did in fact have sexual intercourse with her, was in fact aware of her age. And that the victim was forced to submit to defendant against her will. Now, the state feels it is incumbent upon it to protect the identity and innocence of this victim, to shield her from the glare of the media publicity that is bound to be generated by this case because of the notoriety of the defendant. The state therefore moves that defendant be preliminarily arraigned on the single count of rape, or unlawful sexual intercourse, pending an airing of all charges in the warrant through a grand jury investigation, which the state proposes to conduct immediately. Only by a grand jury probe can all the facts and evidence in this case fairly be developed, and at the same time the victim's identity be protected.'

The magistrate temporarily reserved decision on the D.A.'s motion and asked Polanski's lawyer if he had a case to present. The attorney, after conferring with Polanski, said that his client had nothing to say but to express his innocence of all the charges, and his confidence that a grand jury would absolve him of any guilt in the matter.

The magistrate thereupon granted the prosecutor's motion and held the case over pending the findings of a grand jury.

Polanski, misunderstanding the colloquy between the magistrate and the two lawyers, was suddenly elated. He thought he was about to be freed. His elation was quickly punctured, however, when the discussion at the bench turned to bail.

The district attorney made the obligatory pitch for no bail, arguing that the crimes with which Polanski was charged called for up to fifty years in prison, if he was convicted, and pointed out that Polanski was a foreign national with no allegiance to America or to the California system of justice.

Polanski's attorney countered by saying that his client was presently under contract to a major Hollywood movie company to direct three motion pictures, that his livelihood depended on his American employment, and that he was so confident of vindication that he would never consider fleeing the jurisdiction of California. He referred to Polanski's involvement with the Los Angeles police and district attorney's office, 'during the investigation of the tragic murder of his wife in 1969 and 1970,' and assured the magistrate that his client had every reason to believe that 'these law-enforcement agencies are motivated to treat him with fairness and justice and will eventually exonerate him of the distasteful offenses he has been charged with.'

After further haggling, the magistrate set Polanski's bail at $2500. The lawyer arranged for a bondsman to put up the bail, and Polanski was released on the proviso that he remain within the immediate reach of the court pending the findings of the grand jury.

It was now 'The People of California, Plaintiff, vs. Roman Polanski, Defendant.' As they left the courtroom in the early morning hours of Saturday, 12 March 1977, Polanski said to the attorney, 'What do I do now?'

'They're out to fry your ass,' answered the lawyer. 'What you do now is find an attorney who can get you out of this mess.'

CHAPTER 4

IN HIS first term at the drafting school Polanski did well, impressing his instructors with his talent for realistic, detailed drawing and dismaying them only when, during an occasional exercise in a life class, he would grotesquely distort the subject so that it was not only unidentifiable but fiendishly macabre.

Recalled one of his teachers in 1968 when talking to a European film quarterly, 'He took a certain childish glee in turning what was supposed to be a still-life of apples, pears and flowers into a collection of gruesome, surrealistic animals, crushed and gushing with blood . . . Or a nude into a human figure without skin, just a collection of bloody organs spilling like Dali watches into a puddle of scarlet ooze, with figures of strange, emaciated dogs lapping up the blood. Where he got his ideas I don't know.

'There was always something sly and devious about the boy . . . . He had a clear talent for drawing and color, but he refused to follow the main stream. We were trying to turn out artists and draftsmen for the state so that the state would give us more money to expand the school . . . It became evident early in his stay with us that Roman had no interest in our needs. He had a genius that was solely devoted to upsetting the status quo and in some mysterious way gratifying his own needs. We thought at first that he engaged in this bizarre behavior in order to get himself expelled from the school. But then it became clear that he was content to be there . . . He just enjoyed being different, like some of the actors he associated with. He scoffed at rules, but always obeyed them except when he could circumvent them without being detected. Yes, now that I think of it, I would say that much of his behavioral deviation came from the influence of his actor friends.

'In many ways, Roman was without direction, squandering his talents and opportunities solely for the sake of being different and getting the momentary approval of his classmates. But on the other hand he had a singleminded self-direction and self-discipline. Often it was compulsive and childish and impenetrable to the rest of us. But it was there. It was like an invisible band of iron that ran through his being.'

By the fall of 1950, the Soviet Union had forged neighboring Poland into its primary communist satellite. The Cold War was in full bloom and the Russo-Polish authorities had sealed off Poland from just about all Western, and particularly American, cultural influences.

At seventeen, Polanski had been thoroughly steeped in communist dogma after his four years at the technical school. His exposure would continue at drawing school. Hardly any academic course was presented that didn't have a daily reminder of its relationship to communist doctrine and ideals. In the beginning stages of his education, Polanski had responded eagerly to the indoctrination. As he was later to say, 'The communists were the saviors of Poland from the Nazis. We were all so grateful that we were willing to do anything in the service of communism.'

Part of Roman's continuing rift with his father stemmed from his adolescent devotion to communist ideology. He frequently criticized his father for his continuing pursuit of 'private initiative'. Not only did his father's private-enterprise activities expose Roman to ridicule among his schoolmates and teachers, they were contradictory to strict communist policy.

89

Roman was thus developing into a model communist youth, his potential marred only by his blood tie to his father, as he entered the drafting school in the fall of 1950.

His fervor for communist doctrine and the communist way of life would soon begin to change, however.

The seeds of the change had already been sown during the summer of 1950, when Roman made his second acting trip to Warsaw. Although Poland had shut most of its population off from foreign cultural influences, the country allowed its intelligentsia a limited exposure to Western arts. This was done in the hope of improving the quality of the Polish art, particularly theater and motion pictures. The Leninist dictum that cinema, and secondarily theater, could be powerful weapons in the spread of communist ideology continued to be taken seriously by the Polish authorities.

The immediate postwar period of communist entrenchment was over, however, and the populace was growing bored with the endless round of bleak, simplistic war-inspired stage and film productions. What Poland's stage and film creators needed was some exposure to Western examples of dramatic and comedic writing, stage production and film-making. Not, certainly, for the political and cultural values of Western life they reflected, but for their advanced technical qualities.

As a consequence of this policy decision, the production of Western plays and the showing of Western films, on a severely limited basis, were allowed in Poland's major cities starting in 1949. The plays and films were carefully screened so that only those that reflected or could be related to the evils of Western capitalistic life were permitted. The first films were limited to those of the postwar communist, realist Italian school – films such as *The Bicycle Thief,* which were made as much to foment leftist political sentiment in Western Europe as to entertain. Later, selected French, British and American films would be permitted, but solely those that pictured or satirized the darker sides of the cultures.

As with films, certain Western plays were allowed to be staged by Poland's big-city theatrical companies. Translated into Polish, many of the plays by Shakespeare, bowdlerized to conform to communist notions of the evils of aristocracy and the class system, soon became popular theatrical fare. And even American plays, such as Arthur Miller's *All My Sons* and *Death of a Salesman,* both of which could easily be contorted to serve as damning indictments of American culture, gained favor.

During his visit to Warsaw for the theatrical festival in the summer of 1950, Roman Polanski had his first exposure to Western stage literature. This was in the form of a production of *Macbeth,* put on by Warsaw's National Theater. Another company staged a Polish version of *King Lear,* emphasizing the greed and avariciousness of the royal daughters and turning the Shakespeare classic into a vehicle of state propaganda.

That Roman's Cracow troupe was still mounting turgid postwar native dramas probably doubled the impact the Shakespearian plays had on him. Somehow he was able to peer beneath the state-distorted exteriors of the dramas and perceive a breadth of tumultuous human spirit, however dark and twisted, that others in the festival audiences missed. These two productions made a lasting impression on him, confirming once and for all the power of the theater to hypnotize an audience. They confirmed even more the power of a theatrical director to impose his influence and vision on a group of people. Rushing backstage after the *Macbeth* production to congratulate an actor he knew, he was mesmerized by the way the performers, emotionally drained, fawned over the play's director.

The actor he knew was Zbigniew Cybulski, a native of Cracow who was only six years older than Polanski but on his way to becoming one of Poland's most popular performers. As an actor in Cracow, Cybulski had always been haughty and remote with his fellow actors. To see him embracing the director of *Macbeth* cemented Roman's notion that directing was the noblest of theatrical pursuits. Harking back to what he had been told the year before – 'You must read . . . ' – he went out into the book shops of Warsaw in search of printed plays.

But plays were not the only things that left a sharp impression on Roman in Warsaw that summer. Approved Western films had begun to be shown in the Polish capital the previous fall.

For the first time actors visiting from the hinterlands had a chance to see them, and they soon wore paths to the two or three Warsaw movie houses that screened them with Polish subtitles.

Mostly Italian, these films opened up a whole new world to Roman Polanski. Raised on a diet of German, then Russian, propaganda films, his fascination with cinematic story-telling remained as firm as ever. But it was heightened by what he perceived to be the far more sophisticated use of the motion-picture camera in telling the stories he was watching. Instead of great blocks of time in which the camera remained motionless while a series of events unfolded across the field of its lens, in these modern movies the camera became part of the action, moving in strange new curves and angles, and functioning much more as the central narrative device than in any of the films he had previously seen. When he left Warsaw that summer, he ached to get his hands on a motion picture camera.

Despite his erratic behavior during his first year at drafting school, Roman was chosen to be a member of a group of Polish art and engineering students sent to Vienna in the summer of 1951 for a tour of the Austrian capital's museums and architectural monuments. Vienna had, until shortly before, been under partial postwar Russian control. One of the conditions of the recent Russian withdrawal was a continuing link between the communist-bloc countries and the eastern region of Austria that adjoined several of them. Vienna was the hub of this region.

By the time the group of Polish students arrived in the city, Vienna had shaken off many of the dour effects of the postwar Soviet occupation and was once again taking up its traditional Western European ways. Roman's three-week stay was his first personal exposure to anything even remotely Western. He was captivated, particularly by the theatrical and movie experiences open to him. With a fellow student, Stanislaus Syzmanski, he managed on several occasions to slip away from the group to spend long hours in darkened cinemas watching the latest in the American movies that were so popular in Vienna.

Roman also managed to take advantage of Vienna's postwar

hedonistic atmosphere to have his first adult sexual experiences. He once told a writer for *Cosmopolitan* magazine, with 'gestures and grand-opera delivery,' of the sexual side of his trip to Vienna. ' . . . I was very, very young and naïve, this was in Vienna. I met this mad Viennese promotor who took me out one night with a man I call 'The King of the Laundry,' as he controlled all the laundromats . . . We go to nightclub, which was once ornate old opera house, the dancing girls were available, and at the end of the evening The King of the Laundry makes arrangements for me, and I find myself with tall girl, upstairs in one of the old theater boxes, the drapes of it drawn, the orchestra still playing below. She orders champagne, then washes herself with it, then washes *me* with it! Incredible! Abruptly, the King of the Laundry comes in, draws open the drapes so that all could see, and begins to throw money, great wads of it, large bills, in an elegant slow shower, down to the performing musicians . . . ' *

The tale sounded like one of Polanski's later movie scenes, one that he might have discarded from a script. According to several of his intimates, nothing of the sort ever happened to him in Vienna or anywhere else.

It is likely, though, according to a friend, that during his trip to Vienna he did engage in one or more sexual liaisons with a local showgirl doubling as a prostitute, and that he later chose to fantasize the experience in film-scenario terms.

One childhood friend remembers him returning to Cracow and art school boasting of his sexual conquests in Vienna. 'Polanski was never a great teller of the truth. We knew him as a boy who would make up stories to inflate his own self-importance or to get out of some difficulty. So initially we didn't believe his 'tales of the Vienna woods.' But after he was back for a while we noticed that he was much more daring and brazen with the girls of Cracow. And with some results – they seemed to like his cocky manner with them. So then we concluded that maybe his stories about Vienna were true. Where else would he have learned to deal with women, get what

---

* *Cosmopolitan,* March, 1975.

he wanted from women, in so short a time? Remember that in Cracow in those days it was taught that promiscuity was against state policy. Girls were taught that casual sexual or romantic affairs were taboo unless they were meant to lead to marriage and the production of more children who would grow into workers for the state. As a consequence, Polish girls in the late Forties and early Fifties were very chaste. And as a consequence of that, most boys our age had little or no sexual experience. But suddenly Polanski becomes somebody different. He knew how to approach girls to get what he wanted. So where we at first laughed at his stories about Vienna, we were soon envying him.'

It would not be accurate to say that Polanski discovered the pleasures of indiscriminate and uncommitted sex at the very same time in his life that he discovered the attractions of Western living and Western movie-making. Aside from sex, no one can remember him talking about anything else upon his return from Vienna but his new-found dream of becoming a movie-maker, preferably in the West. It was under the influence of this dream that his personality began to change just after he turned eighteen in the fall of 1951.

Polanski nurtured his dream by keeping it a secret from his father, but few others. During the winter of 1951-52 he continued to act at night while attending school during the day. But his ardor for the theater had subsided markedly. It was replaced by a passion for cinema – not just going to films but talking about them, about the enormously rich variety of films and film-making techniques there were to be seen and experienced beyond Poland's provincial borders. Back in the drab, grainy atmosphere of Cracow, his choice of cinema experience was once again severely limited by government edict. He began to resent the communism of Poland and to lose faith in communism in general for what he now viewed as its excessively paternalistic and spiritually suffocating treatment of the populace. By denying people a wider variety of experience and entertainment, he argued to schoolmates, communism would soon become a prisoner of itself.

Polanski's youthful heresies did not go unremarked by the authorities. Early in 1952, after spreading his enthusiasm for Western films among Cracow's theatrical groups, he was offered a major boy's part in an industrial film to be directed by a member of a rival group. The director had seen Polanski play a similar role on stage and felt that his elfin face would project strongly on screen. The part was that of the son of a factory manager anxious to follow patriotically in his father's footsteps.

Polanski was eager to play the role. There would be no pay, and the ideology the film espoused was no longer appealing, but these aspects of the project did not matter. It was a chance for him to get on a film set and learn first-hand how movies were made, as well as appear in a plum part.

The only trouble was that the film was to be made on location at Breslau, the industrial city on the Oder River, 150 miles north-east of Cracow, which had been renamed Wroclaw after the war. When Polanski applied for a permit to travel to Breslau, it was denied on the ground that he had been creating dissidence and dissension within his school and the local theatrical community by his anti-state, pro-Western remarks.

Polanski was crestfallen. When appeals on his behalf by the film's director were rejected, he grew bitter. But he suffered in silence. He had already begun to think about applying, after his graduation from the drafting school, for admission to Poland's national film school at Lodz. There, he had learned, students were allowed to study a wide variety of international films – the only place in Poland that provided such an opportunity. Thousands applied each year, mostly for that reason, but few were accepted. As a veteran radio and stage actor, he had good qualifications for admission. But, he had been warned, unless he put a rein on his outspokenness he was sure to be rejected. Poland was not in the business of training film artists who publicly disagreed with state policy or national ideology.

'It was at this time that I first began to think about one day getting out of Poland,' Polanski told me in London, at a club called Tramps, in 1975. 'And then, what had only been a thought turned into a dream.'

95

INTERLOG 4

LIKE MOST people who knew Polanski, I learned of his arrest the following Sunday, 13 March 1977. We glanced at our thick Sunday newspapers to see the news of it emblazoned across the front pages.

Roman Polanski Nabbed On Sex Charge

Accused of Drugging, Raping Minor

read the headline in one paper. The story beneath was infused with an undertone of moral outrage. It went heavy on the child molesting, sodomy and oral copulation portions of the charges. It underlined the fact that Polanski had drugged and assaulted the unidentified thirteen-year-old girl at the home of Jack Nicholson. Although it added that Nicholson had not been there when the crimes were committed, it mentioned that his girlfriend, Anjelica Huston, had been arrested in connection with the case, hinting that she may have been involved in the thirteen-year-old's sexual violation. 'Polanski faces up to fifty years in prison if convicted,' the report concluded ominously.

The story was immediately picked up and wired across the world. The press liked nothing better than a good Hollywood sex scandal. Since Polanski was already notorious for his life of

96

Arriving in New York for the first time, October 1963. The occasion was the
New York Film Festival's showing of *Knife in the Water*. *(Wide World)*

With actress Jill St. John in 1966. *(Wide World)*

At the Playboy Club in London, 1972. *(Gamma-Liaison)*

In the south of France during the summer after his flight from the U.S. (*Gamma-Liaison*)

A snowless Christmas ski holiday at Gstaad, Switzerland, 1971. The man on the right is Polanski's screenwriting pal, Gerard Brach. (*Gamma-Liaison*)

At a New Year's Eve party in Paris,
January 1, 1980. (*Gamma-Liaison*)

With two young girlfriends at the nightclub *Regine's* in Paris, Christmas
1978. (*Gamma-Liaison*)

On a brief hiatus in St. Tropez after his arrest in Los Angeles. *(Gamma-Liaison)*

The day after his
arrival in Paris
following his escape
from Los Angeles,
February 1978.
*(Girani-Pietrangeli/
Gamma-Liaison)*

(Peter Borsari/camera 5)

His marriage to Sharon Tate, London, January 1968. (*Wide World*)

Sharon Tate before her marriage to Polanski, 1967. (*National Film Archive/Stills Library*)

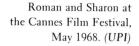

Roman and Sharon at the Cannes Film Festival, May 1968. (*UPI*)

Slot car racing at Polanski's London house, 1968. Sharon Tate is on Polanski's left. The man on his right is Sharon's former lover, and soon to be co-victim, Jay Sebring. (*Gamma-Liaison*)

Polanski posing at the entrance of the death house for *Life* magazine a week after the slaughter. He charged *Life* $5000 for this picture. *(Julian Wasser, Life Magazine, © 1969, Time Inc.)*

Polanski breaks down at Sharon's funeral. The women to the right of him are Sharon's mother and youngest sister. *(Wide World)*

An aerial view of 10050 Cielo Drive the morning the murders were discovered. (*Wide World*)

The infamous murderers
Above: Their leader, Charles Manson

From top to bottom:
Susan Atkins, Patricia Van Houten
Linda Kasabian, Patricia Krenwinkle

(*Wide World*)

Judge Rittenband castigates Polanski to reporters a week after Roman fled the country. (*Wide World*)

With attorney Douglas Dalton after guilty plea, August 9, 1977. (*Wide World*)

The famous photo of Polanski enjoying himself in Munich when, Judge Rittenband thought, he was slaving away at *Hurricane* in the South Pacific. (*UPI*)

Vith his star at the Paris premiere of *Tess*, October 1979. (**Wide World**)

With Natassia Kinski at the May 1979 Cannes Press Conference. (*Wide World*)

The fifteen-year-old Natassia Kinski and Polanski after Polanski's 1977 arrest. (*Tourte/Gamma-Liaison*)

Polanski directing *Knife in the Water*, 1963. *(National Film Ar-
chive/Stills Library)*

In Poland, 1962. *(The Museum of Modern Art/Film Stills Archive)*

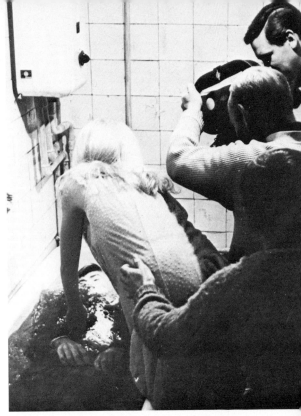

Polanski positions Catherine Deneuve for the gruesome murder scene in *Repulsion*, London, 1965. (*National Film Archive/Stills Library*)

Members of the cast of *The Fearless Vampire Killers* take a break from filming. Sharon Tate is in foreground. (*Hatami/Gamma-Liaison*)

sex and drugs, for the vividly remembered Sharon Tate slaughter, and for his sexually bizarre movies, this one looked like it was going to be an especially juicy one. Reporters began flying into Los Angeles from all over the globe.

The initial media reports were designed to shock. But few people who knew Polanski were even surprised. Just curious to know if it was really true. Phones were ringing that Sunday morning all over Hollywood. 'The kind of life Roman leads,' said one friend, 'this was bound to happen.' Said another, 'I don't know if he has a special thing for young girls or not, but he has a thing for females, period. He subscribes to a punching-bag theory of women. They're put on this earth for only one reason. Which is to satisfy Roman Polanski.'

But a thirteen-year-old girl?

'She isn't the first,' a woman who knew Polanski well in England exclaimed to me. 'That British-American society and showbiz crowd he hangs out with in London has a big thing about young girls. I've actually heard some of those chaps compare notes on who has had the youngest. And when they find what they consider to be a really good one, it's a matter of honor that they pass her around among themselves. To think I have a twelve-year-old daughter. And to think I once left her alone with Roman.'

I was well acquainted with the male circle the woman was talking about. I had always wondered why so many of its members were almost exclusively involved with young girls. I put the question to another woman who I knew existed on the fringes of the circle. 'These middle-aged men are so sexually jaded,' she said. 'They've spent their lifetimes in sexual over-indulgence, so they can no longer relate sexually to ordinary women – their wives, mistresses, their age, what have you.'

Another friend of Polanski's confirmed the movie director's previous interest in young girls but ascribed it to other causes. 'Roman and many of his male friends are in their forties and fifties. They are traditional European chauvinists to the Nth degree. They are basically frightened by mature women because of the hints of their own mothers they see in them. And they are more frightened of them than ever today, when so many women

97

are much more sexually liberated and aggressive and given to unashamedly expressing or demanding their own sexual needs and desires. Even more threatening, expressing themselves critically about the men's sexual abilities. This is why they've gone in so heavily for Quaaludes and other such tranquilizers. A few years ago the word got around that Quaaludes allowed a man to "perform" much longer than most men are accustomed to. Of course, that's a lot of hogwash, but a lot of these men still hang on to that belief. But when they finally realize it's not true – well, that's when they start going for the kids. Young girls who've had little or no sexual experience and who aren't likely to have great expectations or make denigrating comparisons or otherwise hassle them about their abilities.'

Dozens of others who have at one time or another been close to Polanski failed to be surprised at his arrest and the criminal charges leveled at him. But they credited his troubles to more complex causes, ranging from his war-ravaged childhood in Nazi-occupied Poland to an adult life that has been repeatedly marred by tragedy beyond his own making.

There were also those who excused and defended Polanski in his latest imbroglio. 'The arrest was a set-up,' declared one friend in Hollywood who claimed to know the inside story. 'Roman wouldn't knowingly touch a kid. It's the girl's mother. She had the hots for Roman for a year or more and was trying to use him to get into films as an actress. When Roman failed to live up to certain promises the woman fantasized she had gotten Roman to make, she decided to strike back. And she used her unwitting daughter to do it.'

That theory was exploded a few weeks after Polanski's arrest, when he publicly conceded that he had indeed had sexual intercourse with the girl and had given her a Quaalude prior to it. Nor did other friends' explanations that Polanski did not know the girl was thirteen survive the facts: Polanski readily admitted to the press that he had been aware of the girl's age when he imposed himself on her.

What was left to say, then, in the film director's defense? The standard explanation for a while became that the girl herself, mature beyond her years, had enticed Polanski into bed either on the instructions of a vengeful mother or on her own initiative, perhaps in the hope of getting the director to cast her in his next movie. It was an explanation that Polanski did nothing to publicly or privately discourage, although secret grand-jury testimony and a later court-ordered psychiatric examination of Polanski would, if revealed, have exploded it. For a while, though, Polanski would enjoy the luxury of playing the role of the victim in the entire affair.

Once the victim pose was dispatched by the facts, though, what was left to justify Polanski's criminal sexual behavior?

There *was* one final rationale concocted by a close friend and business associate of the director's. It was an ingenious creation, designed to elicit, if not public approval, at least sympathy for Polanski's crimes.

Based on a claim of temporary insanity, it presented Polanski on that fateful day at the Nicholson house as gazing down at the lovely nude body of the drugged thirteen-year-old and suddenly recalling, in impossible agony, his own beautiful slaughtered wife and *in utero* child. The rationale had long-dormant mental circuits suddenly beginning to click together uncontrollably in Polanski's agonized brain. Aided by his own drugged state, it had the circuits forming into mental images of his wife Sharon's killers, amongst whom had been pretty American girls not unlike the thirteen-year-old on the bed. It had Polanski's now crazed mind fantasizing the thirteen-year-old as a clone or extension of his wife's bloodthirsty murderers. It had the fantasy compulsively driving him to commit revenge – not by murder, but by his sexual violation of the innocent girl. Finally, and climactically, it had Polanski's fleeting madness exorcized once and for all by the completion of his act. It viewed the act as, so to speak, 'justified rape'. Once freed of his insane but understandable torment, went the rationale's denoument, Polanski stood ready to return to a sane and normal life. So long, that is, as the authorities understood the madness Polanski had suffered and were willing to let him go without punishment.

It was a scenario that was presented to Polanski that very Sunday, and which he seriously considered following in his legal defense. But then the lawyer he soon acquired pointed out that the recent trials of Patty Hearst in California would make such a defense – a defense based on his having been somehow possessed against his will by an outer force – perilous at best.

The idea was put to rest, although Polanski would retain a residual affection for it and later pass it off half-seriously to his friends as the reason for his actions. It was, after all, good theater. It was provocative of sympathy and understanding as well. Good theater and the sympathetic understanding of friends were the two things Polanski valued most in life, next to frequent sex.

When his legal troubles later intensified, many of Polanski's Hollywood friends would begin to abandon him. But that Sunday morning he was grateful for the commiserating calls he received from many of them at his suite in the Beverly Wilshire. 'He was typically confident, almost joking about it,' according to one. 'But it was clear that this was just something he was doing to mask his concern and anxiety.'

Polanski cautioned his callers that he had to keep their conversations to a minimum. He was awaiting a vital call from the noted Los Angeles criminal lawyer with whom his agent was negotiating at the moment to take the case.

The lawyer was Douglas Dalton, a rumpled but raffishly handsome attorney who was about the same age as Polanski. Expert in a broad spectrum of criminal and civil law, Dalton had recently been in the news as the lawyer representing Groucho Marx's erstwhile secretary and mistress, Erin Fleming, in her fight to wrest control of the senile and mortally ill comedian's property from his son.

Dalton was well-regarded by the local judiciary for his slavish attention to detail in trial preparation and for his courtroom savvy. He was also highly thought of by top motion picture executives. Polanski had polled several of them the day before for recommendations on the best attorney to handle his case, and Dalton had been the lawyer most frequently mentioned. Polanski had had his agent contact Dalton. Now, on Sunday morning, the director anxiously awaited the lawyer's call.

Polanski's anxiety stemmed not so much from his legal plight as from something he had been told the day before. The main reason he had come to Los Angeles a month earlier was to sign a contract with Columbia Pictures and begin work on the first of three films he was scheduled to write and direct for them. The high-paying contract was a personal coup for Polanski, since he had not done any movie work in Hollywood since making the highly acclaimed and financially successful *Chinatown* four years earlier. The contract gave him complete control over the films he would be making, a right he had not been able to secure before with any other American movie company, despite his successes with *Chinatown* and his earlier *Rosemary's Baby*. The Columbia contract provided him with the opportunity to become a major creative force in Hollywood, a status that he had not yet achieved.

But what really made the contract a coup was its lucrative financial terms. Up to that time he had made generous salaries on his pictures. But he had spent all his earnings establishing and maintaining a flamboyant international life-style for himself, with a luxurious house in London, an apartment in Paris, and a perpetual round of travel and entertainment. Although he was wealthy in possessions and property, his cash flow had shrunk to a trickle, forcing him to go into debt to friends. His new contract, which called for payments totaling close to a million dollars during the next few years, would finally put him on easy street. He would soon be able to pay off all his personal debts and become abundantly solvent for the forseeable future. At the age of forty-three, the forseeable future was all that concerned Polanski.

His anxiety that Sunday morning after his arrest was thus understandable. The day before while hunting for a lawyer, he had been told by a Columbia executive on the phone that the company might take a dim view of his arrest, particularly in view of the fact that it had come on a morals charge. His contract with Columbia contained what is known in the business as a 'standard morals clause'. The clause gave the company the right to automatically suspend or cancel the contract, and all monies payable under it, 'if in the company's opinion Polanski behaved in such a manner as to bring discredit

101

on himself or the company'. His arrest certainly fell under the purview of the clause, the executive had suggested.

Polanski had argued that his arrest was a mistake and that he would quickly be exonerated.

'Well, we'll have to see about that,' the executive had said. 'There will be a meeting at the studio on Monday. You know, the company's had so many difficulties in the press of late that we're going to have to be very sensitive to this business about you. A lot depends on what kind of publicity you get when the papers hit the streets tomorrow. We might have to review the situation. We might even have to suspend everything until you do get exonerated. I'm terribly sorry about this business, Roman. I'm sure you're innocent and I'm sure that everything will work out in the end, but I just wanted to put you in the picture. I want you to be prepared for whatever the company might decide to do.'

Douglas Dalton called Polanski at about noon on Sunday and arranged to meet the director at his law office later in the afternoon. When Polanski arrived, he was brimming with indignation and cocksuredness. He was clearly convinced that his troubles, however embarrassing, would only be brief – the able Dalton, he had been told, would see to that.

But Polanski, knew little about the American grand jury system and how it worked. He had little understanding of the American tradition of prosecutorial ambition and rectitude – he was unaware that prosecutors were political beings for whom favorable publicity was a lifeblood. And he was unfamiliar with basic American attitudes toward the crimes he had been charged with, having shaped his own sexual and moral values in the more liberated atmosphere of Europe and the atypical sleazeholes of Hollywood.

As any competent lawyer would, Dalton immediately sought to deflate Polanski's cocky indignation. The director genuinely believed that he had been entrapped by circumstances beyond his ken, Dalton realized. But he did not want Polanski to think that the solution to his problem was going to be simply a matter of legal form. Dalton had read the newspapers that morning. And he knew the people in the District Attorney's office. Even before he got Polanski to begin telling his version of the story, he knew that his new client was in for a tough time.

Polanski's story was this.

His initial picture for Columbia was to be based on his own screenplay, called *The First Deadly Sin.* It was to be a tale of lust and bloodcurdling terror of the kind Polanski was famous for. With horror movies having become the vogue in the commerical marketplace of America, Columbia Pictures had signed Polanski in order to capitalize on his unique and proven talent as a director in this genre.

Since arriving in Hollywood in February, Polanski had divided his working time between polishing his screenplay in his suite at the Beverly Wilshire and attending pre-production meetings at the Columbia studios in Burbank, where he had been given an office and a secretary.

As a diversion, Polanski told Dalton, he had come to Los Angeles with a photographic commission from the French magazine *Vogue Homme.* The assignment was to produce a pictorial feature on the beautiful young girls of California. He had done other work for the magazine. Louis Malle, the celebrated French director, was in the process of making a film in the United States that featured a twelve-year-old heroine in a turn-of-the-century New Orleans whore-house. The girl who had been cast to play the heroine, American child-model Brooke Shields, had received a great deal of publicity in France. *Vogue Homme* wanted to capitalize on the publicity. Its editor had asked Polanski, whose reputation in France as a purveyor of pubescent girls was legendary, and who had suitable contacts in America, to carry out the assignment.

Which was what, Polanski told Dalton, had brought him for the first time to the home of the thirteen-year-old in Woodland Hills, two weeks before.

He had met the girl's mother a year earlier, Polanski explained when he had come to Hollywood for initial negotiations on the Columbia contract. He had gone slumming one night with a group of European male friends, including a pal named Henri

Sera. They had ended up at a Hollywood bar called On The Rocks. The woman was there drinking. Sera knew her and introduced her to Polanski. One thing led to another and they ended up spending the night together. Polanski conceded to Dalton that he might have led the woman to believe he would help her in her acting career. As he later informed a court-appointed investigator, the woman 'was an actress, was trying to get another agent.'

But he would never lead a woman on by promising to put her in his next movie or anything like that. 'I do not mix my work with my private life. Ask anyone who knows me.'

Polanski told Dalton that he learned about the woman's daughter through his friend Sera. Sera was going out with the girl's older sister a year later. 'I was talking to Henri regarding the project of photographing young girls for *Vogue Homme*. Henri told me about this girl, that I should photograph this sister of his girlfriend. I called the mother, who was excited. She knew about it from Henri. I said I'd come over to see the girl. A few days later I was there. I saw the mother, her boyfriend, the girl . . . I said I'd come back to photograph.'

Polanski informed Dalton that after several more phone calls he returned to the girl's house in Woodland Hills to take some test pictures. He claimed that they had gone out behind the house to a hill and that the girl had changed clothes in front of him several times without embarrassment. So he asked her if she would pose topless. She agreed, and Polanski took some quick topless shots. 'We discussed her possible career as a model,' Polanski later told the court probers. 'The girl said she didn't want her mother to see the photographs.' The photos he took at this session were the ones Sergeant Vanatter found in his room at the Beverly Wilshire.

Polanski arrived at the crucial day in his narration to Dalton. As he later recounted his version to court-appointed probation investigators, 'We went to Victor Drey's-place on Mulholland. He was there with some writers. I realized the sun was almost gone. We hurried with pictures . . . I realized Jack (Nicholson)'s house was near. I called Anjelica. She wasn't there. I talked to Helena, the housekeeper, and told her I wanted to take pictures at the place.'

Driving to Nicholson's, Polanski said, he informed the girl that Nicholson would not be there – that the star was away on a ski trip.

'In the car, she mentioned she liked champagne. She said she once got drunk at her father's house. She was always extremely talkative when her mother was not there. We talked about her modeling. We talked about the use of drugs . . . and she said she had used Quaaludes, which she stole from her mother. She talked about sex and said she had sex at eight with a kid down the street and later her boyfriend.

'We went into the house. The girl was thirsty. I went to the fridge. There was a bottle of champagne. Helena said OK. We filled three glasses. Altogether the girl had about two glasses while we were there.

'While I was photographing her on the deck she saw steam from the Jacuzzi. We went inside. She changed. She took her blouse off, like before, and I took some more pictures. It was dusky. I said we should call her mother. She talked, and I talked . . . She told her mother about the Jacuzzi and that she was going in.

'I found a little box in the bathroom with Quaalude pieces marked Rorer. She took one piece. There was conversation about it but there was no actual offer by me. I said I was drinking and shouldn't take one. I took more pictures, but there was nothing by now on the light meter.

'I jumped in the pool for a swim. I asked her into the pool. She said she had asthma. I heard a car coming, I was apprehensive. Some maniacs used to come to the compound.

'I told her to rest in the bathroom. I went to the bedroom. She never objected. No, we didn't discuss birth control pills there, we discussed them later in the car. There was no discussion about her period. I withdrew before climax. There was no discussion about what to tell her mother. The whole thing was very spontaneous. It was not planned.'

Such was the gist of Polanski's tale as he told it to attorney

105

Dalton and later repeated it to various court investigators. He had not forcibly raped the girl, nor had he drugged her into compliance with his carnal wishes, he insisted. She had acted seductively and he had responded 'spontaneously', as any normal man might. In Europe, such a pattern of seduction was normal, even with a young girl.

Dalton explained that the laws and mores of the United States were different. In certain countries of Europe. a man in his forties might be toasted for seducing a young girl and providing her, in a tender, sensitive way, with her first sexual experience. So long as no one complained about it.

In the United States, such a business was called statutory rape. It didn't matter that the girl might not have resisted, that she might even have consciously provoked it. So long as Polanski had been aware of her age, he had committed statutory rape. And had he not been aware of her age, he could still be held responsible. Particularly if someone wanted to press the issue, as in his case the girl's mother apparently did.

Polanski cursed the girl's mother, claiming that she had deliberately set the situation up to get back at him.

'Can you prove that?' asked Dalton.

'I have many people who will say what the mother is like.'

Dalton patiently lectured his new client on the niceties of evidence and proof in a California court of law.

The realization that his problem was not going to go away with the magic wave of a lawyer's wand began to sink in on Polanski, and his righteous indignation dissolved.

'I am in serious trouble, then?' he said to Dalton.

'For now let's just say you're in trouble,' the lawyer answered. How serious it would be depended on what the district attorney intended to do. At the moment Polanski was only charged with unlawful sexual intercourse, the modern name for statutory rape. That was trouble enough, but it could be neutralized if evidence of extenuating or mitigating circumstances could be developed in Polanski's behalf.

However, if the DA intended to use a grand jury to indict Polanski on the rash of other charges he was open to as a result of the girl's original complaint, then things could become stickier for the director.

Dalton would have to wait until the morning, when he could get a better sense of what the DA was going to do, before he could properly tell Polanski what he might be in for. He was only sorry that Polanski had already conceded so much to the arresting officers. Had he had sense enough to keep his mouth shut, the girl's complaint, no matter how riddled with falsehoods and exaggerations it might be, would not carry the weight that it now did. And the prosecutors would not have the advantage they now had.

'What is the worst that could happen?' Polanski asked.

Dalton looked at him, his face creased in a thoughtful squint. 'Let's not worry about that now,' he said.

'I must know. The papers this morning – they said fifty years in prison.'

Dalton laughed. 'You mustn't believe everything you read in the papers. I can't tell you what the worst could be. But it's not going to be fifty years.'

CHAPTER 5

POLANSKI HAD kept his promise. For more than a year he had been on his best behavior. He had worked diligently at the drafting school. He had muzzled his impulses to criticize the government. He had done everything he could to please his father.

Now, early in 1953, he announced to his father that he intended to try to get into the national film school at Lodz after his graduation from the drafting school.

His father had other ideas, however.

Riszard Polanski had prospered in his private business. But he still feared the government. The elder Polanski was still distrusted by the authorities, particularly so because he was a Jew who had made good. Riszard Polanski's success had fed the Polish anti-Semitic stereotype of Roman as an unfairly privileged youth because of his father's status. It was time for him to make a contribution to the state that permitted such status. There could be no better contribution for him to make than to serve in the army. For less privileged young men, particularly non-Jews, army service was unavoidable.

Roman thought he could circumvent such a fate by

persuading his father to turn his plastics business over to the government and then manage it for the state. Riszard Polanski angrily rejected the suggestion. He did not particularly want Roman to go into the army. But he was not against the idea either, since he believed that if his son submitted to military service, it would take a certain amount of government pressure off him and his business. He had been operating the business at the sufferance of the government – the authorities could take it over at any time and had indeed made veiled threats to do so in the past. Despite the endless red tape he was forced to wade through and the taxes he was required to pay in order to operate privately, he desperately wanted to remain a private enterprise. Anti-private enterprise feelings were on the rise in Poland, as was once again anti-Semitism. By submitting voluntarily to the Polish draft, Roman would be demonstrating the Polanski family's patriotism. At the same time he would be helping his father's business interests. Riszard Polanski felt that Roman owed him this as son to father. Later, after army service, Riszard would find a place for his son in the business.

Since Roman had not yet reached the age of twenty-one, he was still legally under his father's dominion. But Roman had made up his mind that he would never voluntarily submit to the draft. And he had no interest in joining his father in business. His ambitions were set firmly on film school and a career in cinema. So, the two fought and argued through the spring of 1953.

By May it was time for Roman to make his formal application to the film academy at Lodz. When his father saw that he could not deter him, he put out the word among the authorities that his son was acting in defiance of him, and that he would appreciate it if Roman was summarily rejected. Army service, he hinted, might be just the thing to teach Roman to obey his elders.

For his part, Roman single-mindedly gathered a pile of recommendations from theatrical and cinema figures in Cracow and Warsaw recommending his acceptance to the film school. He was a bright and talented young man with great initiative, the admission board was told in chorus, and he stood to make a

109

greater contribution to the state by being trained as a film actor than as a soldier.

There was to be a certain irony in this. Although his sights were set on someday becoming a film director, Roman had been told he was too young to apply to the film school as a directing student. Moreover, he had had no directorial experience. He was advised that his best chance for admission lay in his application as an acting student.

Despite all his letters of recommendation, early in August he was rejected as an acting student at the school. Having graduated from art school and with no further schooling available to exempt him from army service, he bitterly sat back and waited to be drafted.

But then he had a stroke of luck that was fueled by his self-assertiveness. Once more he traveled to Warsaw with his Cracow acting company to participate in the 1953 summer stage festival. While there he again came across Zbigniew Cybulski from Cracow, by then one of Poland's leading young actors. Roman confided his problems to Cybulski, exaggerating the role his father had played in his rejection by the film academy. Cybulski told him to re-apply and promised to personally recommend that the school accept him. Roman re-applied in September and was once again promptly rejected.

Cybulski felt some responsibility for his fellow-Cracowian, and was offended that the school overrode his recommendation. He was due to start filming soon in a major Polish motion picture about wartime Poland and its resistance fighters. The film, to be shot by one of Poland's up-and-coming directors, Andrzej Wajda, was called *A Generation.* Cybulski had an important part in it, and he promised Polanski that he would talk to Wajda about getting him a job on the production crew. Director Wajda was a graduate of the national film school as well as an occasional teacher there. Perhaps if he got to know Polanski, suggested Cybulski, he would use his influence to help him get into the school.

Polanski's hopes skyrocketed. But, after a few days had passed he heard nothing more from Cybulski. He impatiently decided to take matters into his own hands. He located Wajda in Warsaw and began to pester him for a job on the production of *A Generation,* claiming that Cybulski had already promised that he'd be hired. When the irked Wajda checked with Cybulski, he learned that the actor had only said he would try to get Polanski a job, not that he had promised him one. Now Cybulski was angry with Polanski for having misrepresented what he'd said, and he recommended that Wajda forget about him. But Wajda had been impressed by Polanski's aggressiveness and lack of fear in approaching him. There was a small part in *A Generation* that called for such a personality. Polanski was astonished, then, when Wajda called him in and offered him the part. The most he had expected was a job moving lights and heavy equipment.

Working for no salary, Polanski remained with the film company during October and November as the movie was shot at various locations around Warsaw and in Poland's beautiful but somber north-eastern lake country – an area he had never seen before. Playing a young but rebellious resistance fighter, he performed his few brief scenes well, particularly a fight scene with Cybulski. Moreover, he exhibited a discipline and responsiveness to Wajda's direction that further impressed the director. To cement the favorable impression, Polanski slavishly devoted his spare time to running errands and helping with the sets and lights, all the while eavesdropping on Wajda's conferences with his principal actors and studying his directing style.

A Generation turned out to be among the first in a new wave of postwar Polish films and was highly acclaimed when it was released in 1954. Although about the war and the struggle of communist partisans against the occupying Germans, it was relatively free of the ham-handed propaganda that up until then had been the bane of younger movie-makers. Yet it did have censorship problems before it was released. Indeed, Roman Polanski's most important scene – the fight with Cybulski, who played the leader of a partisan band – had to be cut from the final print. It would not do to show internal strife within the resistance, not even in the Poland of the mid-1950s. Like many a film actor the world over, Polanski's greatest moment in the film ended up on the cutting room floor. As a consequence, the few brief scenes he did appear in were hardly noticed.

He was undaunted, however. The experience of being part of the production had more significant rewards. 'It was my first contact with serious, or let's say enthusiastic, cinema,' Polanski told the British magazine *Films and Filming* in 1969. 'The whole crew were young people, mostly from the national film school. After working with that group, I knew there was nothing that would keep me out of Lodz.'

Polanski redoubled his efforts to get into the film school. During the filming of *A Generation,* he had startled Wajda by his knowledge of electricity and electronics, and also by his spontaneous portrait-drawings of the various actors. He even did a detailed drawing of Wajda and presented it to him when the filming was over.

But there was one occasion during the shooting when his presence had been invaluable. Wajda was experiencing difficulty in setting up a scene – a tableau of several actors set against a skyline. He could not find the right angle from which to shoot it. Polanski, after eavesdropping on the director's fruitless discussions with the camera operator and others, silently dashed off a sketch that put the actors in a different arrangement and solved the technical problem. Hesitant for once about approaching Wajda directly, he gave it to Cybulski. When Cybulski handed it to the director, Wajda's eyes widened in recognition. He acknowledged the solution and re-set the scene according to Polanski's sketch.

Thus, when Polanski went back to Wajda after the filming was over and asked him to help him get into the film school, the director promised to see what he could do. Wajda did not seem surprised when Polanski said that he was no longer interested in going to the school as an acting student. He now wanted to be accepted into the much more rigorous director's course.

The national film school had been instituted by the Polish government shortly after the end of the war in recognition of the Leninist doctrine about the importance of film-making in the communist scheme of things. At its core was a group of talented, intellectual, experimental left-wing film-makers who, before the war, had met with little success in Poland. At that time, Polish cinema was neanderthal in its quality, producing only cheap exploitation movies and barring its production facilities to serious film-makers – particularly those who had 'progressive' political ideas. Many of the progressive film-makers had escaped to Russia ahead of the Nazi occupation of Poland and remained there for the duration of the war. In Russia they were kept busy making Soviet propaganda films, which had highest priority. When the war was over, most of them returned to Poland. Because they were now acceptable politically, they were commissioned and subsidized by the new communist government to establish a national film school at Lodz for the training of actors, writers, technicians and directors.

The school quickly gained form and substance in the late 1940s. It built most of its early philosophy on the influences of such prewar Russian realist film-makers as Eisenstein, adding the acting notions of Stanislavski and focusing its work on the great Russian social novelists and playwrights. The school was provided access to the prewar Polish film archives, however. Once its solid communist-tinged curriculum was established, films from other parts of the world were allowed to be screened, studied and criticized.

This was one reason why, in 1950, the Lodz film school was flooded with applicants. It was the only place in Poland where young people could watch movies from all over the world, particularly the West. It was also the reason why most applicants were not even considered for admittance unless their communist political credentials were impeccable. Only those who were able to prove an unerring devotion to the state could be trusted to exposure to the seductive materialistic lures of Western European and American films.

By 1953 the Lodz school – because of the range of its technical facilities, the proficiency of its faculty, and the extent to which it had the government's support – was celebrated throughout Europe.

Although rejected twice in 1953 as an acting student now,

early in 1954, Roman Polanski's sights were set firmly on getting into the film school's directing program. With the influential Wajda committed to helping him, he grew confident of his chances, despite the fact that Wajda had warned him the school usually did not accept directing students as young as Polanski. He would have to excel on the examination given to all directing applicants to gain even the routine attention of the admissions board.

The long, exhaustive examination was scheduled for two days in the early spring of 1954. Such was his determination that Polanski spent weeks prior to it in intensive study, using as a guide a sample of an earlier exam he had obtained from Wajda. The exam was designed to measure the prospective student's historical knowledge and scientific aptitude. Much of it was technical, testing the applicant's practical skills in such subjects as electronics, the chemistry of paints and pigments, optics and scenery design, camera mechanics and film processing.

Polanski hitchhiked from Cracow to Lodz in March to take the two-day test. Afterward he was sure that he had done well, particularly in its technical aspects. Next came the month-long wait to learn if he would be admitted.

He hid his anxiety behind a facade of boastful confidence. 'Roman was sure he'd been accepted,' a friend from Cracow later recalled for me. 'He came back from Lodz telling everyone that he'd soon be returning there to study cinema. If he had any doubts, he didn't show them. In fact he lorded his assurance over us, bragging of his connections with people at the film school and how they would guarantee his admission. Some of us did not appreciate Roman's cockiness. We were trying to get into Lodz too, but we didn't have any connections. We were awaiting our answers with our nerves on edge.

'The day the decisions were released, some of us were at the theater rehearsing. The decisions came through the theater's director, since we had all had to apply as members of the theater. He stopped rehearsals and called some of us in. Roman wasn't there – he was late or something. Anyway the director read each of us the decisions. One fellow had been accepted, and he was delirious with joy. The rest of us, five or six, had been turned down, and we were so gloomy that the director suspended the rehearsal. He also had the decision on Roman and knew what it was, but he wouldn't tell us. He was waiting for Roman to show up.

'Roman came in later. As soon as he heard the decisions were in, he ran to the director's office. When he came out a few minutes later, it was clear that he had been rejected. I'm afraid to say that it gave most of us a lot of secret pleasure to see what had happened to him. Not only because of his boasting, but because it made our own rejections a little more palatable. Even with all his so-called connections he could not get in.

'Somebody made a wisecrack to Roman. An argument started. He claimed that he had passed the tests and that the only reason he'd been rejected was his age – he was too young. I found out later that this was true. But whoever he was arguing with kept baiting him. Roman was already obviously shattered, and now he became hysterical. He leaped at his tormentor and they started fighting. The other fellow gave him a whipping. This was his second tremendous humiliation of the day. He ran out and went into hiding, and we didn't see him for days. When he finally reappeared, he claimed that he had only been rejected because he was a Jew. One minute he cursed the film school for having it in for Jews. The next he cursed his family for being Jews and himself for being born a Jew. Although he was not at all religious, he began to hate the fact that he was a Jew. After that he went to great extremes to shed this Jewish image people had of him.'

In the meantime, the military draft was closing in on Polanski. The Polish army did not discriminate against Jews, and he had received a notice to report for conscription in June. 'Roman blamed his father for the mess he was in,' said the same friend. 'He hated his father anyway, but now he believed that his father was behind the pressure to get him into the army. They had furious fights over this. His father tried to tell him that army service would be good for him, good for the family. Roman shouted back that he would never go into the army. He would run away and cause his father embarrassment and trouble with the government.'

115

Instead of running away, Polanski sought out Andrzej Wajda again and begged him to do something. Wajda queried the film school and learned that Polanski had indeed done well on his examination. The board of admissions had decided, however, that since Polanski was subject to the draft and so many other applicants had completed their army service, he would have to do his stint in the military first. Afterwards, he would be reconsidered for admission.

According to what Polanski later told friends, Wajda for some reason decided to put his official relationship with the school on the line in order to get the board to change its decision. Wajda argued that Polanski was too promising to be shunted off into the army. He would be of much more use to the army, and therefore to Poland, as a trained cinematographer in five years than as an unschooled soldier then. If the school admitted him now, Polanski would still have to go into the army after his graduation. But then he would be able to make a much more valuable contribution.

Wajda's arguments impressed the board, and in June it changed its decision. Polanski was at the theater in Cracow when the news came down from Lodz.

'Roman had come back. Except for his denunciations of his father and his being a Jew, he had been pretty subdued. He had lost all his cockiness, he was depressed, and he did not expect Wajda's efforts on his behalf to amount to anything. He was not even trying to figure out a way to avoid army service anymore. Then the director came running out into the theater, waving a sheet of paper. It was the announcement that Roman had been accepted at Lodz after all and that he was to report immediately.

'Roman was stunned, so stunned that he was unable to show any pleasure. He was matter-of-fact in his reaction. Despite his sometimes obnoxious manner, most of the people at the theater liked him. So we were more happy for him than he seemed to be for himself. We had forgotten our own disappointment and bitterness and had gotten to the point where we could at least share Roman's pleasure. But he showed no pleasure. Like he usually did, he became officious and pompous. "It's about

116

time,'' he said, or something to that effect. Then he turned on us and said, ''You see, you idiots, I told you I would get in.'' Then he walked out, just like that. He stopped very theatrically at the door, like he was playing a part and was pausing before making his exit. He turned and said something sarcastic again, like, ''Enjoy yourselves, you bastards, I hope I never see you again.'' Then he was gone.'

Polanski immediately traveled back to Lodz. When he showed up at the elite film school, he learned to his greater satisfaction that his military service had been officially deferred until after his graduation, five years hence.

A late addition to that year's apprentice directing class, he had a lot of catching up to do. By then he was so intent upon making good that he let nothing distract him. With a small allowance from his still-benevolent uncle, he moved into a broomcloset flat in Lodz with two other new students but spent almost all his time in the school's library in an effort to make up what he had missed. 'That first year I was like a monk,' he later said. 'It was all new and strange to me and I didn't dare get into trouble.'

In addition to all the technical training given over five years to students in the directing course, such as camera operation, film editing, lighting, sound reproduction, and the like, the school also had compulsory courses in the history of art, acting, literature, scriptwriting, music, philosophy, optics and aesthetic theory. The first year's course was introductory and general, designed to steep the students in all the arts and give them a background against which to develop their cinematic sensibilities. Although films were studied and discussed, the first-year students were not allowed to engage in actual film-making. The closest they came to it were courses in still photography, where they learned the rudiments of lighting, camera function, framing, composition and film developing. Polanski was later to say that 'the techniques of still photography are essential to anyone who hopes to be a cinematographer.'

Polanski proved to be an eager student of the technical side of his beginning education. But the mightiest impact on him that first year came through his cultural courses. When he

117

arrived at Lodz, he had had little exposure to the history of thought and art. Now he was inundated by centuries of cultural and intellectual ideas, and he had to struggle to keep up.

The school was an intellectual cauldron. Suddenly thrust into an environment in which his older fellow-students were as intelligent, inventive and disputative as himself, Polanski at first kept a low profile. He did his work quietly, was usually prepared for an instructor's question, and was always ready to volunteer for the classroom or laboratory clean-up duties that the other students most of them older, shunned.

At the beginning of the second year, however, he began to assert himself, arguing technical points with other students and impressing his teachers with the aggressiveness and originality of his opinions. 'Roman was not very articulate,' one instructor later recalled. 'That is, he did not speak with ease or confidence. But despite that, what he was able to communicate usually had a touch of original insight. One could see that his brain worked at a more intense level than most of the others. The others could out-talk him, usually. But they could not out-think him.'

And a former student at the school, Eugene Gorski, says, 'Roman was very good at talk outside the school environment. But within the school, in academic discussion, he was not so good at the beginning. This probably had to do with the fact that he missed out on a lot of early education. There were large gaps in his basic thinking process – an inability to proceed logically from one point to the next. So this caused him difficulty in expressing himself coherently, in making people understand what he was getting at. Because of this he was often teased, or an impatient teacher might pass on to someone else before letting him finish what he was trying to say.

'This would make him angry and frustrated, sometimes ashamed, and he would turn moody and sullen and refuse to talk for a long time. Yet he had a very intuitive brain. You could see that he was seeing things that were important and original but could not quite express in intelligible terms. As he was longer at Lodz, he would strike back at those who teased him by cursing them, saying, "Look, it is simple, this is the way it is. If you can't see what I am saying, it is because you are dumb, not me. You don't need a lot of fancy words to explain or understand a simple concept. If you don't understand what I am saying, it is your problem, not mine.''

'That became Roman's hallmark in his later years at Lodz. He grew to have utmost confidence in his insights and ideas. Rather than try to explain them anymore, he simply stated them with some vehemence and dared you to challenge him. If one challenged him, or expressed a doubt, a verbal battle would follow. In the end he would usually win. No matter how elegantly the other spoke in trying to demolish Roman's position, he would refuse to budge. He would win by pure tenacity, even though he could not defend his ideas through logical speech.'

Polanski himself described the atmosphere of discussion and dispute at the film school in an interview in *Playboy* magazine in 1971. 'An important part of our education was a baroque wooden stairway in the school building where we would sit for hours arguing about films, which sometimes we were screening all day and all night. Occasionally the discussions became rather heated. In fact, I have a scar under my eye from one of them.'

Polanski has said that at Lodz there were 'schools within the school'. There were those who subscribed to the Russian school of film-making, while others championed the neo-realism of the postwar Italians. As he got to view more and more prewar American movies from the Polish film archive, to which the school had almost unlimited access, Polanski began to develop an avid interest in the richly varied 'Hollywood' approach to film direction. 'With the Russians it was the same thing every time,' he was to say. 'The same style, every Russian director imitating the officially approved model, which was a film like *Potemkin*. And the Italians – everything in the style of *Bicycle Thief*. But the Americans – well, from what we saw of American films we could watch so many different approaches, so much visual imagination, so much imagination in lighting and color and framing and camera work. And the writing, the dialogue – so much in the good films was left to the imagination.'

Polanski, somewhat to the consternation of the film school's faculty, became an early enthusiast of American, and later French and British films. Which was partially why he encountered so much difficulty in communicating with students and teachers. Western films were screened primarily so that their intrinsic values could be criticized in the light of communist principles, so that the 'decadence' of capitalistic Western life which they reflected could be made object lessons for the Lodz students.

'It was not expected that the students find things to be admired in these films,' Eugene Gorski says. 'The students were being trained to be communist film-makers. Most were proper conformists, eager to show the school authorities that their political values were in line with the official doctrine. When Roman came along and began to have insights and to utter things in praise of a Western film, they fell on him like a pack of wolves in their zeal to rebut his political deviancy and display their own conformity for the authorities to see. Not that Roman at that time was advocating the cause of capitalism. Truly he didn't give a damn about political systems. But when he argued in favor of some cinematic virtue he saw in a Western film, he was accused of advocating Western values or Western culture or something. A young man who had already been alienated to a certain degree from society by the events of his life, he was made to feel further estranged by his originality, by his failure to always conform to doctrinaire principals in school.'

There were two American movies that Polanski was particularly impressed by in his second year at Lodz: *Citizen Kane,* which was directed by and starred Orson Welles, and *Of Mice and Men,* Hollywood director Lewis Milestone's film of the celebrated John Steinbeck novel and play. Both were powerful studies of individuals functioning in a world in which they did not fit – Kane, a power-hungry tycoon whose passions went against the grain of all the democratic impulses in America; George and his dimwitted sidekick Lenny, a pair of outcasts in the society of California farmworkers. Polanski responded to this theme.

He was particularly impressed by the subtlety and complexity of the characterizations in these two films as developed through the lenses of their directors' mobile cameras and their film-editing techniques. They were techniques of characterization that communist-oriented film-makers seldom strove for; most communist directors relied on actors alone, performing at a remove for their stationary cameras, to make the impact.

In addition, Polanski was captivated by the two or three suspense films of Alfred Hitchcock that were permitted to be screened at the film school. Again, it was the way that Hitchcock spookily established elements in his stories which did not quite fit into the reality of the films' scenarios that captivated Polanski. Having experienced much real-life alienation and terror in his own life, he readily identified with the alienation and terror depicted in these pictures. He learned to admire their cinematic methods as well as the stories they embraced.

During the second year at Lodz, each directing student was assigned to an experienced and established film director, under whom he would study for the next three years and who he would serve as a general assistant in the making of that director's regular state-financed films. Polanski was assigned to the veteran documentary director Andrzej Munk, a man whose imperious temperament was unbending and whose film erudition was encyclopedic.

Andrzej Munk would become a powerful father-figure for Polanski, as well as a demanding and inspirational mentor. More important, he would eventually provide Polanski with the opportunity to fulfill his dream of leaving Poland for the West.

INTERLOG 5

ON MONDAY morning, 14 March 1977, Douglas Dalton got the news from deputy district attorney Roger Gunson that the Polanski case would shortly be brought by him before a grand jury for a determination on whether to proceed with prosecution of the director.

Dalton was not surprised at the adamant tone in Gunson's voice as they spoke on the phone. Although the prosecutor tried to disguise his fervor behind the bantering tone lawyers often use between themselves, it was clear to Dalton that he was out to pin Polanski to the wall. Dalton understood. It wasn't every day that a prosecutor got to share the headlines with a celebrity and get cornered by television broadcasters frantically seeking the latest sensational developments.

Dalton also understood the tactic of the grand jury. Ostensibly it was to protect the identity of the girl and her mother – Polanski's accusers. What it was *really* for was to ensure that the case would stay in Los Angeles, to neutralize any court motion Dalton might later make for a change of venue due to the prejudicial publicity Polanski was receiving from the media. Monday's papers were even more lavish in their coverage of Polanski's arrest than Sunday's, featuring sidebar stories that described Polanski's connection with the Sharon Tate murder case and painting lurid pictures of his general lifestyle. By processing the case through a grand jury, the prosecutor could successfully rebut a change-of-venue motion by arguing that the state's case against Polanski was proceeding not because of the unfavorable publicity, but in spite of it. The need to prosecute would be shown to derive not from any prejudicial whims or motivations on the part of the police and district attorney's office, but solely from evidence dispassionately assessed in secret by a grand jury isolated from the ongoing publicity.

After speaking with the deputy prosecutor, Dalton had his secretary put in a call for Polanski at the Columbia studios, where the director had gone that morning to take part in a casting meeting, as though nothing had happened.

The meeting had gone badly. Although most of the people working on pre-production tasks for *The First Deadly Sin* had greeted Polanski with sympathy, one woman, a costume assistant and the mother of a retarded thirteen-year-old daughter, who had recently died, reacted in anger at the joke he made to open the meeting.

'I want to warn all of you to keep your children off the set of this picture,' he had cracked. 'Particularly those of you with sex-starved daughters.'

There were six people at the meeting. Several chuckled. But not the costume assistant. She had already had some tense scenes with Polanski over his dictatorial demands of the costume department and was thinking about asking for re-assignment to another production. Now she seethed, and her bile rose even higher when a fawning assistant director, quipped, 'Tell us, Roman, is it true what they say about thirteen-year-old girls?'

'What is it they say?'

'They have no pubic hair?'

'Ah,' smiled Polanski, 'this one did.'

The costume assistant could contain herself no longer. 'Goddamn you!' she shrieked at Polanski. 'You dare to make jokes about this? I don't care who you are. You're an animal!'

With that she got up and, collecting a pile of sketches, stalked out of Polanski's office.

Polanski studiously ignored the outburst and the meeting went on. But the others present grew dispirited, feeling a bit ashamed at having laughed at Polanski's crack. They were not without worry either. When they had come into the studios that morning, they had immediately heard rumors that the company's top brass were meeting to decide whether the production would go on. Most of them were free-lancers and would be out of jobs if the picture was shut down.

Polanski continued to make joking references to his arrest. According to one who was present, his voice became increasingly nervous and strident as he received less and less response to his jokes. When the meeting broke up, the room cleared in an instant, leaving Polanski blinking in perplexity.

The director put in a call to the Columbia executive he had spoken with on Saturday. The executive, he was told by his secretary, was in a meeting and could not be disturbed. A call to another studio higher-up found him also unavailable. Growing fidgety, Polanski was about to phone Douglas Dalton when a call came in for him from Dalton's secretary.

'Mr Dalton would like to see you in his office as soon as possible,' she said.

'ANJELICA NO ANJEL,' read the headline in one of Monday's Los Angeles newspapers. The story beneath cleared up the question of whether Anjelica Huston had been directly involved in Polanski's rape of the thirteen-year-old Woodland Hills girl: she hadn't, the story assured the paper's readers. But it went on to say that the district attorney's office now viewed her as the key to its prosecution of Polanski. 'Sources within the police department indicated that Miss Huston was in the house at the time and can place Polanski inside the bedroom with his victim,' the reporter wrote. 'The district attorney believes he has an open-and-shut case against Polanski and expects to get an indictment this week. An assistant D.A. hinted over the weekend that Miss Huston will be asked to testify against the

124

accused director in exchange for a reduction of the drug charges currently pending against her.'

This is what Dalton wanted to talk to Polanski about. He had learned that the newspaper report was accurate – prosecutor Gunson intended to co-opt Anjelica Huston by offering her a deal whereby, if she testified against Polanski, the charges against her would be reduced, possibly even dropped. Despite the evidence Gunson might present to his grand jury – testimony from the girl and her mother, testimony from the arresting officers, testimony from Helena Kallianiotes – all of which would get him the indictment he was seeking, the evidence was basically circumstantial and therefore insufficient to assure him of getting a conviction when the case came to trial.

Gunson in effect had no case without Anjelica Huston. Dalton wanted Polanski to tell him about Anjelica. Could she be persuaded to resist the district attorney's blandishments? If not, then Polanski's problems were indeed serious.

Gunson, in the meantime, was organizing the people and material he intended to bring before the grand jury the following day. He had statements from the girl and her mother. He had the police-lab reports about the semen on the girl's panties. He had Sergeant Vanatter's descriptions of what Polanski had said to him and his partner when they arrested him. Vanatter had described Polanski as 'extremely hyperactive,' and had said that from the things the director talked about, 'I had no doubts that the acts with which Polanski was charged occurred.'

Gunson had the photos and Quaalude pills that had been confiscated from Polanski's room. And he had the statement of Helena Kallianiotes, the Nicholson neighbor-housekeeper.

Interviewed again by the police on Sunday, Kallianiotes had confirmed that she was at the house when Polanski arrived with the girl the previous Thursday. 'Roman, the girl and herself went into the kitchen area of the house,' read the investigators' report of their questioning of Kallianiotes, 'where Mr Polanski asked for something to drink. He was directed to a refrigerator where he found a bottle of champagne and asked if he could open the bottle . . . Kallianiotes stated that she then removed some long-stemmed wine glasses for the champagne. Mr Polanski and witness Kallianiotes poured some champagne for themselves, but the witness did not see the victim take or drink any of the champagne. The witness stated that she only looked at the girl one time and thought that she was approximately eighteen years old and felt she was a girl trying to get into the movies. She also stated that Mr Polanski and the girl acted as if they were lovers . . . '

Gunson decided to avoid any questions about Helena Kallianiotes' impressions of the girl when he summoned her before the grand jury. He would merely ask her to testify as to the time of Polanski's arrival with the girl at the Nicholson house, and the time of her own departure. Her testimony would be the next to last link in the chain of independent evidence he expected to construct to get an indictment, and later a conviction, against Polanski. But to complete the chain, he would definitely need the testimony of Anjelica Huston.

Anjelica had already told the police that she had arrived home to find Polanski in the bedroom, and that the girl was also in the bedroom. Except for her annoyance at 'Roman's presumptuousness at using the house for his sexual adventures,' she hadn't thought much about it. As she would later say in a sworn deposition, 'I wasn't thrilled about [finding Roman there]. He wasn't in the habit, you know, of coming over without, you know . . . people aren't in the habit of coming over without my knowing.'

Gunson had already talked with Anjelica's lawyer and sounded him out on a possible deal: her voluntary testimony in exchange for a possible reduction of the drug charges against her. The lawyer had told him that, at the time, Anjelica was not in the mood to testify. For one thing, her loyalties were in conflict. Anything she might say would only serve to get Roman Polanski deeper in trouble, and Polanski was one of her boyfriend Jack Nicholson's best friends. Also Nicholson and Polanski had been planning to capitalize on their *Chinatown* success with another movie, and a lot of money could be at stake if she said something that damaged those prospects or drove a wedge between Polanski and Nicholson.

126

Perhaps even her relationship with Nicholson would be at stake. Nicholson had rushed back from Colorado, and he seemed to be more concerned about Polanski's arrest than about Anjelica's – perhaps because he already sensed that Anjelica could cause Polanski problems.

Gunson decided not to press the issue for then. He was confident of an indictment without Anjelica Huston's grand jury testimony. In the meantime, he would see that she and Nicholson were made to understand what she had to lose by exposing herself to prosecution on her arrest. If Polanski went to trial, Gunson intended to have her there.

On Thursday, 24 March 1977, Roman Polanski was indicted by a Los Angeles County grand jury on all six felony counts of the original arrest warrant: furnishing Quaaludes to a minor, child molesting, unlawful sexual intercourse, rape by use of drugs, oral copulation, and sodomy. Once again the local papers plastered the news all over their front pages when the indictments were announced.

'How can it be?' Polanski cried to Dalton when he heard of it that afternoon. 'I did nothing, you know that.'

Dalton tried to explain the grand jury process, explaining that an indictment was merely an official accusation, not a conviction. But Polanski wouldn't listen. 'This place is barbarian!' he shouted.

The case was immediately removed from the jurisdiction of the city court system and placed on the calendar of the Santa Monica branch of the Superior Court of the State of California. Polanski was notified that his arraignment in Superior Court was scheduled for the following Tuesday.

The director spent the weekend huddled with Dalton, going over possible defenses. On Monday he made an unannounced visit to Nicholson's house to learn what Anjelica Huston was going to do, but neither she nor Nicholson were there. Then he drove out to Woodland Hills, ignoring Dalton's warnings not to, to confront the mother of the thirteen-year-old. When he found no one home, he waited outside the house for an hour. A

127

neighbor noticed his car and called the local police. Soon a cruiser turned into the street and pulled up next to the director's Mercedes.

'Whatch doin', buddy?' the policeman called through his open window.

'I'm waiting for the people to come home,' Polanski answered, nodding at the house.

'Say, aren't you . . . ?'

'Yes, yes, I am Polanski – so what?'

'Uh oh,' said the cop. 'I don't think that's a very good idea.'

'Why not?'

The cop's voice suddenly turned hard. 'Get outta your car and put your hands on the roof, legs spread wide.'

'You're joking,' said Polanski.

'Out!' barked the cop as he reached for his radio.

'Okay, okay,' said Polanski. 'I go.'

By now the cop was out of his cruiser. 'Too late,' he said. 'Come on, get out.' He backed away from the door to let Polanski out of the Mercedes. 'Okay, hands on the roof, legs apart.'

'But I have done nothing, what is this?'

'Quiet!' shouted the cop as he frisked the director. He squeezed Polanski's crotch, causing the Pole to jump in reflex.

'Just thought I'd see what all the excitement is about,' said the cop, backing away.

'You son of a beeetch!' cried Polanski.

'Okay, Mr Polanski, you don't seem to be armed,' said the cop, suddenly polite. 'But I got to tell you there's such a thing as intimidating witnesses, threatening witnesses, that kind of thing. You know about that?'

'I don't know what you're talking about.'

'Well, it seems you're sitting here in front of the house of the girl you're accused of raping. Now how do you suppose that looks?'

'I just want to talk to the mother, I just want to know what she has against me.'

'Mr Polanski, I'm gonna give you some advice. Get your ass outta here pronto. You don't say anything about this, I won't say anything. I'm gonna drive around the block one time. If I find you here when I come back, I'll have to take you in. Understand?'

'But I . . . '

'No buts,' said the cop, getting back into his cruiser.

Fighting his way through the circus of shouting photographers and reporters, Polanski appeared at Santa Monica Superior Court the next morning, 29 March to be arraigned before Judge Laurence J. Rittenband. Tired-looking and angry, he wore a heavy rumpled blazer and open-necked shirt as he stood defiantly next to Douglas Dalton in front of Judge Rittenband's bench.

Rittenband was not the ideal judge for the case, Dalton had warned Polanski. An acerbic, white-haired man in his late fifties, Rittenband had a reputation among lawyers as a defender of the establishment and a jurist given to harsh sentences. He had a tendency to lean over backwards to show fairness and even sympathy in criminal trials then slap them with heavy punishment when convicted. He was believed to be very publicity conscious.

Rittenband had gotten the Polanski case through the rotation system that applied to all cases before the Santa Monica Superior Court. He had a busy case load that day, so he rushed through Polanski's arraignment. He ordered a hearing in the same court for three weeks hence, at which time, he said, he would take Polanski's plea to the charges and set a trial date. Then he agreed to Dalton's request that Polanski be allowed to remain free on bail.

Emerging from the courthouse minutes after he had entered, Polanski was besieged by the mob of newsmen. The blitz of questions was relentless and soaked with ribaldry. Polanski, his eyes blinking against the morning sun, tried to proclaim his innocence, but before he could answer one question he was bombarded with a dozen others.

'Did you rape the girl?'

'No, I merely . . . '

129

'How does it feel to be accused of such terrible crimes?'
'What is so terrible . . . '
'Are you guilty?'
'What do you mean, I just told you . . . '
'What was she like, Roman?'
'She is a nice . . . '
'So why did you drug her?'
'I didn't drug her, she . . . '
'Was she one of Jack Nicholson's girls?'
'Jack didn't even . . . '

Nudging Polanski, attorney Dalton finally intervened. 'Gentlemen!' he shouted. 'There is only one question my client is interested in answering at this time, and that has to do with his innocence.'

'What do you have to say, Roman?' called out a voice from the silenced throng.

'I have to say that I am innocent of these charges,' Polanski replied, as though reciting from memory. 'I have trust in the American system of justice, and I know this justice will' – he stumbled over the next word – 'exonerate me.'

'So why are you accused of raping and sexually abusing a kid?' exclaimed a woman reporter.

'Is all a stupid misunder . . . '

The rest of Polanski's answer was lost in the din of further questions.

Dalton whispered to Polanski and broke a path through the crowd toward his car. His diminutive client followed, smiling and seemingly confident. (Later newspaper reports would have him 'leering and winking at reporters, as though he didn't have a care in the world.')

When he reached the car and was about to climb in, Polanski was peppered with a final barrage of questions. He picked out the one that asked, 'Can you tell us how you feel, Roman? You've had a lot of grief in this country.'

'I am used to grief,' he answered. 'This is just a trifle.'

As the car inched away from the curb, Polanski turned to Dalton. 'Animals,' he hissed. Then he turned and shouted through the car's window, 'fucking animals! all of you!'

The next day one of the reporters wrote a withering column about a pot – Polanski – calling the kettle black.

CHAPTER 6

A<small>T THE</small> start of his second year at the Lodz film school, Roman Polanski fell in love with a young actress who had stabbed two previous lovers.

'I don't remember her last name,' a former student and friend of Polanski's told me. 'But her first name was Flora, and she was quite insane. She was a redhead, bright orange-red hair that was curly all over. She was small, thin and wiry, with freckles. And she was very emotional, very dramatic. Not at all attractive, plus she stuttered. There was always a kind of wild look in her eye, like a caged animal. She had started out as a ballerina. She was very promiscuous, and the male students were attracted to her because she had this awesome sexual agility, I mean, she had more positions than the Kama Sutra.

'But most of all, she was crazy. She had been out of school two or three years when Roman met her. Her last two boyfriends she had stuck knives into, literally. The first time it happened, it was overlooked, put down to a lover's quarrel. But the second boyfriend, he had gone to sleep in her bed, and the next thing he knew he woke up with a knife sticking in him. Almost died. For that they put her out of the school for a while

132

and told her to get treatment for her head.

'Roman knew nothing of her history when she appeared back at the school. She was supposed to be cured of her craziness. But those of us who had known her before knew as soon as we saw her that she wasn't cured at all. So we kept away from her. Since she had never seen Roman before, she zeroed in on him. He hadn't made much headway with girls up to then. When Flora let him go to bed with her, he took an immediate shine to her. With her agility, it wouldn't surprise me if she taught him more about sex in one night than he'd ever imagined existed. In the event, pretty soon he was in love, following her about the school and bristling with jealousy if anyone else so much as looked at her. Nobody told him about her. We were all waiting to see what would happen. And then it happened.

'One day Roman came in and he was as white as a sheet, trembling. We asked what had happened. At first he wouldn't say. Finally he confessed to someone that Flora had tried to stab him while he was asleep. He would have been dead, for sure, except she had the habit of going through some crazy incantation before plunging knives into her lovers. Her moaning had woken Roman just in time to see the knife coming at him.

'Flora was finally carted off to a mental ward and nothing was heard of her again. But she left quite an impression on Roman. Whenever I've seen the films he's made, the ones with the crazy women, I think of his experience with Flora. But except for Flora, Roman's first couple of years at the school were not very eventful. He was generally quiet and unassuming. He didn't start to make himself felt until after Andrzej Munk took him under his wing. Then, within a few months, he became a big shot, talkative and aggressive.'

After the annexation of Poland by the Soviet Union in 1945, Russian was installed as a compulsory language in all the country's schools. As a result, Polanski learned Russian during his technical and art-school years. Andrzej Munk was an aficionado of French culture and gloried in speaking French in private and when he directed. Polanski had learned a

133

rudimentary French from his parents as a child. When he saw that his new mentor preferred French, he signed up for a concentrated course in the language. Between the course and the French he was able to retrieve from his memory, he was able in a few months to converse with Munk. This gave him an enormous advantage over the older students assigned to work under the director. The normally aloof Munk quickly took the twenty-two-year-old Polanski under his personal wing.

In the summer of 1955, Polanski was called upon once more by Andrzej Wajda to play a small role in another of Wajda's feature films. This turned out to be the highly acclaimed Polish film *Kanal,* which was about the 1944 Polish uprising against the Germans in Warsaw. Glossing over history, the film did not note that the uprising failed because of Russian perfidy. Yet it was riveting in its portrayal of human agony in the sewers of Warsaw. Polanski again played a young resistance fighter. Over the next few years he would act in several more Wajda pictures while at the same time studying under and working on Munk's films at Lodz. With his rising prominence as a film actor and the special relationship he enjoyed with the revered Munk, he soon became the envy of his fellow students.

Polanski wasted no time in using his eminence to become a leader in the film school. Yet he remained something of an *enfant terrible.* He began anew to refuse to hew to rigid political policy. He had less and less hesitation about advancing aesthetic ideas of his own, based on his Western-movie influences and on the political iconoclasm of Andrzej Munk. Often he shocked and angered the school authorities.

By late 1955, though, Polanski's daring began to be viewed as somewhat visionary by many of his schoolmates. There had been a massive spontaneous uprising that summer in the city of Poznan, by young people and factory workers, in protest against the harsh political and working conditions of western Poland. The protest turned violent and countless students and workers were killed when the Polish army was sent in, guns blazing, to quash it. Nevertheless, the demonstrations spread. Soon the violence toppled the Soviet-controlled regime and brought in a new one headed by the more independent communist, Wadislaw Gomulka. By fall, the Gomulka government began to revise the restrictive communist party philosphy and to allow the populace of Poland more freedoms, intellectual as well as physical. Suddenly the intellectual impertinence Roman Polanski had been demonstrating at the film school was no longer shocking, but more-or-less acceptable. Polanski, would not allow himself to become part of the pack, however. Having had his notions vindicated by the events in Poznan, he strove to express ever more daring ideas in order to sustain his sudden student eminence at the school. His principal vehicle became the student films he was allowed to make himself.

Starting at the end of the second year, each directorial student was required to make one or two very short films – to write, cast, shoot, edit and carry out all the other technical tasks involved in the making of a film. These films were final examinations and were judged by the faculty mainly for their visual and technical execution. A passing grade was required before the student could advance to the school's next level.

Polanski made two brief films in 1956, and they were by far the most acclaimed and discussed of any of the student shorts. One lasted for only one minute, the other for three, but they had a visual impact and reflected a technical inventiveness far beyond what anyone expected. What debate there was about their merits centered around their substance. The 'stories' they told, like the pictures he once drew in drafting school, were eerie and symbolic, as though they were projections of Polanski's most deeply buried and repressed thoughts. They were gloomy and gory, mock-comedies of a tortured, even insane, soul. Yet they were abstract, nothing like the personality of Polanski himself, who was caustic, vibrant, rational and pragmatic in his approach to life.

Despite the films' technical precociousness, Polanski was severely criticized for 'artistic meretriciousness' and for 'fabricating counterfeit visions meant solely to stun and shock . . . to draw attention to himself.' This was no way to go about filmmaking he was told. His exercises contained no recognizable social content. They were all 'self-aggrandizing form without any redeeming substance,' and were 'immature attempts to attract attention and . . . foster a reputation for the bizarre.'

The criticisms notwithstanding, Polanski was promoted to the next level. Andrzej Munk had come to his defense. Although he, too, had been 'disturbed by the films' idiosyncracies,' he insisted that their technical qualities were the sole standard by which they were meant to be judged. And on this account, Polanski had acquitted himself with distinction.

The experience of finally making films on his own, however brief, captivated Polanski, and he would spend the next three years at Lodz in almost constant work on further projects. Before he was promoted to the school's next level in 1956, though, he would endure another life-threatening experience.

One day in the summer of that year he was racing with a group of other actors from Lodz to reach the location of a film being shot near Warsaw by Andrzej Munk. The crowded car in which Polanski was riding spun out of control on a rain-slickened road and hurtled into a tree. He suffered the second fractured skull in his life, and when he was found he was near death. Only skilful surgery saved him and prevented severe brain damage. A steel plate was inserted in his head to protect his brain while the shattered bones of his skull knitted.

Polanski was transported back to a hospital in Lodz to recover. He remained there for three weeks. During this time, visitors from the school detected a radical change in him. One of his visitors was Wojtek Frykowski, a schoolmate who would later achieve the dubious fame of being slain with Sharon Tate. About his visit, Frykowski once said, 'Roman came out of that crash with severe head injuries. The injuries seemed to do something to his personality. While he was recovering, lying in that bed, he became hyped up. He had always had a lot of energy and ambition, but now it was super-energy, super-ambition. He used to tell me later that lying in that bed gave him time to think. He reflected on his life and realized that he was lucky to be alive at all. He figured he had used up all his luck and would die at a young age. He became a confirmed fatalist. He was sure his fate was to die long before the rest of us. But before he died he would do the things he really wanted to. And he became a cynic. 'Screw this world,' he said. 'It has treated me like shit, so why should I care about it. I will use the world for what I want and to hell with the consequences. The world will get me in the end, anyway.'

'Like I say,' Frykowski went on, 'this change in him happened suddenly. In some ways he was more brilliant than ever. It was as if the shock to his head had shaken up his brain and cleared it of any doubts and confusions about himself and about life. He brooded more, but he laughed more too. And he became much more daring. It was this new screw-the-world attitude. He dropped all inhibitions. Inhibition was the chain that all men were forced by society to wear around their necks, he used to say.'

The plate has remained in Polanski's skull to this day. He has always claimed that he is unaware of it, and that it has had no effect on his behavior. 'I am me,' he has said, 'and it is my brain that makes me who I am, not a piece of steel that covers it.'

Another Pole who encountered Polanski around the time of his car accident was the young anti-communist Jerzy Kosinski. Born in Lodz, Kosinski would flee Poland a short time later. He would eventually become a famous novelist in America as well as a frequent guest of Johnny Carson on television's *Tonight Show*. At the time, Kosinski was studying to become a teacher of political science, but he was also obsessed by photography. He took some courses at the film school and struck up a friendship with Polanski – a friendship cemented by the common bonds of their childhoods. Kosinski too had lived a life on the run from the Germans during the war, and much of his family had been wiped out in the concentration camps.

Highly intelligent and mordantly intense, Kosinski was every bit as cynical and intellectually combative as Polanski. Although they became friends, they also became rivals for the attentions of the less gifted students at Lodz. One basic theme pervaded their arguments: the primacy of literature versus film as the most effective medium of the narrative form. Kosinski took the side of literature, dismissing cinema as a counterfeit artistic vehicle. Polanski, of course, argued for cinema. Their arguments often raged for hours.

Kosinski once told me that Polanski at this time had 'a very sharp mind, but what is even more, a powerful ambition to prove himself. Like many a young man who had grown up during the war under the worst of conditions, he felt an outcast. He felt dreadfully insecure in the world in which he had been born, and felt as if the world was ever waiting to crush him once again, to cast him out once more, even kill him. The only way to beat the world was to get control of it, to prove oneself to the point that that world would not dare mess with you any more. The more he got the hang of things at the school in Lodz, the more he believed that he had found a way to prove himself, to make himself so valuable to the world that it would not dare touch him.

Of course, to carry this out demanded a certain arrogance. And Roman was not without the gift of arrogance. He rapidly constructed a shell around himself that made him safe from any rejection, any attack. This shell – call it cynicism if you want – made him used to living a life of superficial emotions. Surface pleasures, surface displeasures – these were all he would allow himself. He wanted nothing in the way of deeper, more lasting emotions, whether pleasurable or not. Which is why I think he was so attracted to acting and film-making.

Kosinski has often been criticized for writing cold, emotionless literature. He himself is a man who shields his feelings behind a wall of trenchant wit and offhanded intellectualism. Yet his words give the hint that he probably understands Polanski better than most.

'A man makes himself like a piece of film – all slick images and surface feelings. When you see a film projected against a screen, what you really see are one-dimensional images flickering on a barrier, which is what the screen is. Without the barrier, which is put up to intercept the beams of light through which the film is projected, the beam of light would extend into infinity and the images would never be seen. So – the barrier, the screen, is absolutely essential for the film to be seen.

'This is very much how Roman formed himself once he began to understand film. He made of his personality and character a screen – a hard, inpenetrable screen – against which he projected the image of himself he wanted the world, the viewer, to accept.'

But what about feelings?

'Then he developed feelings with which he shaped the image. Since he could not use deep feelings, which are not easily controllable and imply the same vulnerability he had as a child, he substituted superficial feelings and, you might say, appetites. In fact I would describe Roman even today as a man of deep appetites rather than deep emotions. Not that you should infer that he is shallow or superficial. On the contrary, he is a very complex man. It is just that he is dominated by appetites rather than emotions. Appetites cannot be hurt. They can only be satisfied or denied.'

Kosinski's first novel was *The Painted Bird,* a harrowing account of a boy struggling to survive on his own in Nazi-occupied Poland during the war. Based on his own experiences, which had been considerably more perilous than Polanski's, the book was published to wide acclaim in the United States in 1965 and in several European countries shortly thereafter. It was a time when Polanski was beginning to gain public attention in American and Western Europe. When asked by interviewers about his childhood in Poland, Polanski declined to talk about it. He hinted that anything anyone wanted to know about it could be found in *The Painted Bird.* Much of Kosinski's novel, he implied, was based on his (Polanski's) life as a young boy.

Was this so?

No, said Kosinski, it certainly wasn't.

But the writer did not resent Polanski's co-opting of his own life. In fact he understood and sympathized. 'You notice that Roman has never attempted to deal with his own childhood in any of his films. How terrible it was I don't know for sure, but I do know that it must have been pretty terrible. Yet he has pointedly avoided portraying it in his work. Taking the boy in my book as himself was his way of avoiding ever to have to make it part of his work. But that wasn't the only reason. He's a good friend, and like a good friend he wanted to plug my book. He figured people who were interested in him would buy

139

The Painted Bird and I would make a little more money.'

Many of Polanski's friends disagree with Kosinski's whimsical explanation. 'It was all part of Roman's trying to create a myth about himself when he first started to become famous,' says one. *'The Painted Bird* came along at just the right time. By claiming that the boy in Jerzy's book was himself, Roman was able to avoid talking about his childhood to interviewers, which was distasteful to him. But he soon learned that interviewers took him seriously, so he decided to keep doing it because it was an easy way to pull the wool over people's eyes and form this myth about himself. And what really counted after a while was that the myth was a great help in getting him girls. Girls, he learned, fell for the idea of this.'

Polanski's long stay in bed in the early fall of 1956, and the several months thereafter of limited physical activity, left the muscles of his body atrophied. His already small figure appeared even more shrunken, causing him to lose a role in another Wajda film being shot that fall. To rebuild his body, he took to weightlifting and exercise programs. By the beginning of 1957, he had restored his body to its normal configuration and improved it. He enjoyed his added bulk and the inner sense of power it gave him. He had always been well-coordinated, quick and agile. But he had never had an opportunity to exploit his native athletic ability except in neighborhood soccer games.

Kosinski played a vital role in Polanski's physical rebirth. Lean and lithe, Kosinski was extremely athletic and an expert boxer, soccer player and skier. Since their friendship was based in part on a sense of rivalry. Polanski sought to equal Kosinski's physical prowess.

Friends who have described the change in Polanski's personality resulting from the automobile crash also credit the accident for the sudden and visible change in his sex life. By all accounts, including his own, up to the time he turned twenty-three he had had limited sexual experience. Much of this stemmed from the fact that he was self-conscious about his size and looks, say some. Others insist that his small stature had nothing to do with it – after all, he was not that much shorter than the average Pole. They claim that having grown up without a mother, he did not know how to deal with females. Despite his boasting about his experiences in Vienna several years before, Polanski seemed to have lost interest in girls after his first round of sexual experiences in Cracow. Once at Lodz, except for his brief affair with the psychotic Flora, he was hardly ever seen in the company of a female – this despite the fact that girls were numerous at the film school and on the motion picture sets. 'Whenever he was in a one-to-one situation with a girl at the school,' a male contemporary of Polanski's recalls, 'he was awkward and timid. The only time he would reveal himself to a girl was to make a cutting remark, to say something clever but cruel so as to push her away.'

'He was not comfortable in the company of females before the car crash,' remembers another former student at Lodz. 'I think he had this fear or abhorrence of women because he had lost his mother, and all the other women he had encountered growing up were unpleasant. But after the crash, while he was building himself up with his exercises, he suddenly started chasing girls. He told me the reason for it was that while he was in the hospital, there was a young nurse who fell for him. His head, you see, was all swathed in bandages, and his neck and chin. All you could see of him were his mouth, nose and eyes. His eyes had developed into a most attractive feature. Brown and deer-like, they were quite appealing. The nurse took pity on him, I suppose, fell in love with his eyes, he said. She would come into his room and be very kind to him and tell him what great eyes he had. I think he had a brief affair with the nurse when he got well enough to have sex. Ever since then he was very conscious of his eyes and the effects he thought they had on women. As he was building himself up with his exercises, he took to flirting with the girls in Lodz and, as he called it, 'seducing them with his eyes'. And he had quite a bit of success. The more he succeeded, the more daring he became. Soon he was a regular Lothario. But the girls, many of them, wanted more than sex from him. They wanted – companionship, I guess, trust, a relationship. But he wasn't interested. Oh, he tried, but he just couldn't or wouldn't commit himself. For one thing, the girls he went with were not all that attractive. Nor smart. Nothing like Roman. It bored him talking to them.'

Others insist that, more than any other factor, it was again Jerzy Kosinski who was responsible for the radical change in Polanski's conduct with regard to the opposite sex. Kosinski was courtly and darkly, almost menacingly, handsome. When he arrived at Lodz, he instantly established himself as a Lothario. Polanski soon picked up on this and, again motivated by his sense of rivalry, sought to emulate his friend.

Polanski's reputation at the film school flourished after his automobile accident and the development of his friendship with Kosinski. His principal cinematic exercise in 1957 was an eight-minute short which he called *Break Up The Dance*. It was a more restrained venture than his initial efforts of the year before. Nevertheless, during its making, there were complaints by the actors and technicians who worked on the project about the way Polanski directed. 'He was doing a bad imitation of Andrzej Munk, who was notorious for his ruthless, dictatorial manner on the set,' said one. 'When Munk wanted tears from an actress, he would bully her, shout at her, insult her until she broke into sobs. Everyone was afraid of Munk on a film set. But he was revered at the same time because he made such good pictures. When Roman tried to style himself after Munk, he received a lot of antagonism. As a result, *Break Up The Dance* was not very interesting. In fact no one at the school liked it, and especially not Munk.'

Polanski was undaunted. Around him at the school had formed a small clique of admirers. Some of them were talented and original, while others were simply sycophants who sought to attach themselves to Polanski's rising star in the expectation that they would be able to share in his glory once he became an important film-maker in Poland, as, they now believed, he would.

Among the talented was Jakub Goldberg, a young writer who had survived the concentration camps and whose intellectual fires burned with a flame of the macabre and absurd. In Goldberg's fevered and disordered mind, the real world was an illusory place in which the usual was unusual, and the unusual was ordinary. Goldberg was a man without passion, though, all feeling having been sucked from him by the horrors he had witnessed as a child. He thought and felt in symbols, in often cruel and wry symbols that personified for him the absurdity of life. He wrote that way too, and the student scripts he turned out, although deficient in the technical niceties of screenwriting, appealed to Polanski in their sinister ambiguousness.

At this time, Polanski was not a screenwriter; his passions were centered solely on the directorial process and the power – creative and personal – it provided him. He became fascinated by Goldberg's ideas, in large part because of his own growing affection for enigma as it related to film. It was much easier, in Polanski's view, to photograph an abstract story than a realistic one – to leave things dangling, to float several non-essential elements through a film without having to resolve or explain them – than it was to, say, put one on the stage. Film by its very nature was mysterious and enigmatic, and it lent itself, like painting – indeed, like life itself – to the imprecise. It much more readily accommodated itself to subtex than conventional literature or drama.

Jakub Goldberg had come under the spell of Eugene Samuel Beckett, the Irish dramatist, and then Ionesco, the French-Rumanian dramatist whose plays had become immensely popular in Europe – plays such as *The Bald Primadonna* and *The Chairs*. Ionesco wrote in surrealistic subtext, the architecture of his scripts serving only as frames for the mysteries and enigmas he sought to impart. And he wrote cryptically. His scripts were like poems, bereft of the conventional stage directions or instructions regarding character emotions, devoid of set scenes, of time, of space. They were truncated monologues and dialogues that evolved out of a situation – for instance, a man contemplating the carcass of a dead bird or two women encountering each other on a path.

Early in 1958, Goldberg handed Polanski a short script about two men who emerge from the sea carrying a giant wardrobe between them. The ensuing dialogue was, in Goldberg's Ionesco-influenced style, by turns mysteriously philosophical and animalistically crude, but always murky and unfocused.

Polanski, who had also studied Beckett and Ionesco, decided to use the script as the basis for his new student film. He reworked the script into a more clearly definable fable and filmed it during the spring of 1958. He entitled it *Two Men and a Wardrobe,* and when he screened it at the school in June it captivated the judges and student audience alike.

Retaining Goldberg's basic idea, Polanski pictured the wardrobe, carried between them by the two men as they emerged from the sea, as a symbol of apartness. As the film unreeled, the two laboring men carried their burden through a world of cruelty, conformity, and self-interest, where they were unable to make any human contact. Defeated in their quest, they returned into the sea again, still lugging the wardrobe between them.

The film was considered daring, Polanski later said of it, 'but it came at just the right period when the new more liberal trend was starting in Poland and more and more people were saying what they wanted to say, in the press, in books, in the cinema. There were certainly still difficulties in doing what you wanted to do in a feature film, but not in the short films made in the school.'

The theme of disoriented individuals in conflict with a hostile society was not an unusual one. What was unusual was the coherence Polanski had given it in the film. The camera work was highly inventive and the film's technical qualities impeccable for the time.

What was even more significant was that Polanski had discovered a subject matter he felt comfortable with as a way of cinematic storytelling. His embellishments to Goldberg's original symbolic idea of alienation and disorientation, and the way in which he carried the film off technically, prefigured the work Polanski would eventually become famous for.

Two Men and a Wardrobe secured Polanski's reputation as one of the film school's foremost talents. He was inflated by the acclaim he received and was driven to better himself. He teamed with Goldberg again to make two more shorts, one of which they presented as their graduation exercise in the spring of 1959. Called *When Angels Fall,* it was the monologue of an elderly female toilet attendant recalling her past – a past that was half-dream, half-real. Polanski made the film more to show off his technical virtuosity than to impress the judges with his narrative talents, since, he says, it was his graduation film. Although it was criticized for its lifelessness and cleverness, it passed the judges' muster and Polanski was given his diploma.

During his last two years at Lodz, Polanski had had several casual romantic relationships with actresses in the school. Most Polish women, even actresses, were brought up in the tradition that men were superior beings and that their desires and needs had priority over their own. They were generally pliant and submissive, and they were conditioned to suffer what in modern Western terms would be seen as male exploitation, sexual and otherwise, with stoic acceptance. Polanski learned from his school relationships that women, usually, were an easy device through which to express his manhood, gain sexual self-esteem, and earn the social esteem of his male peers.

There was one young actress in the school, however, who was not like the others. At twenty-four, Barbara Kwiatowski was not only attractive and talented, she was independent and assertive and, when necessary, aloof. During his last spring at Lodz, Polanski became intrigued by her inaccessibility and began to pursue her. When she proved not to be the easy mark he had become accustomed to, his intrigue turned to desire.

Barbara, who had taken the acting name of Barbara Lass, was also ambitious and, it has been said, a bit of an opportunist. When she perceived that Polanski had a good chance to rise quickly in the Polish cinema hierarchy, she began to respond to him.

In Poland at the time of Polanski's graduation, the state-subsidized cinema was comprised of eight separate production units. Each was headed by an eminent producer-director, who was required to submit scripts to the central cinema board for approval before he could hope to receive money to make a film. Recently named to head one of the eight companies, called KAMERA, was Andrzej Munk, Polanski's film-school mentor.

Upon his graduation from Lodz, Polanski, now twenty-six, once again faced a call-up to the army. Munk, however, arranged for a further brief deferment in the summer of 1959 so that his protegé could join KAMERA as an assistant director. The reasoning used, again, was that Polanski was more valuable to the state as a movie-production worker than as a soldier.

KAMERA was located in Warsaw. When Polanski arrived there in the early fall of 1959 after a brief visit to Cracow, he brought with him Jakub Goldberg. Since graduation, the two had been collaborating on a script for a full-length film. It was their hope that through Munk they would get financing from the film board and be able to make the picture in short order.

The script had its origin in a short script Goldberg had crafted, while still at Lodz, about two men who kill each other through some absurdist existential verbal misunderstanding. Although he liked the idea, Polanski had felt the work was too static for cinematic rendering and had gone to work during the summer on improving and expanding it. The two toiled together and separately up to the time they reported to KAMERA, but the improvements were few. Polanski's main contribution at the time came in changing the setting from a coffee house in Lodz to Poland's starkly beautiful northern lake country, which he remembered from the filming of *A Generation*.

Upon arrival in Warsaw, Polanski was immediately put to work as an actor and assistant technical director in a film being shot by Andrzej Wajda. His ambition to make his own film did not abate, however, and he spent most of his spare time on the Goldberg script.

Polanski encountered another budding writer-director who worked for KAMERA. His name was Jerzy Skolimowski, and as the two became friends and started trading ideas, Polanski showed him the bulky script. Skolimowski, several years younger than Polanski was impressed by the theme of how enmity between two men develops in a world in which everything is slightly off center and not really the way it seems. But he too felt the story of the two old characters – friends now sharing a boat in a northern lake and carrying on an interminable conversation that leads to disagreement, then disaster – was static and without suspense.

Skolimowski, who had already written one full-length film

for Andrzej Wajda, was enlisted in the script collaboration. He changed the setting from the boat to a car and made the men strangers – one the driver of the car, an older man, the other a hitchhiking youth he picks up. The two men were to symbolize the younger and older generations of Poland, the car and passing landscape the rapidly changing world in which they lived. The drama's conflict would lie in the clash of values between the two men as they tried to understand each other on their ride to oblivion.

Skolimowski's changes improved the script and made it cinematically more taut. But it continued to lack the suspense necessary to carry a full-length film; it was still a twenty-minute short.

In the meantime, the military authorities were once more breathing down Polanski's neck. This time they seemed determined to force Polanski to serve his time. As an unmarried man in his mid-twenties, and with several deferments behind him, he had long been at the top of the list of those eligible for the draft. The fact that he hadn't yet been inducted was becoming an embarrassment to the authorities in charge of his case. They let him know in no uncertain terms that once his present deferment expired at the end of 1959, he would be compelled to report for his three years of military service.

As summer turned to fall, Polanski grew desperate. He persuaded Andrzej Munk to apply for a continuance of his deferment, but that was summarily rejected. He got others to write letters on his behalf, claiming again that his conscription into the army would nip the beginning of an important film career in the bud. They were ignored. He even persuaded a middle-level official of Poland's ministry of culture – the ministry that controlled the film industry – to intercede on his behalf. The official suggested to the military authorities that Polanski be allowed to remain a civilian in exchange for making several military training films each year. The suggestion was declined.

But Polanski would not give up his quest for a way to continue avoiding military service. Much of his time that fall was spent in trying to find a way out. Finally he discovered it.

147

His salvation came in the form of Barbara Kwiatowski-Lass.

Upon his graduation from Lodz a few months before, the aspiring actress had rewarded Polanski by allowing him to go to bed with her. There followed an impassioned week-long sexual affair before the two were forced to go their separate ways – Polanski back to Cracow and then to Warsaw to take up his job at KAMERA, Barbara Lass to Poznan to join an acting company. The passion had been mostly Polanski's, and when they separated he was convinced he was in love with her.

Polanski's ardor grew more intense and pained as the summer passed. By August he began to write her tortured love letters, pleading with her to come to Warsaw and promising that he would get her film roles in KAMERA productions. Impressed by his promises, Barbara Lass showed up in Warsaw in late September.

Polanski was so grateful that he immediately introduced her to Andrzej Munk and several other directors, insisting that they consider her for film roles. Munk, despite his fondness for Polanski, was taken aback by his protegé's demands and rebuked him. The others simply ignored them.

Embarrassed but undaunted, Polanski did not tell Barbara Lass about the rebuffs. He convinced her instead that Munk and the other directors had agreed to use her as soon as the right parts came up. In the meantime, he promised to make a reel of screen-test film of her and declared that he was going to write a screenplay which he would direct and in which she would star.

Polanski had been promised by Munk an opportunity to direct his first feature-length film once he produced an artistically acceptable script that was also approved by the ministry of culture, whose imprimatur was required for all Polish films. Polanski had originally hoped that the script he had been laboring over with Goldberg and Skolimowski would be the one that would launch his directing career. But with that project still bogged down in conceptual difficulties, and inspired by his feelings for Barbara Lass, he immediately set out to develop a story that would have as its main character a woman who Barbara could portray. It would be romantically fitting, he convinced her, that they make their professional film debuts together.

This new writing project quickly bogged down as well. Polanski was not only distracted by his continuing efforts to avoid army service, but was handcuffed by his basic lack of understanding of, and insight into, women. As a result, his attempts to create a convincing female character were repeatedly frustrated. They were particularly frustrated by Barbara Lass herself, for whom Polanski was trying to tailor the character. Since she had such a vital interest in the script, she was unhesitating in her willingness to point out the flaws in Polanski's writing.

By this time, mid-October of 1959, Barbara Lass had moved into Polanski's tiny flat near the KAMERA offices. Two people who knew them well later told me that Barbara Lass was never in love with Polanski. She moved in with him partly because she had no money for a place of her own and partly because she was impressed by the efforts he was making on her behalf. Becoming Polanski's full-time lover was her way of expressing her gratitude.

Polanski, on the other hand, was clearly in love with Barbara, although 'it was a typically male adolescent kind of love,' as one of their friends later put it to me. 'She was good-looking and aggressive, very modern in her outlook and intense in her ambition. Roman adored her, mostly because being with her made him look good. Barbara was very sophisticated sexually, Roman wasn't. She was teaching him things about sex that he never imagined existed. But the real attraction for Roman was that being with her made him look good with his male friends. Barbara became like his badge of honor – none of them had such good-looking girlfriends. So to Roman, this became love.

'Barbara, though, was not so much in love with him as she was with the idea of what he could do for her career. Usually it is the men who are the exploiters in these situations and the women who are the exploited. But here Barbara Lass was the exploiter and Roman the victim. Of course, this was not to say she didn't have an emotional feeling for him. She did get involved with him emotionally. She had to. After all, in many ways she came to believe that her success depended on his. She

149

wanted him to succeed. That was the emotional investment she made in him.'

Polanski, as it would turn out, was not beyond exploiting Barbara Lass, however. As the end of his military deferment approached in November and he continued to be thwarted in his increasingly desperate attempts to renew it, he learned through his friend at the culture ministry that a freeze had been put on the drafting of married men because there were so many unmarried men who had not yet served in the army.

Suddenly Polanski found himself with an unexpected opportunity to once more beat the Polish draft. He wasted no time in begging Barbara Lass to marry him. She was at first unwilling, since marriage to Polanski was not something that had figured in her plans. But Polanski kept after her. He claimed that it had always been his hope that they would marry once their respective careers were launched. He argued that if the promising beginnings of his cinema career were interrupted by three years of forced military duty, hers would suffer as well. He needed only a little more time, he implored, to get their joint film project off the ground. If he was drafted, the entire project, all the work he had done, would go down the drain. Indeed, he insisted, most of his problems, in putting together an effective script stemmed from his anxiety about being drafted. Once free of that worry, he would be able to devote all of his concentration to his work and would produce a stunning screenplay for her. When translated into a feature film, it would make them both cinema luminaries.

Barbara Lass finally caved in under Polanski's pressure. 'She had misgivings still,' says one of her friends of the time, 'but I think she genuinely felt sorry for Roman. She felt he was obviously going places and did not want to be responsible for preventing or delaying his success. Of course, she trusted that his success would be hers too.'

Polanski and Barbara Kwiatowski-Lass were married just before Christmas in December of 1959. Polanski immediately presented his marriage certificate to the military authorities. His name was grudgingly taken off the list of priority draft-eligibles and put on a reserve list. He was warned, however, that when married men were once again eligible, probably the following year, he would be at the top of the list.

His marriage was certainly a significant event in Polanski's life, but something considerably more significant took place during the same period.

At the time Polanski was trying to convince Barbara to marry him, Warsaw was visited by a group of left-wing French film-makers headed by the noted director Jean Drot. Andrzej Munk, the Francophile, had arranged for the visit so that his French counterpart, Drot, could film some documentaries about Poland. As Munk's only French-speaking assistant, Polanski was assigned to interpret for Drot and his contingent of writers and technicians. The facilities of KAMERA were theirs to use as needed.

Polanski quickly ingratiated himself with Drot, who was a homosexual, by procuring a couple of willing young Polish actors for his leisure-time pleasure. The French director repayed the favor by agreeing to sit through a screening of Polanski's student film, *Two Men and a Wardrobe*. Impressed, Drot offered to take a print back to France, where he would offer it to several film festivals. Drot also introduced Polanski to a young French film publicist and novice screenwriter who he had brought on the trip to Poland. The writer's name was Gerard Brach. According to Drot, Polanski and Brach had complementary cinematic ideas.

Brach, an effusive and intense Frenchman, was as impressed as Drot had been by *Two Men and a Wardrobe*. He and Polanski quickly became friends, and Brach began to tell Polanski about life and film-making in France. Between them, Drot and Brach convinced Polanski that his film future lay in France where the opportunity for experimentation and free expression was much richer than in Poland. A reciprocal visit by a group of Polish film-makers to France was being arranged for the following spring. Drot and Brach promised to try to get Polanski invited, along with his soon-to-be wife Barbara Lass.

The promise would be partially fulfilled. Barbara Lass did not make the list, but with Munk's approval Polanski was allowed to leave Poland. He arrived in Paris, the city of his birth, in March 1960. His six-month stay there would be another major turning point in his life.

INTERLOG 6

POLANSKI'S INDICTMENT on 24 March 1977, unleashed a new round of media publicity, much of it leering and irreverent.

One newspaper, New York's *Village Voice,* printed a doctored photograph that pictured a surprised-looking Polanski cheek-to-cheek with Amy Carter, the much-in-the-news nine-year old daughter of the new American president. 'The Romance That Might Have Been,' read the caption, while superimposed on the photo was a balloon that had Polanski asking: 'She's *Whose* Daughter?'

Another paper printed an item about Polanski having dinner the night after his indictment at *Ma Maison,* Hollywood's 'in' restaurant. When he was spied from across the room by a producer, a man known for his mordant wit, the producer sent over a complementary bottle of Polanski's favorite French wine. 'It was a 1964 vintage,' went on the item, 'the same age as another recent Polanski favorite.'

These are examples of the milder forms of media ribaldry that followed in the wake of his indictment. Polanski ignored it all, and he refused to go into hiding. Instead, he carried on his public life as though nothing had occurred, attending parties and film screenings and continuing to work on *The First Deadly Sin*. He remained his old cocksure self and seemed to go out of his way to be seen in the company of young actresses of indeterminate age. Much of Hollywood found this fascinating, the way the director for the first week or so appeared to be thumbing his nose at the law and his critics in the press. Only the nervous Douglas Dalton counseled him against it, but Polanski wouldn't listen.

'I am not guilty, so why should I act guilty,' Polanski said.

All well and good, Dalton told him. But if and when his case went to trial, he would be facing a jury of people who would remember his behavior. They would be certain to see it as arrogance on his part, as an unforgivable flaunting of convention. If they didn't see it by themselves, the uncompromising prosecutor would certainly point it out. In America, when a man was indicted for felonies, he was supposed to declare his innocence and then maintain a somber mien and low profile until he was exonerated in court. If Polanski kept carrying on in public as if he didn't have a care in the world, a jury would be likely to consider it worth punishing him, regardless of his innocence. It was unfair, Dalton said, but that, unfortunately, was the way the system often worked.

'There is nothing fair about this whole business,' Polanski retorted. His voice was uncontrite, his words spilling out almost too quickly to be understood against the harshness of his accent, which always became more pronounced when he was angry. Dalton gave up trying to argue with him on the subject.

The director's defiance was short-lived, however. Although he refused to express public concern over his legal plight, he grew secretly more worried about his position with Columbia Pictures. After his indictment, matters became confusing at the studio, with executives still declining to answer his phone calls and production workers studiously ignoring him when he came into his office in the mornings. Then came the dreaded news: Columbia announced that it intended to suspend further work on *The First Deadly Sin* and hold Polanski's contract in abeyance until he was cleared of the charges against him.

Polanski had good reason for concern. Not only was the

movie shut down, but his generous monthly contract payments were cut off. He was asked to leave his office at Columbia and told that the company would no longer foot his bills at the Beverly Wilshire Hotel.

As always, Polanski was now in need of ready cash, if for no other reason than to pay for his defense. According to Dalton's estimates, the defense would be costly. Dalton charged well over $100 per hour, and in addition to his fees there would be enormous expenses for pre-trial preparation and investigations. Polanski's entire defense, not including the cost of appeals if he was found guilty, could set him back in excess of $100,000. And there was no guarantee that it would succeed.

Polanski had never worried about money, but these figures were staggering. With the Columbia contract suspended, he was barely able to give Dalton a token down payment. With the director's shrunken finances in mind, Dalton suggested that Polanski consider plea-bargaining. Dalton was sure that he could negotiate a deal whereby the district attorney, in exchange for accepting a plea of guilty to one of the lesser counts in the indictment, would drop the other charges. A guilty plea would preclude a costly and sensational public trial, and the consequences would probably be less onerous than if Polanski were found guilty of one or more of the more serious felonies in a jury trial.

Dalton's suggestion was one that any conscionable lawyer would give to a client in such a situation. Polanski, however, found it unconscionable. 'I did not rape her,' he said over and over. 'It's all a stupid misunderstanding. She did it willingly. Why should I plead guilty to something I'm not guilty of?'

The girl was thirteen, Dalton reminded Polanski. The lawyer then outlined once again the various statutes that exposed him to trial and punishment. It really didn't matter that the girl might have been willing. Polanski had still had sexual intercourse with a minor. If she testified that she had been unwilling, there would not be much he could do about it.

Polanski would have none of it. 'I don't care,' he told Dalton. 'If I plead guilty to something, it will make it seem that I *was* guilty. That will give Columbia the excuse to terminate my contract altogether. I can't let that happen. I'll take my chances on a jury. A jury will see that I was not at fault.'

Dalton had fulfilled his obligation. He shrugged resignedly and settled down to prepare as competent a defense as he could under the circumstances. But, he wondered aloud to Polanski, how would he get paid in view of the director's sudden financial drought? Was Polanski willing to put some of his property in hock? He wasn't. He had a better idea, but he would need Dalton's help.

Before he had signed his Columbia contract, Polanski had been offered a directing job in England and France by two producers representing a syndicate of German investors. He had declined the offer, partly because the Columbia contract was soon to be confirmed, but also because, as he announced at the time, 'I will not work for German money.' Although he regularly drove Mercedes-Benz automobiles, he had long claimed to despise everything German.

Now, the German money was his only financial lifeline. He called Paris to learn if the offer was still open. It was, and it was made even more attractive by the sensational publicity Polanski's US troubles were receiving in the European press. If Polanski would come to Paris, he was told, a contract would be ready.

On 19 April 1977, Polanski appeared before Santa Monica Superior Court judge Laurence J. Rittenband to enter his formal plea of innocence and to have a date set for the trial. Rittenband set the trial down to begin on 11 May and continued Polanski in $2500 bail.

Then, Douglas Dalton made a motion that his client be allowed to travel to Paris for a week to conduct urgent business. He had explained to the judge privately, and to District Attorney Gunson, that the trip was required so that Polanski could sign a contract and obtain some money to help pay for his upcoming legal expenses. With no objection from Gunson, Judge Rittenband granted the motion.

This was the first of several developments in the case that caused newspapers to wonder whether Polanski was getting special treatment. Had he been 'an ordinary person charged with the crimes attributed to him,' wrote one paper, 'no judge in California would allow him such personal latitude – surely his passport would have been confiscated.' What was going on here? Why was Polanski deferred to by the court when an ordinary citizen would probably be in jail, unable to make bail. Rittenband's judicial competence, and his motives were severely questioned.

'It's essential that Mr Polanski travel to Paris to take care of a business matter,' Douglas Dalton had explained to the press at a raucous news conference. 'It is quite important for him to make the trip.'

Important for Dalton too, guessed one newspaper. The reason D.A. Gunson didn't object was because 'lawyers look after each other when it comes to collecting their fees, even when they are adversaries.' And, went the speculation, judges look after lawyers too.

Asked if he wasn't afraid Polanski might just stay in Paris, never to return for trial, Judge Rittenband had claimed that he had Dalton's assurances that his client would return.

Polanski had jumped in with his own vow at the news conference. 'I wouldn't [flee the country],' he told the Los Angeles *Herald-Examiner*. 'First of all, I have confidence in the judicial system. I know I am innocent and I am not going to shy from it.'

As the trial date neared, fewer and fewer people expected it to begin on 11 May. Gearing up his defense, Dalton announced to the press during the last week in April that he intended to file a host of pre-trial motions that were guaranteed to delay the start of the trial.

Polanski flew to Paris at the end of April. There he signed his contract, which called for him to direct a costume movie in England based on Thomas Hardy's nineteenth-century British novel, *Tess of the D'Urbervilles*. It was the story of a young innocent girl, Tess, who is trapped and possessed by a lecherous older ne'erdowell, Alec D'Urberville; later, she kills D'Urberville and is sent to the gallows.

The irony of this was not missed by the press when it learned about it. 'What is it about Polanski,' asked a columnist for the *Hollywood Reporter*, 'that compels him to make himself the laughingstock of Hollywood. You would have thought that he'd have the good sense to make a war movie or something.'

The start of the picture would have to wait the outcome of Polanski's legal problems in California. But at least now he had a $50,000 cash advance with which to help finance the beginnings of his defense and maintain his lifestyle for a few months.

While Polanski was in Paris, Douglas Dalton was busy opening up the discovery process available to criminal defendants in California – the process that requires the prosecution to disclose to the defendant the evidence it intends to use in mounting its case. The chief document of discovery was the transcript of Roger Gunson's grand jury investigation. Judge Rittenband ordered the contents sealed from public view in order to continue to protect the identity of Polanski's victim, whose name was freely mentioned. But the transcript was made available by law to Dalton. In it he found the material upon which he would attempt to establish Polanski's defense: the girl's credibility and her past sexual history.

The doctor who examined the girl at Parkwood Hospital on 11 March had appeared before the grand jury. He testified that the girl had told him that she had engaged in sexual intercourse on two occasions prior to her encounter with Polanski. When she was called to testify, the girl was asked if this was true. She replied that it was. She was asked no more about it.

In response to the questions put to her before the grand jury, the girl was alternately certain and uncertain, or vague, about the events she described during her afternoon with Polanski. Whether this reflected nervousness or calculated obfuscation on her part could not be determined by seeing her answers in print. But Dalton believed that her occasional vagueness gave him an opening to attack her credibility.

What convinced him was the testimony of the girl's boyfriend. The grand jury proceedings revealed that the boyfriend had been questioned about what the girl had said to him the night Polanski returned her to her home. Buried in his answers were statements that reflected the boyfriend's disbelieving reaction to what the girl had told him about Polanski. The girl was 'always acting,' the boyfriend had testified. At first he had thought she was making up the story of what had happened to her at Polanski's hands in order to make him jealous.

With this knowledge in hand, Dalton went into court on 11 May – the date set for the beginning of the trial – without Polanski but with a twenty-five page motion for summary dismissal of the charges against him. Failing that, he demanded an opportunity to question the girl. 'I seek to ascertain if she is truthful about her previous episodes of sex,' he said in his motion. 'It is possible that she fantasizes or lies about previous sexual experiences.'

Where had Dalton come up with such a possibility?

He was not ready to reveal it yet, but he had not just relied on the grand jury transcript to perceive a possible lack of credibility in the girl's story. He had hired a private investigator to do some quick research into the girl's background. The report he had received indicated that the girl might well have had more than two sexual experiences in the past. If so, she had lied to the grand jury. He wanted to question her in order to confirm his reports and thereby be in a position to impugn her testimony at trial.

All Dalton would claim in his motion, however, was that the failure of the district attorney to question the girl further about when, where and with whom she had had her previous sexual experiences, 'deprives the defendant of vital information' that could be used to attack the girl's credibility. Dalton conceded that California law generally bars the exploration of an alleged rape victim's sexual history in court. But he contended that the prosecution had 'opened the door and waived any objection' to such questioning as he wanted to do by introducing the matter before the grand jury.

Dalton then referred to the boyfriend's grand jury statements, claiming that the boy's characterization of the girl as 'always acting' was sufficient to raise doubts about her

159

believability. And the testimony of the girl herself indicated, Dalton heatedly claimed, 'that she is barely able to remember events that she alleges occurred to her.'

Dalton then presented a separate sixteen-page discovery motion designed to force the district attorney to turn over 'all physical evidence,' including the panties the girl claimed to have worn, for independent analysis by the defense. Sergeant Vanatter's grand jury testimony showed that the girl 'was not wearing the garment at the time the [police] officers arrived,' Dalton argued. 'She went to another part of the house, got the garment, and gave it to the officers.' The panties, Dalton went on, which police said had tested positive for semen, could not be legally connected to the case since the girl did not remove them from herself and hand them to the officers. Thus they should not be permitted as evidence.

Why did Dalton want the panties, then?

Since the girl had left the officers' presence to get them, they could have belonged to anyone. They could have belonged to her sister, and the traces of semen could have belonged to a man with whom her sister had had sex. Or, if indeed they were hers, she might not have worn them for some time before her meeting with Polanski. The semen traces might have gotten there from a prior sexual encounter she had with someone other than Polanski. If the court denied the defense access to the girl's undergarments, it would be depriving the defendant of his right to determine the true ownership of the panties and his ability to discredit his accuser's credibility.

District attorney Gunson announced to Judge Rittenband that he would oppose any attempt to scrutinize the girl's sexual history, not only because the law proscribed such scrutiny but 'because it is plainly not relevant to this case.'

Judge Rittenband reserved decision on Dalton's motions and agreed to delay the start of the trial until 29 June. He called another hearing for 20 May, at which time he promised to rule on Dalton's motions.

Polanski was still in Paris at the time of the 11 May hearing. His absence was noted with annoyance by Rittenband, since that had been the date set for the trial and Rittenband was growing angry with press criticisms of his treatment of the director. Dalton promised to have him in court for the 20 May pre-trial hearing.

True to his word, Dalton appeared on 20 May with Polanski in tow. The director, dressed in a stylish new suit, was looking confident once again. Not only had he signed the French contract, but upon his return a few days earlier he had been offered an immediate directing job by Dino de Laurentiis. The picture was to be an expensive South Sea island epic called *Hurricane*. Already chosen to star in it was Mia Farrow, a devoted friend of Polanski since the time he had directed her in the hit *Rosemary's Baby*, almost ten years before.

Farrow had her own troubled history. She had made a name for herself in the early 1960s as one of the featured players in the long-running television series *Peyton Place*. A brief, turbulent marriage to Frank Sinatra followed. After her divorce from Sinatra, she met the noted musical conductor Andre Previn and his wife. Previn married her after obtaining his own divorce. The two settled in London and Mia had two children and then adopted two more. By 1977 she had broken up with Previn and had accepted the role in *Hurricane* to put some distance between Previn and herself. When she heard about Polanski's problems she prevailed upon de Laurentiis to give him the job of directing *Hurricane*.

The only trouble was that the movie was scheduled to be shot in the South Pacific and pre-production work was already behind schedule. Would Polanski be able to work on it there while in the midst of his legal troubles in Los Angeles?

The 20 May hearing lasted for almost two hours. Polanski sat expressionless at the defense table while Dalton jousted over procedural matters with prosecutor Gunson and Judge Rittenband. Rittenband testily denied Dalton's crucial motions for summary dismissal and for the right to question the victim before trial. 'It is clearly contrary to law,' said Rittenband, 'and I therefore have no authority to grand your request. And even if I did, I would not, Mr Dalton. It is not my function to serve as your pathfinder.'

Dalton countered with another motion – this one seeking to introduce independent evidence testimony regarding the girl's previous sexual conduct.

The newspapermen present buzzed about this. Dalton, it was becoming clear, although arguing procedural points, was out to make the girl the focus of the case, not Polanski. Perhaps he hoped to pressure her, or her parents, into persuading the prosecution to drop the case. After all, went the speculation, what parent would allow his or her child to be cast into the role of villain in such an affair?

Gunson attacked Dalton's strategy of this in his objections, vehemently repeating his argument that the girl's sexual history was irrelevant, whether testimony came from the girl herself or from independent sources. Gunson, as he later explained, didn't know whether Dalton's private investigations had turned up more than two people who would testify to having had sex with the girl. But he didn't want to find out. Of course, he thought, it might be just a procedural bluff to intimidate the girl and her mother. Dalton, he knew, was an accomplished courtroom strategist.

Next came arguments over the girl's panties, and here Gunson had a surprise for Dalton. He downplayed the importance of the panties as he disclosed that he had other, more significant physical evidence which he intended to produce at trial. The evidence was the group of topless pictures taken of the girl by Polanski and found in his room at the Beverly Wilshire by the arresting officers on 11 March. And Quaalude tablets, one of which Polanski had tried to discard upon his arrest. These separate items of evidence, Gunson told the court, 'substantiate almost every point [the victim] testified to before the grand jury.'

That was an odd twist. How could Polanski's pictures of the girl, or the fact that he possessed Quaaludes at the time of the arrest, prove that he had drugged and raped the girl.

They couldn't, of course. But Gunson was a trial lawyer. Like Dalton, like most lawyers, he would seek to stuff the record with as much 'evidence' as he could, no matter how inconclusive it might be. Every bit of evidence that might substantiate minor or even irrelevant details of the girl's story was worthwhile. If the girl could be believed on minor points, she could be believed on major ones – the points before the bar. Did Polanski actually feed her drugs and then rape her? Or was she a willing victim? It was essential to Gunson that the girl's story – despite the inconsistencies it might contain – hold up. Shreds of secondary evidence, such as the pictures and pills, would help that cause.

But the really vital corroborative evidence Gunson had was not physical. It was the testimony of Anjelica Huston, who would place Polanski in the bedroom with the girl.

A few days before, the district attorney had finally made a deal with Huston and her lawyer that he had been holding in abeyance. She would not be prosecuted on the narcotics charges. In return, she would testify for the prosecution in the Polanski case.

Polanski had learned about this upon his return from Paris. The news came in a phone call from Jack Nicholson, who apologized and tried to explain. Polanski shrugged it off, saying that he understood and had no hard feelings.

Douglas Dalton could not be so cavalier. Anjelica's testimony could not corroborate the state's charges that his client had sodomized the girl or forced her to submit to oral copulation or even that he fed her drugs, since she had witnessed none of these. But the basic and most damaging charge against Polanski remained the one pertaining to unlawful intercourse, or statutory rape. All Huston had to do was testify before a jury that she had ascertained that Polanski was in the Nicholson bedroom with the girl and had later seen them emerge together. That would be enough to get a jury to convict Polanski on the rape charge at least, since the girl was underage. The only way he could ameliorate Anjelica Huston's testimony was to show that the thirteen-year-old girl had a record of sexual promiscuity. But it was clear Judge Rittenband was not going to allow him to try to establish this.

After the hearing, Dalton brought Polanski back to his office and again raised the subject of a plea bargain. He had heard that day through the grapevine that the girl's father had hired a lawyer. The lawyer was trying to find a way to prevent the girl from having to testify, thereby suffering public exposure and embarrassment. Perhaps, counseled Dalton, the D.A. would agree to accept a guilty plea by Polanski to contributing to the delinquency of a minor, a misdemeanor, and would in exchange drop the six felony charges and avoid a trial. Such a ploy might work if he, Dalton, could get the girl's lawyer to put pressure on Gunson. If Judge Rittenband went along, chances were that he would give Polanski only a token sentence, maybe just a fine.

By now, Polanski was in a better frame of mind. His trip to Paris had refreshed his spirit, as had the *Tess* deal and the *Hurricane* offer. He was tempted to agree to Dalton's proposal so that he could have everything over with and quickly get to work on the new movies. The two pictures would take up the financial slack left by the suspended Columbia contract. And, Dalton told him, Columbia would probably reinstate the contract should he get out of his troubles with nothing more than a misdemeanor charge. All things considered, a plea such as the one Dalton was urging on him would be the simplest, neatest quickest and cheapest solution.

But one thing still nettled Polanski. It was the mother of the thirteen-year-old. Had it not been for her and her vicious crusade against him, Polanski thought, none of this would have happened. He had been publicly humiliated by women before in his life and had vowed never to let it happen again. Although he had kept up a front of indifference throughout most of his latest ordeal, inwardly he had been seething with rage and a growing obsession for revenge against the woman. He yearned to confront her in court, no matter what it cost him, so that the world could see for itself her twisted nature.

'The newspapers have always made me out to be the evil one,' he declared to Dalton. 'But it is she who is really evil, trying to get this phony pound of flesh from me.'

Dalton told Polanski that the woman probably would not even have to appear. Gunson would surely keep her off the stand, and he himself could not call her as a defense witness.

'You would never see the woman in court.'

'Then what kind of system is this, when an accused man cannot face his accuser?' Polanski demanded to know.

Technically, the woman was not his accuser, Dalton said. The girl was.

'I don't wish to hurt the girl.'

All the more reason to go the plea-bargain route as he had outlined it, Dalton replied. That is, if he could get the district attorney's office to agree to it.

'I will think about it,' Polanski said.

CHAPTER 7

POLANSKI ARRIVED in Paris in March 1960 and was stunned by its beauty and luxurious ambience. He had read a great deal about it, of course, and had seen countless pictures, but he was still unprepared for the effect it had on him. After the drabness of Warsaw, Lodz and Cracow, it was like entering Eden.

He arrived with little more than a change of shabby clothes, a print of *Two Men and a Wardrobe,* and the scripts he had been struggling over – the full-length script he had collaborated on with Goldberg and Skolimowski, another shorter script he and Goldberg had sketchily developed, and the screenplay he had tried to write for his wife.

Barbara Lass had bitterly resented his departure for Paris without her and they had had a furious argument just before he left. In an attempt to soften her anger, he had promised to spend much of his time on improving the screenplay so that it would be in shape to film when he returned. He had also promised to try to get her clearance to join him in Paris as soon as possible. But he had grown tired of her constant complaining and criticisms, particularly over the script. Although he still thought he loved her, he looked forward to the time away from

166

her.

Within a few days in Paris, Polanski was taken under Jean Drot's wing, introduced to his film company and exposed to the *nouvelle vague* style of film-making that had been invented by a group of documentary directors and had become the rage of feature films in France. He was fascinated but at the same time disoriented by this strange new method after being trained in the classical rigidity of Lodz and the Soviet-influenced cinema. Hand-held cameras, scriptless productions, improvised scenes and dialogue – all were foreign to his basic film-making instincts. Yet after a month of soaking up techniques and theories, when he was invited to create and direct a short film in the new style, he leapt at the opportunity.

Polanski polished up the short, sketchy Goldberg-inspired script he had brought with him and turned it into a shooting script which he called *Le Gros et le Maigre* ('The Fat Man and The Thin Man'). It was a typical enigmatic Goldbergian parable on man's struggle to survive in a brutal world. Conceived in the style of a surreal black comedy, it portrayed a bone-thin servant wearing himself out trying to please his grotesquely obese master. When the servant finally protests, his master pacifies him by making him a gift of a goat. The goat, however, is tied to the servant, which makes it even harder for him to rush about at the fat master's bidding. When the master removes the goat, the servant's relief and gratitude are so great that he works faster than ever before, eventually killing himself with exhaustion.

Polanski's script was seen as a brilliantly mordant fable of the inequalities of the capitalist class system by J.M. Drot's left-wing followers. He was immediately given access to Drot's studio facilities and urged to film it at once – in the *nouvelle vague* style. Polanski cast himself as the servant and employed dozens of cinematic tricks to enhance the story's one-joke idea, including a frenetic, Chaplinesque, speeded-up pace at the end to underline the comedy of the servant's destruction.

Polanski did not handle the *nouvelle vague* method well, though. The short film was an artistic trifle, interesting in spots but generally pretentious, derivative and dull. His own acting contributed to its failure – his colloquial French was at that time awkward and his hesitancy fatally marred the action.

Nevertheless, the film was hailed as a minor masterpiece by Drot's followers and was later released commercially in France's second-run theaters as a prelude to the main bills. In the meantime, Polanski screened *Two Men and a Wardrobe* to as many French film-makers who would watch it. Eventually, it found its way to a film festival in Brussels and won a prize for 'experimental' short films.

During his shooting of *Le Gros et le Maigre* in the early summer of 1960, Polanski renewed his friendship with Gerard Brach. Paris was a revelation to the young Polish director, especially as he began to learn the city through Brach's sensibility. Brach introduced Polanski to countless girls, most of them ambitious actresses. The Parisian social atmosphere was as bohemian and sybaritic as Polanski had been led to believe from books. Although he made a brief attempt to remain faithful to his new wife, presumably pining away for him back in Poland, the overpowering attractions of his surroundings were too much for him. The material abundance, the availability of women, plus the wild and wide variety of sexual practices and customs that were indulged in, sent Polanski into a kind of culture shock. Like a child allowed an hour on his own in a candy store, he was soon running amok. One of his favorite activities became participating in the shooting of the private pornographic films that were made almost nightly at various parties around the city. At first he just went along to the parties. Then he started serving just as a light-holder or camera operator. Finally he was allowed to join in as a performer. He had never seen anything like it before. Compared to the stiff morality of Poland, Paris was like Sodom and Gomorrah. What's more, as he quickly learned to shed his inhibitions, he liked it. Although as his visit would end in the fall and he would have to return to Poland, he knew for sure that he would never be able to remain there.

The most significant aspect of Polanski's stay in Paris, however, lay in the effect it had on the bulky script about the man and the hitchhiker he and his two Polish collaborators had wrestled with during the previous year. Before Polanski left for Paris, Andrzej Munk had told him, along with Goldberg and Skolimowski, that he would help them get clearance and money from the state film board to make a movie of the script – but only after they had solved its problems. Back home, Goldberg and Skolimowski had done some further work on the story and sent their rewrites to Polanski in Paris. But the problems remained. It still might make an interesting, off-beat short film, but it lacked the focus and interest-sustaining suspense of a full-length project.

In his frustration, Polanski turned to Gerard Brach, Drot, and others he had met in the French film world, for advice. He translated the script into French and circulated it among his friends for opinions.

It was Gerard Brach who provided the most perceptive advice. Brach had long been intrigued by the abstract and real correlations he saw beteween sex and violence, sex and death. Most of his so-far unsuccessful screenwriting had addressed itself to this theme. He pointed out to Polanski that although such playwrights as Ionesco, Beckett and Genet were popular on the stage, their work did not translate well to the screen. What made French cinema so popular was its emphasis on – almost preoccupation with – sex and terror. Whether it was husband-wife conflicts, *ménages-à-trois,* or boy-meets-girl situations, the comedy and drama of most successful French films derived from their handling of the sexual equation. Brach pointed to the enormous French hit *Diabolique* and its successors. The world knew much of the violence of war, so much so that movies about violence *per se* had become trite and uninteresting. But sex – sexual tension and the emotional terror that emanated from it, whether real or implied – was of ever-expanding fascination to the public, particularly since the postwar acceptance of Freudian psychology.

All this was a prelude to the specific suggestions Brach had to make about Polanski's script. Polanski had said that its initial impetus came from a desire on his and Goldberg's part to make a film having only two characters – no one else would appear in it, not even as background. Their intent was not only to

169

portray isolation, but to see if they could sustain such a conceit through a feature-length film.

'Fine,' said Brach. 'But the idea of making a symbolic, quasi-philosophical film about two men, representing two conflicting generations, as they set themselves on a path to violence, is passé. Why not two soldiers confronting each other across a battle line? Or two boxers?' Brach's point was that showing two men in conflict, no matter how brilliantly symbolic they were, was a relic of the nineteenth century, a dated, hackneyed concept. And that was the reason the script had no tension. 'Perhaps the audience will be curious to know the outcome. But the curiosity will be abstract, intellectual. The audience will not become involved because there is no 'real tension' to bind them to the action.

What, Brach added, is the kind of real tension that excites audiences in modern cinema? He answered the question for Polanski: 'sexual tension'. Almost every good original movie, comedy or drama, was built on sexual tension. Why? Because modern life was built on sexual tension. People related most immediately in films to the things they experienced most immediately in life.

Brach finally got to his point. 'Introduce a woman into your scenario,' he told Polanski. 'Let the woman become the focus of the conflict between the two men. Let the story develop from there, and you will have a film of great excitement and compelling fascination.'

Polanski initially resisted Brach's ideas. The kind of sophisticated sexual conflict he was talking about was a French notion. 'In Poland,' he argued, 'sexual conflict is not a significant factor in life. Men do not agonize over sexual competition between themselves, and they do not particularly care about how their women feel.' The only threat a Pole would feel would be if another man tried to invade his home, tried to harm or take his woman away. This was a territorial threat, though. The man would not care so much about the woman, but about the reflection on himself if he allowed his territory to be invaded . . .

'Exactly,' said Brach.

It slowly began to dawn on Polanski that Brach *was* talking about territory and self-esteem, and how men react to it. He was simply putting it in sexual terms.

Polanski had by then had enough experience in the sexually hedonistic world of Paris to have observed the patterns of sexual rivalry and conflict that existed, and to feel some of their effects himself. While involved in pornographic movies he had witnessed scenes of sex that often verged on violence and certainly contained the promise of it. He had seen mock-violence acted out in terms of sex. 'Sex and violence,' Brach had told him, 'are two sides of the same coin. Sex is a different kind of conflict, a different kind of tension. Violence is often expressed through sexuality – the rape, the castration. And sex is often expressed through violence. Sex is usually a controlled violence. But often the tension inherent in it turns it into uncontrolled violence.'

Brach's ideas eventually filtered into Polanski's consciousness over the course of several more discussions about the script during the summer. By the time he left Paris in the early fall of 1960 to return to Warsaw, Polanski's resistance was gone. Indeed, he had already begun to rewrite the script, incorporating Brach's ideas on the inclusion of a woman character to serve as the catalyst of the conflict between the two men. The woman character became particularly appealing when Polanski realized that he had found a way, finally, to provide his wife with a movie part. Accordingly, as he shaped the character, she became a young beautiful woman. He expected Barbara Lass to be pleased.

But Barbara Lass wasn't pleased. In fact, she was no longer living in their flat when he returned. She had undoubtedly heard about Polanski's sexual escapades from others who had made the trip to Paris and returned earlier. In his absence, she had become romantically involved with another actor in Warsaw. When Polanski returned, she was living with him.

Her affair with the actor had been going on for two months, and the entire Warsaw film and theatrical community knew about it. When Polanski learned of it the night of his return, he became hysterical with rage. He suddenly found himself

171

confronted by a real sexual-territorial crisis of the kind he and Gerard Brach had talked about so often in Paris. What enraged him even more was the realization that he had been publicly cuckolded and humiliated.

Polanski stormed the flat of the actor the next day and found his wife there alone. A furious confrontation followed, with Polanski first beating Barbara Lass and then collapsing in tears.

'How could you do this to me?' he sobbed.

His wife was battered but unbowed. 'You are scum,' she hissed at him. 'You betray me in Paris over and over again and you expect me to wait. Don't deny it, I know for a fact what you have done. I want nothing more to do with you. Get out.'

But Polanski would not get out. He beat her again, then pleaded with her to return to him.

'Never!' she cried, through swollen, bloodied lips.

Then her actor-lover appeared, a hefty man named Karol Wyzslaus. Polanski attacked him, but he was no match for his size. Now *he* was on the receiving end of a beating. Finally the police were summoned and Polanski was ejected from the apartment.

Polanski laid low for two days, afraid to show his battered face to his friends and plotting revenge. As time went on, though, he gradually realized that he had no recourse to revenge. He accepted the fact that the marriage was over and vowed never again to allow himself to trust a woman. When his bruises were healed a week later, he returned to KAMERA and threw himself into work.

As humiliating as the experience was for Polanski, it had the positive effect of coalescing the Brach-inspired ideas about sex and violence he had been trying to digest. He tried them out on Goldberg and Skolimowski, and the three turned to revamping their script.

The idea of a driver, an older man, picking up a younger hitchhiker was kept as the story's starting point. But now a beautiful young woman – the driver's wife – was placed in the car. As soon as the three writers put the hitchhiker into the car, they were able to build a sexual tension between the driver, his wife, and the young man.

172

The husband in the story was drawn as an intellectual, the hitchhiker as a coarse but sensual peasant-type, and the wife as a magnet to both for their separate reasons. The wife would become the source of the eventual violent conflict between the two men. 'The part is tailor-made for my own wife,' Polanski joked to Goldberg.

While reworking the script, Polanski was given an opportunity to do his first full-scale directing job for KAMERA. It was to be a short film, and the script was based on another of Jakub Goldberg's conceits in the style of Ionesco and Beckett. Called *Mammals,* it portrayed two male characters travelling across the snowy Polish landscape. One sits on a sleigh while the other pulls it. Then they change positions and continue to take turns. The one who pulls tries constantly, by faking different ailments, to take the seat in the sleigh – to be pulled and not have to do the pulling. Finally they fight, and while they are preoccupied with this a third man comes along and steals the sleigh.

The assignment was given to Polanski by Andrzej Munk in order to divert him from the depression he continued to suffer over Barbara Lass, according to Jerzy Skolimowski.

Polanski altered and rewrote Goldberg's original idea to make the script a secret fable for his own recent experience: a man becomes so preoccupied with other things that he loses his wife. His alterations brought about a falling-out between himself and Goldberg, who was already upset by the changes being made in his full-length script. But Polanski lost no sleep over the break with his friend – it was his first professional directorial opportunity in Poland and he would do it his way. 'An artist,' he said at the time, 'cannot have friends if those friends stand in the way of his art.'

Polanski had another friend who did not stand in the way of his art. He was Wojtek Frykowski, who had been among the less talented of the clique that had formed around Polanski several years before Lodz. A would-be director-actor in his twenties, he was a man who forever sought to curry Polanski's favor. It was he who had first informed Polanski about his wife's affair while he was in Paris. Polanski rewarded him by

173

casting him in the role of the man who steals the sleigh in *Mammals.*

Polanski shot the brief film during the first two weeks of January, 1961. As usual, it turned out to be a technically slick affair but a film without any seeming directional conviction or point of view. (It would, however, later win Polanski a minor French award.) According to Skolimowski, speaking not too long ago, 'Roman rushed with *Mammals,* not only the filming but the editing.' He rushed because he and Skolimowski, now without Goldberg, had completed a new version of their full-length script and submitted it to the film board for clearance. They received word that if they agreed to make some changes, it would be approved for filming under the auspices of KAMERA and be given the necessary finances.

With the changes, the final screenplay had the three characters – the man, the wife, the hitchhiker – drive to a boat at one of Poland's northern lakes, to which the man and his wife had set out for a weekend holiday before picking up the hitchhiker and inviting him along to work as a deckhand. The characters had been expanded, mostly by the politically minded Skolimowski, so that the man, a journalist, was seen as a rigid conformist addicted to status symbols, and the hitchhiker as a young man who scorned convention and authority. Skolimowski had accepted Polanski's idea of the basic sexual conflict between the three characters. But he felt the story should have an underlying social and political meaning to satisfy the film board. Much of the final script's shape was contributed by him.

Skolimowski and Polanski gave the screenplay the title *Knife in the Water* to signify the weapon upon which the violent climax of the story turned. After several more demands for minor changes by the film board, money was finally released. Polanski led a group of KAMERA actors and technicians into Poland's lake country during the summer of 1961 to shoot the tense, closely contained little melodrama against the ironic serenity of water and sunshine.

Knife in the Water would prove to be Polanski's passport to success, celebrity and a permanent life outside Poland. The

174

picture, with its sinister sexual overtones and stunning visual impact, took Poland by storm when it was released late in 1961. It represented a radical departure in film-making in a country where sexual passions and their portrayal had long been suppressed, first by the church, then by the state.

Several years later, when he was asked to explain his film-making philosophy in the light of *Knife in the Water,* Polanski said, 'I am . . . interested in studying the behavior of people under stress, when they are no longer in comfortable, everyday situations where they can afford to respect the conventional rules and morals of society. You can really learn something about a person when he's put into circumstances in which civilized values place his own identity, even his very being, in jeopardy. In a way, *Knife in the Water* was my . . . example of this. I took three people and put them in a situation that subjected them to stress, due to their confinement on the yacht and the competition between the two males.'

The subtle, understated violence of *Knife in the Water* gave no hint of the exercises in graphic movie violence Polanski would later engage in. But the sinister mood of the film, the sense it imparted of everything being slightly forebodingly off-center, was prophetic.

About the film's ending, which was enigmatic and failed to resolve the drama, Polanski said, 'What I want is to finish a film without giving the audience a feeling of being satisfied.'

When *Knife in the Water* was first released in Poland, Polanski was not there to enjoy its success. The ministry of culture had recently become intent upon achieving international recognition of the Polish film industry with a view to exporting some of its better pictures for exhibition abroad. Moreover, Andrzej Munk, Polanski's mentor, had just been killed in an automobile crash. Polanski, disconsolate, lobbied to get out of Poland once again. Consequently, because he spoke French, he was sent back to France in the spring of 1962 with a print of *Mammals.* His orders were to screen it at a film festival in Tours and then return to Warsaw. Instead, after winning an award at Tours, he headed for Paris with the travel expenses he had been given and the remains of the small salary he had earned from

Knife in the Water.

Polanski holed up in Paris with his stepsister for several weeks to experience more of the city's material and physical pleasures and to do some soul-searching. Gerard Brach and other French film figures assured him that he would easily be able to work in the French cinema and urged him to stay for good. Then he learned in a letter from a friend in Warsaw that Barbara Lass had applied for divorce and informed the military authorities that Polanski would soon be single again. It was this news that made him decide once and for all not to return to Poland. Because he had been born in France, he would have the protection of the French government. The only drawback was that if he remained there, he would sooner-or-later become subject to conscription into the French army. Polanski decided to face that problem when he came to it.

Within days of his decision he moved into a tiny, cheap flat with Gerard Brach. Brach had met with little success as a screen-writer in France up to then. His preoccupation with sexual themes expressed itself, in his scripts, in graphic excesses. Although he was inventive and articulate in his theories about the role of sexuality in people's lives as a correlative of bestiality and violence, his writing invariably focused on the darkest side of these passions. As a result, much of his work had been rejected by film-makers because of its outlandish shock value. The French public's tastes were too sophisticated for the kind of writing he was doing. And besides, there was the problem of whether the French censor would pass his work.

Just as Brach had been instrumental in expanding Polanski's vision for the script that resulted in *Knife in the Water,* so too did Polanski have a leavening effect on Brach's ideas as the two men developed their friendship. On the strength of his *Mammals* short and on the word-of-mouth out of Poland about *Knife in the Water,* Polanski was invited to direct another short film that would be part of a French omnibus production featuring the work of promising young directors. Brach had been partly responsible for getting Polanski the assignment and the two, almost as though they had an unspoken agreement between them, began to work in partnership on developing an

176

original screenplay for Polanski's episode.

In the meantime, the Polish ministry of culture decided to make *Knife in the Water* available for exhibition in the West. They started by showing the picture at the 1962 Venice Film Festival, where it won the Special Critic's Award. With this laurel behind it, it was picked up for commercial distribution in Italy, France and several other Western European countries.

Any anger the ministry of culture might have harbored toward Polanski for failing to return to Poland was set aside so that he could make an appearance at the Venice Festival without fear or reprisals. Indeed, once *Knife in the Water* won its award, he received the Polish government's tacit approval to remain out of the country so that he could help publicize the picture in Western Europe. In its commercial distribution, the film had a mild success in Italy and a considerable one in the Scandinavian countries and Britain. When it premiered in Paris, however, it was generally ignored. The chauvinistic French critics were generally conditioned to discount any movie not made in the French *nouvelle vague* style, and they adjudged *Knife in the Water* to be dated, awkward and tedious. Nevertheless, they acknowledged Polanski as a film-maker of promise.

This was the first wide-scale notice Polanski had received in Western Europe. Yet back in Paris with Gerard Brach, even after *Knife in the Water* began playing there, he remained relatively anonymous. Aside from the modest salary he had earned the year before for directing the film for KAMERA; he received nothing from its commercial exhibition in Europe. And although he was preparing with Brach to write and direct their short film for the French omnibus picture, for this they would only receive expenses once they began filming. Thus at the beginning of 1963, with Polanski soon to be thirty, he was barely getting by financially.

'. . . Gerard and I were living in miserable conditions,' Polanski told *Playboy* in 1971. 'We were penniless and living in little hotels and places like that, ducking out of one to the other when we couldn't pay the rent. Once we were stuffed into a broom-closet sort of room where in the eighteenth century, I think, they used to stash one domestic because two wouldn't fit.

It was virtually a cupboard . . . Whenever we got together 100 francs, we were happy as kings. The first thing was to run to the cinema to see a movie. The second thing was to have dinner in one of the little restaurants of St. Germain de Pres. And the third thing was to try to get some girls.' The *Playboy* interviewer was naturally interested in the last item. Was it difficult for Polanski to get girls, in view of his lack of celebrity and money, he asked?

'It was much harder,' Polanski said, 'not only because of the lack of notoriety but also because I didn't have the necessary experience. I wasn't so cool. I was too eager.'

Polanski went to Amsterdam in mid-1963 to shoot his short film for the French omnibus picture, which was to be called *Les Plus Belles Escroqueries,* or *The Beautiful Swindlers.* His episode, scripted by him and Brach, was called 'A River of Diamonds'. Struggling to balance his traditional notions of film-making against the avant-garde French style, he soon ran into a directional dilemma.

'For me, a film has to have a definite dramatic and visual shape,' he later said, 'as opposed to the rather flimsy shape that a lot of films were being given by the *nouvelle vague* . . . It has to be something finished, like a sculpture, almost something you can touch . . . It has to be rigorous and disciplined.'

Polanski was describing the difficulties he had with 'A River of Diamonds'. His French film crew and the actors were all veterans of the *nouvelle vague,* and they began to grumble when he resorted to the conventional camera set-ups and lighting methods he had learned at Lodz. Every time Polanski tried a French technique in photographing a scene, he would feel no longer in control of the scene but a spectator. His habit had been to make sketches of the scenes he intended to film and then set them up in strict accordance with the sketches. One of the things French critics had taken *Knife in the Water* to task for was the 'self-conscious rigidity' of the composition of many of its scenes. Scenic improvisation and visual spontaneity were the hallmarks of the *nouvelle vague.* The mobile hand-held camera freed the actors to move about in much more natural ways and enabled the director to follow them, so that the viewer got the

178

impression not of distance but of intimacy, of participation in what was happening on the screen. This was the primary virtue of the *nouvelle vague,* and although it often resulted in sloppy film-making it was thought by many to possess a much more immediate 'truth' than more conventional, neater methods.

In his efforts to strike a balance in his work on 'A River of Diamonds', Polanski managed to achieve neither neatness nor spontaneity. Although the film would eventually be released as an episode of *The Beautiful Swindlers,* when he returned to Paris he knew it would be an artistic disaster. Indeed, the word that he had botched it up preceded him. When he returned, he found that certain potentially important friends he had made among the Parisian cinema community were no longer interested in seeing other scripts he and Gerard Brach were developing.

Polanski turned thirty on 18 August 1963. One person who had gotten to know him at the time, today a well-known American writer, recalls him as 'a curious amalgam of man and child. He spoke no English, but his French was very good. He could and would converse with great intelligence and sobriety about the thorniest of philosophical subjects. He read a lot and was well-informed, albeit a bit naïve in his perceptions. He saw most issues in black-and-white terms. He had no timidity about expressing himself, but he was a bit of a verbal fascist.

'By that I mean, if you didn't accede to his point-of-view immediately, he would either have a tantrum or curse you out for being stupid, or would just shut up and never talk to you again. He was very combative intellectually, but did not like to lose. And, he was a bit paranoic. If someone outreasoned him in a discussion, he would often take it as an attempt to humiliate him, to 'get' him. Roman would be quite compulsively ugly, and offensive in his relations with people, but when the mood struck him he could also be quite charming, even endearing.

'What I'm describing is basically a social profile of Roman – when he was in the most adult situations. When the situations became less adult, he would revert more and more to childish behavior. He was an unabashed show-off. If you were sitting in a bistro with him, there would be all this ogling and chatting up girls. From an American's point of view, it was the kind of stuff you'd expect, perhaps, from a college fraternity boy or a construction worker on the street – you know, a lot of leering and obscene remarks.

'The only thing that made it all forgivable was that he had a certain elfin quality. He looked a bit like a mole with his coarse Polish-worker's haircut – an angelic mole – and he had obviously developed this gamin charm that, despite his off-center looks, women responded to. I remember one time we were at a party, and he went up to this quite attractive, sophisticated-looking woman. "I lost my mother when I was a child," he said straight out to her. "Would you be my mother tonight?" Damned if the woman didn't take him home with her.'

Another who knew Polanski in Paris was Monique Hugot, the French actress and for a while steady bed-partner. 'Roman was a young man of endless contradictions. Sometimes he was like a serious, dull old man, often times like a giggling child. Sometimes he had great self-assurance, other times he was insecure and timid. He could show great sensitivity, and just when you fell in love with his sensitivity, his caring, he would turn around and be insensitive and selfish.

'I believe much of this contradictoriness was an act to draw attention to himself. He was basically a loner, a very lonely young man who did not know how to draw himself close to people in ordinary, accepted ways. You know, to be sociable and such. So he acted out certain kinds of behavior that would get people's attention. He was fiercely intelligent and at the same time profoundly naïve, dumb, when it came to people's feelings. I do not think he really liked women. Oh, he liked bodies, but he did not like what was inside them. Often, from the way he reacted to me, I would think he was afraid of women as people. He was only comfortable with men.'

Another actress with whom Polanski had a brief affair at the time recalls him more candidly: 'Two things I remember clearly. One, he was unhappy with his sexual equipment. You know how French men are, how they take pride in their size. Roman was exposed to this and felt inadequate because he was -

– well, an ordinary size. He enjoyed sex, to be sure, but he was ashamed to be looked at unless he was aroused. If he was not aroused, he would contrive ways to conceal himself, or else he would secretly stimulate himself so that he would look more formidable between his legs.

'The other is that, in lovemaking, he would not talk. I mean, he was alright in the physical part of lovemaking, but he did not know how to be tender. He could make love for a long time, but he did it all at a distance, without passion, without intimacy. And when it was over for him, it was over. He was finished and immediately wanted to jump up and be on his way. He lacked sympathy, tenderness.'

Polanski was undoubtedly enjoying the fleshly pleasures of bohemian Paris around the time of his thirtieth birthday in August of 1963. He was also learning to covet the material abundance that, although near at hand, was still beyond his financial reach. As he became accustomed to his new life in the West, he reveled in its freedoms and rapidly developed ambitions for an even more expansive existence for himself. However, by October he and Brach were having trouble interesting French producers in a full-length screenplay they had collaborated on. It appeared that Polanski's promising start in France would be aborted. What's more, since he had resided in Paris for more than a year, he was in danger of being drafted. France had recently withdrawn from its war in Indochina but was still involved in a costly colonial conflict with independence-seeking Algeria. As a result, unattached men under thirty-five were fodder for the French army. Military service was once again pressing in on him.

In October, just when things looked blackest and Polanski was glumly considering a return to Poland in order to avoid the French draft, he was visited by a stroke of fortune that would complete the radical transformation of his life.

The Polish-licensed distributors of *Knife in the Water* had managed to make a deal to have the film exhibited in the United States. It opened quietly at a small art-film theater in New York in late October and was an instant hit. Soon it was being shown in other cities around the country. Enthusiasm for the picture mounted, fueled by the glimpse it gave Americans of life behind the Iron Curtain. Toward the end of the year it was entered for the prestigious New York Film Festival. Polanski was tracked down in Paris and invited to attend the festival.

With his expenses paid by the festival's sponsors, Polanski flew to New York – his first visit to America. There he was quickly sucked into the publicity whirl generated by the festival. Like most foreigners whose only exposure to America had come through movies, 'I had imagined the streets of New York to be very wide, very clean, with a very even surface, and surrounded by bright, shiny buildings. I found it dense, dirty and not so smooth at all – but incredibly rich and varied, like nothing I had seen in the world, not even Paris. It was tremendously stimulating. The theaters, the restaurants, the crowds all seemed exciting, and a lot of the New York intellectuals, who didn't seem so left-wing and tiresome at the time, I found very exciting – maybe because I didn't speak a word of English . . . I also found the competition – the rat-race, you call it – very exciting.'

Knife in the Water received the festival's imprimatur and America's film intelligentsia took Polanski to its bosom. Early in 1964, with Polanski back in Paris wondering what it would all lead to, the picture was nominated in Hollywood for an Academy Award as the best foreign language film of 1963.

Living in London at the time was a struggling Polish-American motion picture producer named Eugene Gutowski. He had been born in Poland, knew the life there, and still had contacts. He had heard about Polanski several years before, had gone to see *Knife in the Water* when it was first shown in London early in 1963, and had not been impressed. When it was nominated for an American Oscar, however, his estimation of the film and its director changed.

Gutowski learned from a Polish friend who had seen Polanski at the New York Film Festival that the young director was without an agent and that, because Polanski didn't speak English, he had been unable to make a positive personal impression. With the success of *Knife in the Water* in the United States, the American movie companies should have been vieing for Polanski's services. They seemed to have been scared away

182

by his inability to speak English.

Gutowski took the hint. He managed to find Polanski in Paris and called him. Speaking in Polish, he learned that the director was preparing to return to Poland to avoid being drafted into the French army – this despite the fact that Polanski was now certain to be drafted at home too.

'That's crazy,' Gutowski told him on the phone.

'What can I do?' replied Polanski.

'I'll tell you what you *will* do, said Gutowski, 'You will come to London tomorrow and see me.'

INTERLOG 7

THE DAY after his talk with Douglas Dalton about pleading to a misdemeanor, Polanski came back and said, 'Okay, I'll do it. It goes against everything I believe, but I'll do it.'

Polanski had spent the night before with Jack Nicholson, discussing Dalton's proposal. Nicholson had convinced him that it made the most sense, explaining that Anjelica Huston, although she loathed having to do it, would have no choice but to testify against him. 'They got her between a rock and a hard place, man,' Nicholson had said. 'Her father's on her back, her lawyer, the D.A., everybody. I'm staying out of it, but I can see how she's suffering. She doesn't want to do it, but the alternative is a pack of trouble for her. If she testifies, she's out of trouble but you're in a heap of it. If she doesn't testify, she's in trouble and you still are too, though maybe not so bad. But if you can set it up so she doesn't have to testify and you can get off with a slap on the wrist, that seems to me to be the best way to solve everything. The least damage is done to everyone, you see what I mean?'

Polanski saw. But even if he pleaded guilty to a misdemeanor, he wanted to know, how was that going to affect his future in Hollywood.

'Man,' Nicholson had said, 'I am with you all the way. It's like getting a ticket for speeding. I've got some clout in this town, and I'll make sure it has nothing but a good effect. You and me, we'll work together on anything I do, or I won't work. You've got my solemn promise on that. You don't work, I don't work. I'll go back to New Jersey and sling hash the rest of my life.'

The next day, when Polanski told Dalton that he would agree to a misdemeanor plea, Dalton again cautioned him that it might not work.

Dalton then contacted district attorney Gunson and offered to have Polanski plead guilty to contributing to the delinquency of a minor, provided Judge Rittenbrand would approve.

'No way,' said Gunson. He reminded Dalton that the District Attorney's office, some time before, had instituted a rigid case-settlement policy in criminal matters. The policy dictated that in any felony plea-bargaining aimed at a reduction of charges, the defendant was required to plead guilty to one of the most severe counts against him in exchange for the other counts being dropped.

Dalton was aware of the policy, he said. But he thought an exception might be made in this case in order to avoid exposing the girl to the traumatic publicity that a public trial would bring.

'I'd like to see that, too,' said Gunson. 'But on your terms it's impossible. Get your client to go the guilty route on the furnishing-drugs-to-a-minor count or the rape charge. Then I'll see what I can do.'

Dalton replied that Polanski would never agree to that – the possible sentences were too stiff. And because of the press attention the case had received, Judge Rittenband would undoubtedly feel compelled to come down hard on Polanski. Moreover, on any sentence of over a year for a sex or drug felony, Polanski would be subject to deportation under the US immigration laws. Polanski was in the United States on a visa, and Judge Rittenband had already talked in private about giving him a heavy sentence and then recommending his deportation if he was convicted.

185

'See you in court then,' said Gunson.

Dalton advised Polanski that the D.A. would not accept a plea to a misdemeanor, that he was holding out for an admission of guilt to one of the most serious charges in the indictment. He tried to explain that Gunson was hampered by his office's policy, but Polanski was not interested in hearing it.

'Okay,' he said, 'so all that shit was for nothing. Now, we go to court and prove out our case, eh?'

Dalton suggested they talk again about a guilty plea to one of the felony counts. It would avoid a jury trial, where Polanski could really get plastered to the wall. And the judge, in his sentencing, would surely take into account the fact that Polanski had saved everyone a lot of trouble and time and expense.

'But you've already told me that the judge has it in for me,' Polanski said.

Well, not exactly, said Dalton.

'And that I would be deported.'

Not would, necessarily. Could.

'But if I was deported, I could not work here ever again.'

For a while, at least.

'No American company would hire me.'

Probably.

'And Columbia would have good cause to revoke my contract for good.'

'Possibly. We'd have to take that one to court,' said Dalton.

'More money it would cost me to do that. And years to resolve.'

Dalton could not deny it.

'Then no way will I plead guilty to what I am accused of,' said Polanski. He was shouting now. 'No way! No way! No way!'

On 10 June, Judge Rittenband held another hearing on defense motions in his Santa Monica courtroom. Before the session he met in chambers with Gunson and Dalton to inquire if any move toward plea-bargaining had been made. Gunson's

186

position remained the same, as did Dalton's on behalf of Polanski: the director would only plead guilty to a misdemeanor charge. The judge frowned and made a sardonic but unintelligible remark about the Pole. Dalton didn't catch it, but from the tone of it he didn't like it.

Later, in the courtroom, the rancorous Rittenband denied Dalton's earlier motion to introduce independent defense testimony at trial in regard to the victim's sexual history. Then to the surprise of the press, he announced that because of his present case load, he was postponing the opening of the trial from 29 June to 9 August.

It was only as he left the courtroom that Polanski realized that 9 August was the eighth anniversary of his wife Sharon's murder. It was not a realization that he arrived at himself – it came from a reporter's loudly shouted question. As he drove away from the courthouse, in one reporter's words, 'Polanski seemed to reflect with sadness on the harsh irony of it all.'

'Bullshit,' the director told a friend the next day when he read the words in a local newspaper. 'What I was thinking about was whether the postponement of the trial would make it possible for me to go to the South Pacific for a few weeks to work on the *Hurricane* picture.

Polanski had to give Dino de Laurentiis an answer. He was eager to direct *Hurricane,* mainly for the money. But the original June trial date had prevented him from making a commitment for the summer. Now, however, with the trial postponed for six weeks, he would have time to start work on the movie immediately.

A few days later, Dalton went to Rittenband and persuaded the judge to allow Polanski to travel to the South Pacific to scout locations for *Hurricane.* With that, the director signed a contract with the de Laurentiis organization. He flew to Tahiti the next day.

News of the Pole's departure reached the press immediately and triggered another avalanche of criticism of Judge Rittenband. 'When are you coming back?' a reporter wrote that he had asked Polanski upon running across him at the airport. 'Oh, I may never come back,' he reported the indicted director as having replied.

Judge Rittenband answered his critics by saying, 'The man has a right to make a living. He's not been convicted, and for all I know he may never be. Until he is convicted, he has a right to his normal life.' Rittenband added that he had Dalton's assurance that if Polanski had indeed remarked to the reporter that he might never come back, it was intended as a joke.

Tahiti agreed with Polanski, as did Bora Bora when he traveled there to look for further locations. Far away from Los Angeles, soothed by the tropical climate and the nubile girls he encountered, he quickly shed his troubles. Only an occasional call from Dalton jolted him back to reality, and then only for a few minutes. It was when the time approached for him to go back to California that he seriously began to think about not returning. But then he was told that if he didn't, he would lose the movie job.

While Polanski was in the South Pacific, the young girl he was accused of raping was spending the month with her father on the East Coast. She did not want to return to Los Angeles either – or at least her father did not want her to. For both criminal and victim, a trial was undesirable.

Meanwhile, deputy district attorney Roger Gunson became caught in the middle of a three-way struggle. First, he had begun to get pressure from Laurence Silver, the lawyer who had been hired by her father to represent the girl and protect her interests, to avoid exposing the youngster as a witness at the trial. But without the girl to testify, there could be no trial, Gunson said. Silver was nevertheless urging him to persuade Polanski, through Douglas Dalton, to go the plea-route. By now, Silver informed Gunson, the girl's mother would be content with a guilty plea to any felony count and would be willing to leave Polanski's punishment to the judge's discretion.

Second, Gunson continued to press Dalton for a guilty plea to the most serious charge in the indictment – either rape by use of drugs or providing illegal drugs to a minor. The first carried a sentence of not less than one year and not more than fifty years

188

in jail, the exact term being at the option of the judge. The second called for a sentence of ten years to life, again at the option of the judge.

Dalton was more certain than ever that Polanski was in a corner. With the trial evidence Gunson had against his client, and with his own ability to explore the girl's credibility denied by Judge Rittenband, he would have little chance of saving Polanski from a jury conviction on the most serious counts of the indictment. If a jury believed the Pole had given the girl drugs and alcohol, and had then forced himself sexually on her, they would be likely to believe that he had sodomized and had oral intercourse with her as well.

Dalton hinted to Gunson that Polanski might now be willing to plead guilty to a lesser count in the indictment – one that would not result in so onerous a possible sentence. Sodomy, for instance.

'Can't do it,' Gunson said, reminding Dalton once again of the D.A.'s new policy on plea bargaining – a plea would be accepted only if the accused pleaded guilty to the most severe charge or charges.

Dalton persisted. Otherwise, he hinted, Polanski might decide never to return to face trial.

Gunson used the hint to try to get his boss, district attorney John Van De Kamp, to make an exception to the plea-bargaining policy. Thus began the third phase of his struggle. Gunson had firmly come around to the view that it would be in the interest of all parties if a trial could be avoided. He reported to Van De Kamp that Polanski might agree to plead guilty to a lesser charge in the indictment if Van De Kamp agreed to make an exception to the policy he himself had instituted.

At first, Van De Kamp refused, insisting that Polanski would have to plead to the two most severe charges. 'Rittenband is already getting heat from the press about being soft on Polanski for letting him travel the way he has,' said Van De Kamp. 'Can't you see how the press would jump on *us* if we made an exception for Polanski?'

Arguments over the question lasted into mid-July. Finally, Gunson brought in Lawrence Silver, the girl's attorney, to talk

189

to Van De Kamp. Silver told the chief D.A. of how concerned the victim's father was that exposure of his daughter at a trial would wreak lifelong psychological havoc on her. By making an exception to his plea-bargaining policy, Silver argued, Van De Kamp would not be doing it for Polanski's benefit but for his victim's. If the D.A. would bend in his policy just this once, Silver promised to appear in court and make known the fact that the exception had been made solely to accommodate the young girl and not Polanski.

Van De Kamp finally gave in and authorized Gunson to bargain with Dalton on a single count of unlawful sexual intercourse. Lawrence Silver's role in the proceedings was not over yet, however. In order to persuade Polanski to agree to plead guilty to the charge, the girl's attorney would also have to promise Dalton to make a pitch to Judge Rittenband for a lenient sentence.

After talking separately with the girl's father and mother, Silver agreed. At the beginning of August, with attorney Silver's promise in hand, Dalton was able to persuade Polanski, just returned from the South Pacific, to plead guilty to the unlawful intercourse charge and take his chances with Judge Rittenband. The alternative, he convinced the director – a trial – would be much more perilous.

Not that a guilty plea to the single charge was not perilous, Dalton hastened to add. Having researched the possible consequences, he advised Polanski that the plea of guilty gave the judge a variety of sentence options, ranging from the most lenient, straight probation, to the most harsh, a prison term of one to fifty years. Moreover, the judge would have the power to commit Polanski immediately to custody for the purpose of sex-offender psychiatric evaluation prior to sentencing. Finally, Dalton warned, by pleading guilty to a crime of moral turpitude, Polanski stood the risk of being deported after serving whatever sentence was imposed on him. If he was deported, it was unlikely that any American movie company would employ him again.

Dalton's recitation, coming so soon after his return from Tahiti, threw Polanski into a profound depression. Dalton tried to cheer him up by reminding him that Lawrence Silver, the victim's lawyer, was committed to pleading for the most lenient sentence on Polanski's behalf. Coming in effect from the girl and her parents, such a petition should have a significant influence on the judge. Dalton's only concern was that Rittenband had been making some unfavorable remarks about Polanski of late. There was always the possibility that he'd ignore Silver's request for leniency and throw the book at Polanski. He obviously didn't like the director.

Polanski now began to feel trapped. Short of fleeing the country, he had no practical choice but to agree to the single guilty plea. After a few days he glumly acknowledged this to Dalton. He would agree to the plea, he said, but only on one condition: that district attorney Gunson petition the judge against recommending his deportation. He was willing to expose himself to the risk of a brief jail term if necessary, but not the likelihood of afterwards being unable to make a living in the United States.

When Dalton approached Gunson about this, the prosecutor firmly declined. 'We've already made enough concessions to your client,' he said.

Polanski was thus forced to agree to a guilty plea without his condition. On Thursday, 4 August, Gunson announced to the press that the director, to avoid a trial, would be allowed to plead guilty to one of the counts of the indictment, pending the approval of Judge Rittenband. He was requesting a hearing before Rittenband on 8 August, the day before the intended start of the trial, in order to determine whether the judge would accept the plea and dismiss the other counts.

Judge Rittenband's Santa Monica courtroom was packed as usual with print and broadcast journalists when Polanski appeared with Dalton for the 8 August hearing. The only question in the reporters' minds now was whether Rittenband would accept Polanski's guilty plea to the single count. As one who was present later told me, 'A palpable sense of resentment against Rittenband pervaded the press section. They were afraid that the judge would accept the plea and thereby deprive them of the pleasure of having a juicy trial to write about.

What the reporters didn't know was that the question had already been resolved. Prosecutor Gunson had earlier consulted with the judge, as had Dalton. Judge Rittenband had agreed to accept the plea, provided that Polanski clearly acknowledge for the official record that he knew what he was doing and was aware of the possible consequences.

Once in the courtroom, Gunson explained to the judge, for the record, that Polanski was willing to plead guilty to the unlawful intercourse charge and required 'that the court consider the plea and, if acceptable, dismiss the other charges pending against Mr Polanski.'

Gunson then went on to read a written statement from his boss, D.A. Van De Kamp. 'The choice [to accept the plea of unlawful sexual intercourse] is appropriate in that it may achieve substantial justice with respect to society's interests through the felony conviction of the defendant, yet provide the victim with the opportunity to grow up in a world where she will not be known as the young girl with whom Roman Polanski had intercourse.'

Van De Kamp's statement conceded that acceptance of the plea was a 'difficult choice for the court in that it involved the balancing of competing interests.' But, he added, 'if one is insensitive to the legitimate interests of the victim, and this thirteen-year-old victim in particular, one would disregard her and submit her to the ordeal of trial which, in effect, could victimize her a second time. We chose to side with her . . . '

Next came Lawrence Silver, the girl's attorney. Allowed to recite a statement into the record, he urged Rittenband to accept Polanski's guilty plea on the single count of unlawful intercourse rather than hold a trial on the six counts. Silver said that if a trial were held and the girl had to testify in the glare of world-wide publicity, 'a stigma would attach to her for a lifetime.'

'Justice is not made of such stuff,' Silver went on. 'Whatever harm that has come to her as a victim would be exacerbated in the extreme if this case went to trial. The reliving of the sorry

Directing *Macbeth* a year after Sharon Tate's murder. *(National Film Archive/Stills Library)*

Rehearsing Mia Farrow on the set of *Rosemary's Baby*, 1967. *(Gamma/Liaison)*

Instructing a *Macbeth* actor on the right way to wield a club. *(National Film Archive/Stills Library)*

John Huston, Anjelica's father, and Polanski on the *Chinatown* set, 1973. (*Gérard Vilo/Gamma-Liaison*)

Chewing out Jack Nicholson on the set of *Chinatown*, 1973. (*Ronald Grant Collection*)

A scene from *Two Men and a Wardrobe*, Polanski's prize-winning Polish film school short. *(National Film Archive/Stills Library)*

The Fat Man and the Thin Man.
(National Film Archive/Stills Library)

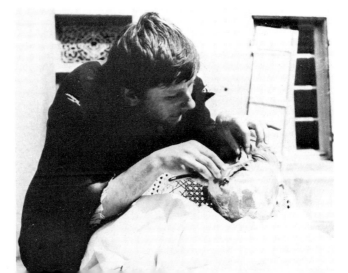

Polanski acting in his spoof, *The Fearless Vampire Killers*.
(National Film Archive/Stills Library)

Polanski and Sharon Tate in *The Fearless Vampire Killers*.
(The Museum of Modern Art/Film Stills Archive)

Mia Farrow in *Rosemary's Baby.*
(Ronald Grant Collection)

Che? (National Film Archive/Stills Library)

John Cassavetes, Mia Farrow, and Ralph Bellamy, the stars of
Rosemary's Baby. (The Museum of Modern Art/Film Stills Archive)

Farrow again in *Rosemary's Baby.*
(National Film Archive/Stills Library)

Polanski in *The Tenant*. *(National Film Archive/Stills Library)*

Polanski slicing open Jack Nicholson's nose in a famous scene from *Chinatown*, 1973. *(National Film Archive/Stills Library)*

A scene from *Macbeth*. *(National Film Archive/Stills Library)*

Natassia Kinski as Tess, 1979.

Polanski in front of the advertising poster of *Tess*, Paris, 1979. *(Wide World)*

ROMAN POLANSK

Tess

events with their delicate content . . . in this courtroom packed with strangers would be a challenge to the emotional well-being of any person.'

Then, keeping his commitment to Dalton, Silver announced that the goal of the girl's family in initiating the action against Polanski, 'does not include incarceration of the defendant.' Instead, the family wanted an admission of wrongdoing from Polanski as the first step in a court-supervised rehabilitation. 'The plea of guilty by the defendant is contrition sufficient for my clients to believe that that goal may be achievable.'

Knowledgable reporters on the scene buzzed to themselves about how well-rehearsed the proceeding seemed to be. And it was, of course, rehearsed. The final act came when prosecutor Gunson called Polanski to the stand and put to him the pro-forma questions the official record required.

The courtroom buzzed when Gunson called Polanski. He had been sitting with his head in his hands. Dalton nodded to him. He slowly stood up, paused, and then walked with what appeared to be reluctance to the stand.

Polanski, his long brown hair covering his ears, wore a neat gray pin-stripe suit and a tie – uncharacteristic garb for a man accustomed to flowered shirts and custom-tailored jeans outfits. His face had a curiously angelic look. His expression was somber, almost contrite, as Gunson briefly questioned him.

Gunson: 'Are you aware, Mr Polanski, of the charge to which you desire to plead guilty?'

Polanski: 'Yes.'

Gunson: 'And are you aware of the possible consequences to you?'

Polanski: 'I am.'

Gunson: 'And you have had the full advice of counsel in arriving at this decision, to plead guilty to the crime of unlawful sexual intercourse?'

Polanski: 'Yes, I have.'

Gunson: 'Very well. Now I ask you, what does a person have to do to be guilty of this charge?'

Polanski, his voice uncertain, hesitant: 'He would have had sexual intercourse with a teenager . . . who was not his wife.'

Gunson: 'Are you in fact guilty of this charge?'

Polanski: 'Yes.'

Gunson took pains to explain to Polanski that if the case went to trial, the director could employ as a legitimate defense his contention that he thought the girl was older than she was. 'Was this in fact your understanding, Mr Polanski, that the young lady was older than thirteen years of age?'

Polanski had already been coached on how to respond. His hands, crossed in his lap, trembled. He looked down at them. Then, his voice barely audible, he said, 'I understood her to be thirteen.'

With that, Judge Rittenband accepted Polanski's guilty plea, dismissed the other charges, and suspended the trial. He ordered Polanski to undergo immediate preliminary psychiatric examination to determine whether he was a 'mentally disordered sex offender,' and scheduled a further hearing on 19 September to take testimony on the findings of the two psychiatrists he would appoint to examine Polanski. He remanded the director to the psychiatric unit at the California State Prison at Chino, and indicated that his sentence would depend in part on the psychiatric findings.

This was an unexpected turn of events. Polanski looked at Dalton in stunned protest at Rittenband's mention of him as a mentally disordered sex offender. Dalton leapt to his feet with an objection and a motion. His client was in the middle of preparing the *Hurricane* movie for filming, he said. Wouldn't Judge Rittenband allow Polanski to complete his work before sending him to Chino?

Rittenband reserved decision on the motion and continued Polanski free on bail.

It was a grim Roman Polanski who waded through the hoard of reporters on his way out of the courtroom. His hair askew, he simply shook his head at the storm of questions. Reporters shouted such queries as, 'I thought you said you were innocent, Roman?' and 'How's it feel to be a sex criminal?' Polanski's expression remained stoic, but when he looked at the reporters his eyes were filled with hatred. And hurt.

Prosecutor Gunson was not so quick to dodge the press.

Indeed, he was expansive as he paused to answer questions. No, he carefully emphasized, averting the trial was not done as a favor to Polanski, but out of a 'human sense of compassion for the victim and her family.' Allowing Polanski to plea to one of the less severe charges in the indictment was 'not really doing him a favor either' – the potential sentences for unlawful intercourse were almost as stringent as those for the two more serious charges. 'It was a way, ladies and gentlemen, to get the matter resolved in the most expeditious manner and at the least cost to the victim of the case and the people of California.'

'Why was Polanski suddenly so ready to admit guilt when he's been steadfastly proclaiming his innocence all this time?' one reporter asked.

Gunson answered by saying that he thought the scheduled testimony of Anjelica Huston was the key factor in Polanski's decision to plead guilty.

CHAPTER 8

LIKE ROMAN Polanski, Gene Gutowski was a survivor of war-ravaged Poland. Ten years older than Polanski and unwilling to live under Russian rule, he made his way west out of Poland during the last weeks of the war and managed to hook up with an American army OSS unit in southern Germany. Since he spoke German, he was immediately put to work assisting in the interrogations of captured German military personnel. A year later, as a reward for his contribution and because he had revealed an aptitude for intelligence work, he was sent to the United States, given an American army rank, and assigned to a top-secret Pentagon intelligence unit.

Gutowski spent the late 1940s in and about Washington, where he became fluent in English and developed a taste for the good life. During this time he met a wealthy young Virginia woman, fell in love and married her. While she was bearing him two sons in the early fifties, Gutowski phased himself out of the military, became an American citizen, and got a job in the motion picture industry. In the mid-fifties he went to London to become an independent film producer. It was a time when the British film industry was flourishing and there was a good deal of cross-fertilization of talent and money between England and America.

The suave, smooth-talking Gutowski and his American wife were divorced at the beginning of the sixties and Gutowski remained on his own in London. By then, the British capital was fast on its way to becoming what *Time* Magazine would later call 'the pleasure capital of the Western World.' The younger generation was breaking out of the country's postwar gloom in a dizzying celebration of mini-skirts, rock music, drugs and sexual hedonism. Gutowski, up to then a modestly successful producer, made the most of his new freedom for a couple of years. But then he met and married a stunning English model named Judy Wilson and settled down again to a life of semi-domesticity in a flat near trendy Montpelier Square. It was shortly after his re-marriage that, early in 1964, he contacted Roman Polanski in Paris and summoned him to London.

'I was thinking of a straight business association,' Gutowski later told me. 'Here was this young, obviously talented film-maker who had won an American Oscar nomination. But he was sitting out of work in Paris. He was a ripe talent just waiting to be plucked by the American studios. But no one in America knew what to do about him because he spoke no English. Since I had hundreds of contacts in Hollywood and spoke Polish, I thought I could be of some use to Roman.'

When Polanski came to London to meet him, Gutowski realized that he could be more than just 'of some use' to him. Gutowski was impressed by his younger countryman's self-assuredness, assertiveness and intellectual acumen, and was intrigued by the juxtaposition of these qualities with what were traits of naîveté and an almost childish insatiable curiosity. It was Polanski's first exposure to London, and he was over-whelmed by the amenities of life there. Paris was as tame as Vatican City in comparison. 'It was like taking your kid to an amusement park for the first time,' Gutowski recalled. 'He was awestruck by the motorcars, the homes, the restaurants, the girls. He had to try everything. And when I took him out to a large movie studio to show him around, he was overcome with wonder at the expanse and the technical facilities.'

What struck Gutowski with the most force was the seeming
contradiction between the Polanski he met and the Polanski he
had imagined he would meet after seeing *Knife in the Water.*
'Here was this brooding, menacing, darkly lyrical film. I had
expected Roman to be somewhat of a fellow along these lines –
silent, brooding, reclusive, phlegmatic, a kind of Polish Ingmar
Bergman. Who shows up but this gregarious, cocksure bantam
with a cheerful, trusting face, a happy-go-lucky personality and
a huge sex drive. The whole picture fascinated me.'

Gutowski and Polanski became instant friends. 'Part of it
had to do with the fact that we had both been through the war –
that was an immediate bond. Part of it had to do with the fact
that we were both in the movie business, although in different
ways. I think Roman was impressed by the fact that a fellow-
Pole had done so well in the West in the movie business. And,
of course, he knew no one else in London, so he sort of clung to
me right off. Yet we would have become friends anyway,
despite the business aspects. As soon as I met him I liked the guy.
I liked him for his enormous vitality and enthusiasm for life.'

Nonetheless, Gutowski detected a dark side to Polanski. 'No
doubt about it, I decided early on that much of Roman's
voluble persona was really a shield he had constructed around
himself. It was as if something was missing in him, something
important, and he knew it was a self-protective covering, and he
had built it to protect himself from himself, from some deep
despair that festered inside him. He impressed me as basically a
loner who was profoundly uncomfortable with his aloneness,
who in fact couldn't stand being alone with himself. So he had
developed this compulsive need not to be alone, but to always
be with other people. There was a lot of what we today call
macho in him – he was very competitive about himself and went
out of his way to impress people, to impose his personality. But
there was an immense amount of charm in the way he did it. A
sort of childish charm – endearing because, at least in the
beginning when his English was halting, it was so transparent. It
was only later, when I saw him at work, that I really got a sense
of his power to create.'

Gutowski quickly abandoned his original intention to serve as a liaison between Polanski and the Anglo-American film industry. Instead, he proposed that he and Polanski join forces to become a producing-directing team. Gutowski would use his experience and contacts to put together American and English deals for films that Polanski would write and direct.

Polanski was quick to agree. Thus began Cadre Films, Ltd, the tiny two-man company that would establish Polanski as a Western film-maker and open the doors of big-money Hollywood to him.

Since Polanski had no funds to speak of, Gutowski advanced him generous living expenses and set him up in a small London flat near his own. Gutowski's next move was to get Polanski better known in the United States. He took him to Hollywood in April 1964 so that he could be present to receive his Oscar in the event *Knife in the Water* won that year's Academy Award. While there, Gutowski announced his and Polanski's exclusive association through ads in the trade papers. Then he took his new partner around to all the major studios to meet key production and financial executives, and threw a giant party for him. *Knife in the Water* failed to win an Oscar, but Gutowski used the publicity the event received to fix Polanski in the mind of the Hollywood establishment as an important new director whose pictures Gutowski would be independently producing in the future under the banner of Cadre Films.

From Hollywood it was on to New York for Gutowski and Polanski, where further publicity was generated, and then back to France in May for the annual Cannes Film Festival. Gutowski practically used up his life's savings to finance the whirlwind trip. But it would soon reap the desired dividends. Upon their return to London in June, the phone in Gutowski's flat – the temporary office of the new-born Cadre Films – 'was ringing off the hook with film offers.'

The trip was a further eye-opener for Polanski. Gutowski interpreted for him, showed him the sights from the perspective of someone who was familiar with them, introduced him to many of the powers in the international film business, and plunged him into the fast and elegant social life of the Hollywood and New York show business sets – a life that included fast cars, the finest in homes and restaurants, and a plenitude of attractive and sexually available women. Polanski found, with Gutowski's help, that the people of this world responded to him with enthusiasm. Although most of it was foreign to his sensibilities, he was immensely excited by it. Poland, even the bohemian life he had lived in Paris shortly before, suddenly seemed light years away. He was ready to become a full-scale Westerner. And with characteristic determination, he set out to do so.

Most of the offers Gutowski received were for Polanski to direct a variety of films being produced by others. Gutowski responded by saying that he was Polanski's exclusive producer and that the two were interested only in doing their own films. They were open to legitimate financing and distribution deals, but were not about to work for other producers as hired hands. 'Polanski's potential was too great to have it squandered by working as an ordinary contract director who would have no control over the films he made.'

Gutowski thus became the orchestrator of Polanski's career. Soon the tone of the offers changed: did Gutowski and Polanski have a film in mind that they wanted to do?

Indeed they did, replied Gutowski.

The film he referred to was from the script Polanski and Gerard Brach had been developing in Paris prior to Polanski's trip to London. The script had curious origins.

Brach was still preoccupied as a writer with his concept of sex and violence as two sides of the same coin. As for Polanski, when he had been directing *Knife in the Water* in Poland in 1961, another Polish director was making a picture that also represented a departure from the film traditions of that country. The director was Jerzy Kawalerowicz, a veteran film-maker whose movies had been among the most popular in Poland in the 1950s. The film he made in 1961 was called, in English, *Mother Joan of the Angels*. It was a strange, mystical, seventeenth-century horror tale about a group of nuns possessed by devils, and when it was released in Poland in 1962 it rivaled *Knife in the Water* in popularity and controversy.

Kawalerowicz was a master of suspense and gory detail. Polanski had studied his previous films and borrowed some of his cinematic techniques for *Knife in the Water*. He had been particularly impressed when he viewed *Mother Joan of the Angels* before returning to Paris in 1961.

Hence, when he and Brach had begun to collaborate on a full-length screenplay in 1963, Brach wanted to write a film of sex and violence, in the style of the French classic, *Diabolique*. Polanski on the other hand was toying with the idea of a Gothic horror film based loosely on the cinematic imagination of Kawalerowicz. Out of their discussions came the draft of a screenplay about a woman 'possessed' by sexual insanity – sex being a modern-day version of the devil, in Gerard Brach's view. Polanski vividly recalling his unnerving experience with the homicidal Flora a few years before, had much to contribute to Brach's portrait of the sex-crazed heroine of their story.

Polanski had summoned Brach to London to meet his new producing partner, Gene Gutowski. Gutowski read the script and expressed his misgivings about it being the proper vehicle with which to launch Polanski's career in the West. Brach and Polanski argued him down, citing facts and figures to prove that movies with sexual themes and movies with horror motifs were among the most popular genres among film audiences. What they intended to do was combine the two into a film of sexual horror. Gutowski, as he later put it, had 'the good sense to concede that they might have something.'

During the summer of 1964, then, when Gutowski was weighing offers in London, the film he had in mind as Polanski's first under his producing aegis was the one based on the Polanski-Brach script.

Several rewrites later, and after its translation from French into an English shooting script, the story became a screenplay that Polanski and Brach called *Repulsion*. It was about a beautiful but psychotic woman whose sexual phobias turn her London apartment into the setting for a carnival of bloodshed. Gene Gutowski made the financial arrangements during the fall and Polanski immediately started filming it. In the role of the mute, mentally dislocated heroine, he cast the up-and-coming French actress Catherine Deneuve, who he had met in Paris the year before. Her cool, exterior blond beauty would

201

act as a stunning contrast to the interior derangement and violence of the character she played.

During the summer and early fall of 1964, before he became fully involved in the making of *Repulsion,* Polanski spent most of his spare time in pursuit of the material pleasures of London and in learning to speak a rudimentary English. Aside from Gene Gutowski, probably the person who got to know Polanski best at this time was Judy Wilson Gutowski, the producer's English wife. She and Gutowski would divorce a decade later; she would subsequently marry another prominent producer and settle in California.

'I was immensely fond of Roman from the very start,' the former Mrs Gutowski recalled to me. 'When I first met him he was really rather innocent and helpless – like a little boy lost in a huge department store. The department store in this case was London. He was a total stranger to the city and at first a bit distrustful, I think, of all the things it had to offer. He was fascinated by it all, but frightened at the same time. A lot of this had to do with the fact that he didn't speak or understand English very well. And perhaps he didn't know what to make of the English reserve. I know he would go out walking by himself, or sometimes with Gene or me, and he'd see a pretty girl and try to say something to her, a come-on compliment. He had no inhibitions about this.

Of course the girl would usually look askance at him and tell him to bug off. Or he'd go into a store and see something he wanted to buy. But he'd get the cold shoulder from the clerk because he couldn't put it into English and didn't yet understand English money.

'This was at the very beginning. After a while he got discouraged, and instead of going out he would hang about our flat all day, working on the *Repulsion* script. I became practically like a mother to him – doing his laundry, cooking his meals, and so on. By then he was so anxious to learn English – to get girls, he said – that he pestered me day and night to teach him words and meanings. I must say I never encountered anyone with such determination. Nor with such an ability to pick up a language in no time at all. He would constantly pick up things around the flat – a dinner set from the dining table, a milk bottle from the kitchen, a toothbrush from the bathroom, whatever. He would ask me what the English words for them were. The same with everything else – he was forever after me to name things for him. Once he got the name right he never forgot it. In a matter of weeks he was speaking intelligible English – stilted but intelligible. Once he could do that, he came out of himself. He started to get his girls too. In fact, after we got him his own flat, I didn't see him halfway as often. He had others looking after him. Once he learned English he never had any difficulty finding female companionship. And then, once he made *Repulsion* and became kind of a celebrity around London, he was overwhelmed by them.'

The difference between Polanski the person and Polanski the film-director astonished Judy Gutowski when she first encountered it.

'I remember going over to Roman's flat one night with Gene during the filming of *Repulsion*. By then, Roman was getting comfortable in London and a few people came over, mostly people involved with the picture. Roman was in seventh heaven. When he was in France he had learned to like fast cars and Grand Prix racing, but he was not yet really able to drive himself. So what he did was to go out and buy himself one of those elaborate automobile racing games – the kind where there is this up-and-down track and several miniature racing cars and you race them by electronic remote control. Slot-car racing. Well, Roman was like a kid showing off his new game to us. We all played, and it *was* fun. But the way Roman was carrying on, you would never have taken him for anything but a sort of devilish little boy with a new toy.

'The next day I went out to the location to watch some of the filming on *Repulsion*. The difference was astounding. Roman still directed in French, and here he was, the little boy of the night before having become transformed into this shouting, cajoling, almost tyrannical adult. He had Catherine Deneuve terrified, and almost everyone else on the set. On the way home I said to Gene, "I can't believe it, I can't believe Roman is like this." Gene didn't believe it either when he first saw it.

'But that was Roman. Film-making was a deadly serious business to him, and everything else in life was for fun. When I saw him a few days later I said the same thing: "Roman, I can't believe that was you I saw directing, you're nothing like that." And he said, "That is the way I work, Judy. I do not apologize for it. It is my method and it is successful for me." '

One of Polanski's 'companions' at this time was Catherine Deneuve. She was to gain her first international fame for her role in *Repulsion*. A few years later she would become even more celebrated for her affair with Italian screen idol Marcello Mastroianni, for bearing him a child out of wedlock, and, in America, for her long-running television commercials on behalf of Chanel No. 5 perfume.

But in 1964, Catherine Deneuve was an icily beautiful, relatively unknown blond French actress. Polanski had learned of her when he was living in Paris. He conceded to friends later that he cast Deneuve in the lead role of *Repulsion* because he wanted to sleep with her.

During the filming, she was a regular visitor to Polanski's flat in Knightsbridge but she too became perplexed by the Pole. 'Roman was a tender, humorous little boy off the set,' she later told me. 'But on the set he was a brutal tyrant. He was a perfectionist director, yes, but an unforgiving, intolerable despot whose temper and impatience knew no bounds. He would scream the most outrageous, obscene things to me when we were shooting. Then, at night, the most endearing words came from his mouth. I would leave the set each day hysterically hating him. Then, when I was with him later, I would love him again. A very complex man, he had the professional ego of De Gaulle, the private humility of a priest.'

Repulsion was released in mid-1965. It provoked an immediate controversy among film audiences and critics. Gerard Brach received little public credit for his contribution to the picture. Polanski, on the other hand, was hailed in some American quarters as a latter-day Hitchcock, while in others he was excoriated for cheap-thrill film-making and a satanic obsession with the grotesque. The film was largely a critical and financial success, however, winning top prizes in Europe at the Venice and Berlin film festivals and profiting handsomely at the box office in America as well as on the Continent.

Gene Gutowski's faith in his judgment of the year before was vindicated. Having a large stake in the profits of *Repulsion,* he and Polanski, in the corporate form of Cadre Films, were launched on the road to show-business wealth and prestige.

No sooner did Polanski finish the final editing chores on *Repulsion* than he and Brach went to work on a script for a quick follow-up film. It was to be based on the bare bones of a story they had discussed for some time. Thematically, it was to be a repeat of *Knife in the Water.* But Brach's ideas about sexuality and violence were to be much more integrated than they had been in that film. Polanski had earlier indicated what they had in mind in an interview he gave at the 1963 New York Film Festival to the magazine *Sight and Sound.*

Asked what he planned after *Knife in the Water,* the director had replied, ' . . . a story of a married couple. He is approximately forty-six or forty-eight and she is twenty-two or twenty-three. They live in a seaside house which is falling apart. He is very rich, but she is ruining him slowly by her extravagance; she is crazy, but he's in love with her. A wounded gangster falls into the house where he finds shelter . . . ' Polanski was again dipping into his personal life for ideas.

After he had been in London for a while and had gained a rudimentary understanding of English, Polanski began to attend the English theater. He became fascinated by the work of British playwright Harold Pinter, whose plays were very much in the absurdist tradition of Beckett and Ionesco in France. Out of this fascination, he, along with Brach, refashioned their initial story into a Pinteresque black comedy. When the screenplay was finished, it portrayed a mad sexual triangle made up of a middle-aged transvestite, his nymphomaniac young wife, and a burly, sadistic gangster who commandeers their home – a medieval castle on a remote English coastline – as his hideout. They decided to call it *Cul-de-Sac.*

Gene Gutowski was able to make another favorable financing and distribution deal on the strength of previews of *Repulsion* early in 1965. Polanski cast the film in London, hiring British actor Donald Pleasance to play the transvestite, French pop singer Francoise Dorleac to play his sex-crazed wife, and American actor Lionel Stander to portray the gangster. Thereafter the company traveled to a real castle overlooking a lonely inlet on the coast of Northumberland to start filming *Cul-de-Sac*.

'It was a disastrous time,' recalls the former Judy Gutowski, who spent much of it shuttling back and forth between London and Northumberland. 'The weather was consistently horrible, there were no amenities for miles around, everyone got cabin fever, and the shouting and arguing were so fierce that people on the crew, who had been friends, became lifelong enemies. Roman himself was particularly difficult. To see him in that unholy environment was to see a mad genius, a maddening genius, at work. *Repulsion* had just been released and he was both elated by the good reviews and crushed by the bad ones.

'There was a lot of backbiting talk about how Roman was becoming a formula director, about how *Cul-de-Sac* was just another *Knife in the Water* with some horror scenes thrown in for box-office reasons. He was upset by the talk, and also upset by people on the technical crew – camera people, lighting people – telling him what he couldn't do. It was an all-English crew, very union-conscious, and they were constantly finding reasons – either work-rules or technical things – why they couldn't produce the set-ups Roman called for.

'His English was just barely getting there. But most of the crew spoke in heavy regional accents so that what Roman was hearing was like another foreign language to him. He also thought the crew was making fun of him behind his back, and with good reason. The more paranoic he became about the crew, the more dictatorial he became, which in turn infuriated the crew more.

'Gene, being the producer, got caught in the middle of it all and was constantly having to bail Roman out of trouble lest the crew walk off and stop production. He wrangled with the unions and had to wrangle with his investors when the production went over budget, he wrangled with Roman, he even wrangled with me. It was a horrible time of endless fights and difficulties between everyone, and it's a wonder the picture ever got finished. Although our marriage did break up later, it almost broke up then. I saw a side of my husband I had never seen before. I still have great affection for Roman, no matter what he's done, but in an indirect way he was responsible for the eventual collapse of Gene's and my marriage. He turned Gene into an ogre for a while, and after that, after only a couple of years of marriage, my feelings about Gene began to change.'

Polanski himself attested to the difficulties he had while filming *Cul-de-Sac,* and the manner in which he imposed his will, in the interview he gave to *Films and Filming* in 1969. There was an important and since-acclaimed beach scene in the picture. During the scene an airplane was to appear on the horizon and approach steadily as the characters on the beach traded dialogue. At the crucial point in the dialogue – a point at which the characters were to react to the fact that the plane was directly overhead – the plane would actually have to be overhead. Polanski could easily have accomplished this by shooting a number of different takes and then intercutting them so that, in the completed film, the plane would be in the right spot at the right time. But in order to capture what he called the 'truer essence' of the scene, and to display his cinematic virtuosity, he decided to film the entire scene as one take.

'There were about fourteen pages of dialogue,' he told *Films and Filming,* 'and the shot lasted eight and a half minutes. Nobody believed that I would be able to do it. I left it until the last day, and by then I had lost the loyalty of the cameraman, who also said I would never be able to do this and that the plane would never pass at the right time, because he had been in the RAF and he knew about things like that. And I really felt by that time very lonely . . . Everybody was doubting me and arguing. So I just told everybody to leave it to me and the radio man. I went through a rehearsal a couple of times and I asked the radio man to keep in contact with the plane and I explained to him exactly when I wanted the plane to pass over. The radio man was in a little shelter with a glass in front, so that when he spoke to the pilot he wouldn't interfere with the recording of the dialogue. But he could see and hear the action, and I taught him

207

how to time it for himself. And so he did one rehearsal and the plane came a little bit too early, and he did another one and the plane came a little bit too late, and then he did another one and it came exactly where we needed it. The plane was flying around out of camera range until we wanted to see it, and both pilots knowing each other very well, had language between them that was much better than any cue I could give. And finally it worked perfectly. We made two and a half takes: the actress, [Francoise Dorleac], fainted in one of the takes. And one other problem was the light. The technical people made me fiddle so long with the rehearsals that finally when I was ready to shoot the light was going and we almost missed the shot because it was evening. The actors were very nervous about it, but it was exciting for them really because they could carry on, as on the stage, which gives a better opportunity of achieving a high performance in acting than doing something which lasts for three or five seconds. And there was no *reason* for a cut in that scene. It would have been easier, of course, to cut to the plane. But *easy* is not a reason. Impossible is a reason.'

Polanski had cast Francoise Dorleac in the film as a favor to Catherine Deneuve. Francoise Dorleac was Catherine Deneuve's sister. Deneuve had been anxious to get her into movies in order to get her out of the French music business and help her break her heroin habit. Polanski never took to Francoise, though. She could not break her habit, and he found drugged women, at least then, repulsive.

According to Gene Gutowski, '*Cul-de-Sac* was a difficult project for all of us, true. But one did not doubt Roman, because he was so sure of himself. He knew exactly what he wanted, and one must respect and support that in a genius. It was my job to take the heat off him and make it as easy as possible. There *were* times when I had to put on a gentle restraint, but seldom. I felt all along that this picture would be a *tour de force,* an *opus magnus* for Roman. I still believe it was, at least cinematically. And it was worth every minute of the problems it caused.'

Cul-de-Sac opened in 1966 to mixed international reviews, but it again won an award at that year's Berlin Film Festival.

Ironically, it became most popular in France, which had ignored *Knife in the Water*. In Britain and the United States it was a financial disappointment, although the airplane scene became celebrated among film buffs for its cinematic daring.

The barely moderate success of the picture dimmed Polanski's star somewhat in the quixotic and fickle world of big-money filmdom. Movie company executives and financiers questioned whether the once-promising director wasn't destroying his potential by his seemingly increasing devotion to movies of the macabre. It was alright to make cheap horror-exploitation films – a long, remunerative tradition in the Western movie industry. But Polanski's films were too complex for ordinary horror-film audiences. At the same time, they were too simple and grotesque for the 'art' market.

They had questions about Gene Gutowski too – why he was allowing Polanski to go off on this tangent? If *Knife in the Water* had been the harbinger of a mighty talent, that talent was being wasted on cinematic trifles. From a pictorial point of view, Polanski was undoubtedly gifted, even commercial. But, the judgment in Hollywood went, the public would soon tire of his films. For all their visual attractions, they were commercially neither here nor there.

Gutowski himself grew concerned. He had hoped to exploit the success of *Repulsion* and *Cul-de-Sac* to engineer a long-term contract for Polanski and himself with a major Hollywood studio. However, the mixed reception *Cul-de-Sac* received caused his negotiations to bog down. Moreover, going well over budget on *Cul-de-Sac*, Polanski had forced Cadre Films to make up the difference, thus depleting the profits that had thus far been earned by *Repulsion.*

Such was the Gutowski-Polanski financial situation when *Cul-de-Sac* was released in 1966. Not that they were on the brink of ruin. But they needed a quick infusion of cash to tide them over until *Cul-de-Sac's* earnings began filling up their coffers again.

It was in that moment of need that Martin Ransohoff appeared on the scene. Ransohoff was an independent American movie producer with his own company, Filmways.

One night in 1966, shortly after the release of *Cul-de-Sac,* he encountered Gutowski and Polanski at a party in London. With him was a young and striking blond Hollywood starlet.

Her name was Sharon Tate.

INTERLOG 8

It was the morning of 9 August 1977, the eighth anniversay of Sharon Tate's murder and the day after his guilty plea. Roman Polanski had driven to the Holy Cross Cemetary in Culver City to lay a wreath at the grave of his dead wife and unborn child. As he stood alone before the grave, he tried hard to focus his thoughts on Sharon. But his mind stubbornly wandered back to his own problems.

'What are you going to do now?' was the last question he'd heard shouted at him the day before as he fled the Santa Monica court. The question had nagged at him ever since. He did not know what he was going to do. The morning papers had been filled with the news of his guilty plea. He was alarmed and depressed by the public rage that seemed to have built up against him in Los Angeles. The guilty plea was a grievous mistake, he was now convinced. Rather than simplify things, it seemed only to have complicated them.

Polanski was angry at Douglas Dalton for having urged it. The day before, Dalton was confident that it was the best way to go. Now the laywer seemed worried over what the judge had in mind for Polanski.

Moreover, Polanski had not had a chance to tell his side of the story. He would be forever branded a child-rapist, would forever be the butt of snide jokes.

As if that was not enough, he was now being thought of as a potential 'mentally disordered sex offender'. That was as ludicrous as calling Adolf Hitler a saint, Polanski muttered to himself. His anger shifted to the mother of the girl he was convicted of raping. If only he'd done something sooner, gotten to her after she first made her complaint to the police, paid her off, if necessary. It was because of her that he was in the fix he was. He might have been able to stop it before it went too far if only he'd . . .

He looked down at Sharon Tate's gravestone. The memories of eight years before suddenly washed over him. The pain of it all became palpable. How could a stupid sexual episode compare to the enormity and bestiality of the crime that had taken her life, Polanski thought? Then he mused about how much more avidly the Los Angeles police had worked to get him than they had to find Sharon's killers.

His bitter reverie was suddenly interrupted by a noise. Polanski turned to see the figure of a man, partly hidden by shrubs, snapping pictures. Polanski was instantly overcome with rage. Shouting obscenities, he charged toward the man. The photographer started to run. Polanski chased him, running him down within a few hundred feet.

The man was a freelance photographer named Curt Gunther. He had staked out the grave that morning in the expectation that Polanski would show up. Now, panting and fearful, he struggled violently with Polanski as the director tried to wrench his camera from him.

In a frenzy of Polish curses, Polanski finally managed to rip the camera from Gunther's grip. He dashed it to the ground. When Gunther tried to retrieve it, Polanski leaped at him and pushed him away. Then, as if it was a soccer ball, he kicked the camera thirty yards across the cemetary's manicured lawn. The frightened Gunther made no further attempt to recover it.

Polanski, breathing hard now, spat at Gunther's face. 'You ever follow me again,' he shouted, 'and I kill you. You understand that? I kill you.' With that he stalked off. He stopped to pick up the camera and then carried it to his car. Once in the Mercedes, he sped off toward the cemetary's front gate.

An hour later, Gunther walked into a Culver City police station and lodged a complaint against Polanski for stealing his camera and assaulting him. Polanski, in the meantime, had made his way to Douglas Dalton's office.

During the next few hours an alarm was out in Los Angeles for Polanski's arrest. The police, finally located him at Dalton's office. When they interviewed him there, he explained what had happened. He said that he had removed the film from the camera and dropped the camera off at the cemetery office. He refused to return the film, citing his right to privacy. Dalton supported him and challenged the police to pursue the matter.

The district attorney's office agreed with Polanski and refused to file charges based on Gunther's complaints. 'The intent of the suspect was to protect his right of privacy without any intent to permanently deprive the owner of his camera,' a spokesman for the D.A. told the press. 'Misdemeanor charges of assault and battery are likewise rejected because there is no evidence the alleged victim suffered any injury.'

How would the incident affect Polanski's standing with Judge Rittenband when the time came for sentencing on his sex conviction, the spokesman was asked?

'As far as we are concerned, it should not have any influence on the other matter.'

To the press and public, Judge Rittenband's conduct in the Polanski case was becoming increasingly vexatious. Especially puzzling were his rulings on 19 September, the day he had ordered a hearing on Polanski's mental condition. The hearing was mostly devoted instead to a petition by Dalton that Polanski be allowed to return to the South Pacific to complete work on the *Hurricane* picture before having to submit to psychiatric evaluation. 'That Rittenband would even consider the motion was odd,' remarked the Los Angeles *Herald*

Examiner. That he would allow Dalton to present witnesses in support of the motion was odder. (Dalton's chief witness was producer Dino de Laurentiis, who claimed that millions of dollars and hundreds of jobs were at stake if Polanski was not allowed to immediately return to the movie's location in Bora Bora.) But that he would assent to the motion and give Polanski a ninety-day stay before he would have to submit to psychiatric evaluation was 'odder still,' said the *Herald Examiner.*

Yet this is what Rittenband did on 19 September. Newspaper editorialists wasted no time in climbing on his back for it. The general attitude of the press was that had Polanski been an ordinary defendant convicted of a sex crime, he would already be sentenced and be on his way either to prison or a mental hospital. Was Judge Rittenband, intimidated by the influence of the film industry, showing favoritism? Or was he simply 'going soft in the head?' asked the *Hollywood Reporter.*

Rittenband, accustomed to press denunciations of his judicial record, refused to respond.

It would be learned later, though, that Rittenband's unusual stay of Polanski was prearranged between him, Dalton, and district attorney Gunson. Dalton went to the judge privately prior to 19 September and, explaining the need for the *Hurricane* picture to be completed in a timely manner, requested a stay – a much longer one than ninety days. Rittenband assured Dalton that he would allow Polanski to finish directing the South Seas film before he ordered him to Chino for the psychiatric study.

On this point a bitter dispute later arose between Rittenband and Dalton. Dalton filed an affidavit, in which he swore that, 'Judge Rittenband told defense counsel not to ask for a long stay such as six months or nine months but for a stay of ninety days. Rittenband stated that he would be subjected to further press criticism for the longer time period, but that after the ninety-day time expired Dalton should come back to court and request an additional stay which would then be granted . . . The judge assured defense counsel that stays would be provided to complete the movie, but that he was not to disclose this to the press.'

Dalton's affidavit was part of his effort, five months after Polanski's ninety day stay was granted, to get Judge Rittenband disqualified from the case.

If Dalton's allegations were true, then Rittenband was indeed granting special treatment to Polanski and was engaged in a conspiracy to keep it from public view. No one could fault Dalton, since he was trying to do the best for his client and himself and was violating no law. Nor was Rittenband breaking the law. But the judicial propriety of his action in granting Polanski a stay was questionable, and he knew it.

Had the press been aware of these behind-the-scenes machinations, editorial puzzlement would have turned to outrage. As one journalist put it at the time, 'Suppose I was convicted of a sex crime against a child. And suppose I came up before Judge Rittenband. And suppose my attorney requested a ninety day stay so that I could complete a newspaper series I was working on. Where do you think I would be today?'

Another columnist conjectured about the reasons behind Rittenband's accommodating treatment of Polanski. 'Could it be that the judge has been reversed so many times on appeal in his career that he is trying to avoid doing anything to give Polanski grounds for an appeal? Or is he simply helping Polanski's attorney, Douglas Dalton, make sure that he gets his fee for defending the director? Rumor has it that Polanski's broke. It's said that he's been forced to pledge a substantial part of his earnings from *Hurricane* to Dalton as a fee guarantee. If true, then Dalton will not get paid unless Polanski is allowed to complete the picture.'

What was district attorney's role in all of this? As of this writing, the deputy prosecutors involved in the case, including Roger Gunson, have refused to discuss it. Apparently, though, the district attorney's office went along with the idea of a stay for Polanski. At least it did not register any objections.

But the negative press comment must have gotten to Judge Rittenband nevertheless. This became evident less than two weeks after he granted Polanski his three-month postponement.

Judge Rittenband later said he understood that after the 19 September hearing at which he had granted Polanski's postponement, the Polish director was to return immediately to the South Pacific to complete his work on the de Laurentiis movie. Yet on 29 September, a photo of Polanski appeared in the Los Angeles newspapers. It pictured Polanski at a nightclub in Munich, Germany, surrounded by a bevy of young women. The caption that appeared beneath the photo was appropriately sarcastic. 'Roman Polanski, convicted rapist,' said one, 'enjoys a night out on the town in Munich, while a certain Santa Monica judge believes him to be slaving away over the Dino de Laurentiis production of *Hurricane* in the Samoan Islands.'

Other newspaper reaction depicted Rittenband as having been duped by attorney Dalton, de Laurentiis and Polanski himself. Furious, he immediately called a special court hearing 'to get some facts straight' about what Polanski was doing in Europe. 'I was startled to see the picture and read that caption,' Rittenband told journalists, 'since Mr Polanski so sincerely indicated to me that his request for the stay was so that he could rush to get his picture done in the South Pacific. It was only on that basis that I gave him the stay.'

The special hearing was called for 21 October. Rittenband ordered Dalton to have Polanski and de Laurentiis in his court-room for questioning. 'I'll put Polanski on the witness stand to explain he was in Munich on business in connection with the movie,' Dalton asserted after emerging from a pre-hearing conference with Rittenband. 'And I'll probably call de Laurentiis to further explain the situation.'

Polanski's attorney added that the director had gone to Munich to discuss financing and distribution of the upcoming movie with a group of potential German investors. Polanski was not even aware that the photo had been taken while he was having dinner with the Germans. The four girls in the background, Dalton said, were seated at a nearby table and were not part of Polanski's party. A fifth girl in the photo, seated next to Polanski, was an actress-girlfriend of one of the members of Polanski's business party.

Dalton pursued this claim when Judge Rittenband's hearing convened on 21 October. Polanski, returned to Los Angeles, testified that he had been sent to Munich by de Laurentiis in

216

order to help sell the film after de Laurentiis was unable to go himself. Since the movie was an independent production and had no backing from a major studio, it was necessary to raise further monies from investors to ensure the picture's completion.

De Laurentiis followed Polanski to the stand. The flamboyant producer had been one of the stellar figures in the postwar Italian film boom, producing everything from the most acclaimed 'art' films to the crudest 'spaghetti westerns'. He was famous in the international film world for his magnetic charm and business dealings. He had recently left Italy, to set up operations in the United States. *Hurricane* was to be his first blockbuster American production. On the stand he corroborated Polanski's story under Dalton's questioning. Polanski had not been vacationing in Munich, he insisted, but was there on business representing de Laurentiis and the movie.

'But just a minute,' Judge Rittenband said to Dalton. 'I gave the defendant a ninety-day stay because you told me he needed it to complete work on the motion picture. Now I'm learning that it was not for him to complete work on the movie, but to serve as a fund raiser for Mr de Laurentiis. He has not yet even begun to work on actually directing the picture.'

That was correct, conceded Dalton.

'Then I've been had,' Rittenband shot back angrily. 'I was misled by the testimony given to me by the defendant and Mr de Laurentiis on 19 September.' With a mighty show of indignation, Rittenband said that he was tempted to revoke Polanski's stay and order him immediately to Chino. On reflection, though, he realized that Chino was not prepared to accept Polanski until the end of the stay. So he would let it stand. But, he warned, there would be no further postponements, and Dalton had better not ask for any. Polanski was ordered to report to Chino on 19 December, 1977, and to remain behind bars there until the state psychiatric and pre-sentencing probation reports were completed – up to ninety days. After receiving the reports, said Rittenband, he would pronounce sentence on the director.

What Rittenband would not learn immediately was that the

217

main reason Polanski had gone to Munich was to be reunited with, and introduce to the picture's German investors, the actress he was promoting to play Tess in the other film he had contracted to direct once his Los Angeles troubles were over.

The actress was Natassia Kinski. The daughter of famous German actor Klaus Kinski, she was a stunning Ingrid Bergman lookalike, though younger and more sultry. Polanski had met her the year before when she posed in the nude for an earlier pictorial layout he had put together for the French *Vogue*. She then obtained Polanski's promise to feature her in one of his next movies and turn her into a star. Indeed, aside from the emergency money it brought him, she was the reason he had signed the contract to make the film of *Tess of the D'Urbervilles*.

CHAPTER 9

SHARON TATE was an American army brat, the oldest of three daughters of Colonel Paul Tate and his wife. Born in 1943 in Dallas, she was raised in several locales around the United States. Early in life, she nurtured a dream to become a movie star. Along with her dream she developed a striking blond beauty which she exploited to win a succession of beauty contests as a teenager. When she was still in high school, her father was assigned to a post near Los Angeles. She would hitchhike into the city and haunt the movie studios in hope of being discovered.

Eventually, Sharon acquired an agent. He managed to get her a few television commercials and then, in 1963, an audition for the television series 'Petticoat Junction'. An aging film and television producer, Martin Ransohoff, happened to see her audition. He was reported to have told her, in the best Hollywood tradition, 'Honey, you've got it. If you let me, I'll make you a star.'

Sharon signed an exclusive contract with Ransohoff and spent the next few years, between acting, singing and dancing lessons, appearing in bit parts in several Ransohoff-produced

219

movies and television shows. According to those who knew her best at the time, although she was being promoted by Ransohoff as a starlet and indeed looked like one, she failed to live up to at least one portion of the standard starlet image. She was not sexually promiscuous. 'Sharon was one of the toughest lays in town,' says a well-known actor of today. 'Strictly a one-man woman.'

The men she was attracted to were the dominant type, like her father. Unlike her father, they also tended to be brutal. Her first serious affair was with a perpetually out-of-work French actor, with whom she lived for two years in Hollywood. He once beat her up so badly, according to Sharon's mother, that she had to be rushed to a hospital for emergency treatment.

Sharon's next affair was with Jay Sebring. Known to the public as the exclusive hair stylist of numerous movie stars, Sebring was also notorious within the film community as a secret leather-and-chains sex freak and a prodigious drug user.

Hollywood had always been in the forefront of adopting the latest in bizarre lifestyles. In 1966, the film capital was aboil with a whole new series of 'sleazo inputs,' as one commentator put it. The burgeoning hippie movement had penetrated the movie community. Its three chief components – ear shattering rock music, indiscriminate sex and illicit drugs – were growing rampant among the younger generation of Hollywood professionals.

The most popular drugs at the time were LSD, mescaline and psilocybin, all hallucinogens, and the 'speed-type' substances. Jay Sebring was one of the early pioneers in drug use. He soon became a dealer, first turning on his hair clients and then serving as their principal supplier.

Although in many ways old-fashioned, the twenty-three-year-old Sharon Tate was in the process of breaking out of her family's strict, Army-oriented sense of values when she met Jay Sebring. The simplest way to prove her independence was to join with the many others of her generation in Hollywood who were taking up drugs. Impressed by the way some of Hollywood's most celebrated stars had grown to depend on Sebring, she fell in love with him. Thereafter she became a

220

regular drug user and his live-in girlfriend. With her innate inhibitions eroded by drugs, she also learned to submit herself to Sebring's jaded sexual practices. These featured such things as bondage, beatings and drug-infused sex orgies, according to several people who knew her.

'It was not a life Sharon really wanted or enjoyed,' one of her friends recently told me. 'But she was a good-hearted gal, and when she became attached to someone she would do just about anything for them. And she was attached to Jay.'

Sharon Tate was living with Sebring when she traveled to London with her mentor, Martin Ransohoff, during the summer of 1966. There, at a party, she met Roman Polanski.

Ransohoff had put Sharon into a featured role in his 1965 film *Eye of the Devil,* starring David Niven and Deborah Kerr. The movie was a weird horror story in which Niven became the victim of a hooded cult that practiced ritual sacrifice. Sharon's role was that of a country girl who had the powers of a witch. With less than a dozen lines, her primary function was to look beautiful, which she did.

Ransohoff wanted to do another horror film, but on a more sophisticated level. Which is why he cornered Polanski at the party. He had seen *Repulsion,* in which the deranged heroine murdered two men. He had also seen an early rough print of *Cul-de-Sac,* in which the inhabitants of the isolated castle each suffered a horrible fate. The gory cinematography was superb. He asked Polanski to do a similar movie for him.

Polanski was interested. He told Ransohoff that he and Gerard Brach were working on a script designed to be a comedy spoof of all the old-fashioned Hollywood horror movies. Ransohoff immediately offered to produce it with Gene Gutowski – on the condition that Sharon Tate be given one of the leading roles. He introduced Sharon to Polanski. The director looked her over appreciatively. Why not, he thought?

In his two years in London, Polanski's personal life had changed markedly. First of all, the profits from *Repulsion* were enormous, and for the first time in his life he had an abundance of money. Second, the Gutowskis had established him in the city's trendy, fast-living show business and society circles.

221

'Always on the hunt for the amusing and offbeat,' as an English gossip columnist put it, they enthusiastically adopted him as one of their own. Third, his English had improved to the point where he was easily able to converse, banter and flirt. His accent and speech idiosyncracies only served to enhance his attraction. Fourth, men liked him. Being all man in his attitudes, yet rather ordinary in stature and looks, he did not pose a threat to them. Finally, women were attracted to him. Despite the manliness he tried so hard to project, he retained an indisguisable boyish appeal that was made up of a combination of forced arrogance and innate timidity.

Not all women liked him, though. Nor all men. 'All that charm was a lovely come on,' says an English woman who had a brief affair with Polanski in 1966. 'I don't mean this to sound bitter or like sour grapes, because it's not – I knew exactly what I was getting. We're still good friends, but I can no longer have any use for the way Roman deals with women on a personal level. He gives nothing and takes everything. It's the conquest that's important to him. Once he has conquered a woman – which means getting her to go to bed with him – it's all over. Maybe not immediately, but as soon as he has drained the woman of all he wants from her. With some it may take only a night, others a series of nights. But it always ends up the same way for the woman. Once conquered, goodbye. Not that I blame him – maybe if I was a man I'd be the same way. But I do blame him, now that I think of it, because it's unfair. It's a way of using people. He entices, then discards. It does tremendous things for his ego, but all in all it's very childish . . . Roman is incapable of making a genuine connection with a woman – I don't even think he did it with Sharon.'

'The quintessential male chauvinist pig,' says another who shared his bed for a short time. 'He treats women like objects, like toys, like his latest pet car. It can be fun to share his limelight for a while, but ultimately it becomes boring.'

Declares a third, 'I still see Roman now and then, and as someone to have around he can be fun, although one gets tired of too much of him. His manner is always the same, always doing things for effect. Even now when I see him coming on to some young girl, I want to warn her, say to her she should give this guy a wide berth. Of course, I don't. I see the girls falling for his style, and I make bets with myself about how long they'll be around.'

A man who was close to Polanski in 1966 says of him: 'After *Repulsion,* Roman began to be conscious of the fact that he was a celebrity. Being a celebrity in London is quite different from being a celebrity in Poland. In London he was fawned over and given practically anything he wanted – whether it was women, money, parties or holidays. He got himself a fancy car, bought a house, surrounded himself with luxuries and became a fixture on the party circuit.

'Nothing wrong with that, but having never been exposed to this kind of life before, he tended to overindulge. I think it also warped his picture of himself. He became self-possessed, self-important and irresponsible. He'd get in a lot of jams – financial jams and the like – but there was always someone around who was happy to bail him out. So in many ways he remained a child, never willing to face responsibility for his actions and always ready to blame someone else when something went wrong. He hurt a lot of people who thought they were his friends that way. It soon became clear that Roman's friends were only those people who were willing to suffer his excesses and endure his diatribes. If some friend resisted or argued, he would no longer have any use for him. Suddenly he would become an enemy. Roman demanded almost blind obedience and loyalty, although these were not qualities he returned in kind.'

'He very quickly became an insufferable show-off, a braggart,' says another male acquaintance of the time. 'I got so I couldn't stand the little twerp and his obnoxious manner. Whether he was bragging about who he went to bed with the night before or was boasting about his physical prowess or was telling about having bested some intellectual in an argument, he was a distasteful character. Life became one long "Look-at-me-I'm-better-than-anyone-else" syndrome. He became a bore, a parody, and the only reason a lot of people put up with it, even encouraged him, was because they got a vicarious thrill out of being close to a celebrity or because he was a meal ticket.'

Because of the abrasive side of Polanski's personality, Sharon Tate found him eminently resistable when she first encountered him in 1966. According to the former Judy Gutowski, who became one of the actress's closest friends, 'Sharon didn't like Roman at all when they met. They met in social situations the first few times, and she was completely turned off by his manner. But then, once she began working for him on the picture, she saw this different man – a man who exuded confidence and dominated his environment. She saw Roman the director. Suddenly this small and not terribly good-looking man was totally in charge of her. And she began to respond to this.

'When I first met Sharon, I expected her to be nothing more than just another beautiful and not too bright American girl. But she surprised me – she turned out to be rather quite remarkable. In a way she was naïve. But she also had this tremendous unaffectedness and sense of decency and loyalty that really impressed people. She never bad-mouthed anyone and was completely free of any of the neurotic ambition one usually associates with actresses.

'But she did have one flaw, which even she recognized and worried about. For all her beauty and goodness as a person, she needed to give herself to a man of authority and dominance. She was very insecure about herself as an actress – even, I suppose, as a person. Directing her, Roman touched a chord in Sharon. She began to enjoy being in his hands.'

Recalls another close observer, 'As a man, Roman was basically weak, which was why he spent so much energy trying to prove to everyone how strong and tough he was. But as a director he was inherently strong. He exuded power and authority and a total lack of nonsense. Perhaps this quality was drilled into him at that school he went to in Poland. I knew Sharon pretty well, and I think what attracted her to Roman was this combination of weak and strong. At least that's what she told me after she became involved with him.'

Polanski himself has described in various press interviews Sharon Tate's initial coolness toward him. 'It took the longest time for me to get her to go to bed with me,' he has said. 'She was not someone who went easily to bed with a man. So when she finally came to bed with me, I knew it was important thing for her. And it was important for me too, because she was so vulnerable and trusting.'

As the filming of Polanski's horror-picture spoof progressed, he and Sharon spent more and more time together. The picture, which would be released in the United States in 1967 as *The Fearless Vampire Killers,* featured Sharon as the beautiful victim of a vampire who ends up biting her lover in the neck, creating another monster. Her lover was played by Polanski.

The two soon became lovers offscreen as well. Polanski had recently purchased and moved into a small mews house off Eaton Place in London's fashionable Belgravia. Sharon moved in with him early in 1967. According to the then-Judy Gutowski, 'This marked a radical new phase in Roman's life. All of a sudden he found himself domesticated, a one-woman man, and he enjoyed it. At least for a while.'

Sharon became a fixture in Polanski's London circle, and for a while life indeed became more domestic for the director. Instead of nightly whirls on the town, in 1967 his routine became a round of small gatherings among show business friends, either at Polanski's house or at the homes of others, interspersed with skiing trips to Switzerland in the winter and visits to the South of France during the summer. For the first time, Polanski has said, 'I was really happy. Except for the first few months of my first marriage, I had never committed myself to anyone. Sharon was the first woman in my life who really made me feel happy. I remember thinking: I am a happy man. It was a sentiment I hadn't known before, because there had always been something missing from my happiness, some little thing that always needed adjusting. I also remember thinking – and here was my middle-European background probably — I remember thinking: "This cannot possibly last. It's impossible to last." And I suddenly got scared . . . I didn't have anything tragic in mind, but I was afraid, being a realist, that such a state of happiness could not last indefinitely.'

Polanski and Sharon celebrated their love affair by

consenting to have some nude pictures of the actress, taken by the director during the shooting of their movie, appear in the March 1967 issue of *Playboy*.

The only unhappiness Polanski was to encounter in 1967 had to do with *The Fearless Vampire Killers*. It was greeted with the critical scorn it deserved and failed miserably at the box office in America. Polanski blamed this on Ransohoff, who he said 'took it away from me and cut twenty minutes out of it and redubbed it and changed the music. When he was through, no one could understand it anymore . . . Until that time all my films had been made as I wanted them to be . . . And suddenly I found I had made a film which had been butchered . . . What I made was a funny, spooky fairy tale, and Ransohoff turned it into a kind of Transylvanian "Beverly Hillbillies".'

Although he had a contract to make another two pictures for Filmways, Polanski refused to work for Ransohoff again and the contract was canceled. Which was another stroke of luck for the Pole, since a bigger and better opportunity lay just over the horizon.

Ira Levin's best-selling novel *Rosemary's Baby,* a tale about a young Manhattan woman who gradually discovers that she has been tricked by her husband into having a child by Satan, had been purchased for filming by Hollywood horror-movie director William Castle and Paramount Pictures. Robert Evans, Paramount's production chief, offered the directing job to Polanski. Paramount could not get the Pole without getting Gene Gutowski, along with his and Polanski's company, Cadre Films. As a result of negotiations between Gutowski's Hollywood agent, William Tennant, and Evans, therefore, Paramount signed the Polanski-Gutowski team to a multipicture contract. The first film would be *Rosemary's Baby.*

The Gutowskis, Polanski and Sharon Tate moved from London to California in mid-1967. Burned by Hollywood's Martin Ransohoff on his last picture, Polanski insisted to Evans and Castle that he not only write the film's screenplay, but that he be given complete control in making the picture. 'I told them how I was going to do the film and I said that I hoped it was for

226

this quality that they called on me and not because they thought it would be easy to change my work. And they said that was exactly why they wanted me there and left me complete freedom.'

The making of *Rosemary's Baby* was by-and-large a happy experience for Polanski. His relationship with Sharon Tate had mellowed him somewhat, and although he was as demanding and meticulous as always on the set, he expressed himself with more grace and patience than ever before. It was the first time he had worked in Hollywood, and Gene Gutowski impressed on him how important it was to make a good impression.

Mia Farrow, the film's star, later said that 'Roman was the best director I'd ever worked for. He always knew what he wanted and he created a tremendous sense of security for the actors on the set. He was demanding in his insistence we do things his way – for instance, say a line with the stress on the word he wanted, not the one we thought was natural. But he inspired awe because he always seemed to know exactly what he was doing. He was so young-looking, like a high-school boy. But he exuded an authority that most older directors would've given their right arms to be able to do.'

During the filming, which shifted between Hollywood and New York, Polanski and Sharon lived in a rented house near the beach in Santa Monica. After he completed his major work on the picture late in 1967, the two returned to his house in London for the Christmas holidays. They had been together for almost a year. As Polanski told *Playboy* in 1971, 'At the beginning of our relationship I was afraid of getting too deeply involved and losing my freedom. But she was extremely understanding, tactful and clever. Being around me, she still made me feel absolutely free. She did not make demands, and she made it clear that she was not going to engulf me. I remember once her words, "I am not one of those ladies who swallow a man" . . . After a while, I realized that she would like to get married. She never asked me, never said a word about it. So finally I said, "I'm sure you would like to get married," and she said she would. So I said, "We'll get married then," and we did. By that time I wasn't nervous about it at all.'

227

The marriage took place in London on 20 January 1968, with Gene and Judy Gutowski in attendance. After a skiing honeymoon in the Swiss Alps, the two returned to Los Angeles.

Although Sharon had been 'understanding, tactful and clever,' in allowing Polanski his freedom up to the time of their marriage, she obviously had different expectations about his behavior after they became man and wife. According to a close friend of Sharon's, 'Once they started living together in London before they were married, Roman stayed faithful to Sharon for about six weeks. But then he started playing around again on the side, mostly with old girlfriends, whenever Sharon went back to Hollywood for a part in a picture. Then, when they returned to Hollywood for *Rosemary's Baby*, Roman found a whole new field of girls that interested him. Sharon soon learned that he was playing around. It hurt her, but she ignored it. At least she tried to, but it eventually began to show. She was in love with him, no doubt about that, and inside it pained her deeply that he was being unfaithful. Roman asked her to marry him, I think, because he began to feel guilty for what he was doing to her. And she agreed to marry him because she thought it was the only way to bring him around to being faithful to her.'

If true, Sharon's hope was an idle one. After their return to California, where she was to play her first really major role in the film version of *The Valley of the Dolls*, Polanski resumed his extracurricular love life.

The Valley of the Dolls was author Jacqueline Susann's blockbuster bestseller about a group of famous women in Hollywood, modeled on real-life stars, who compulsively destroy themselves through twisted ambition, career-advancing sex, alcohol and drugs.

While Sharon was working on this, *Rosemary's Baby* was released and became an instant financial and critical success. Most reviewers agreed that the movie represented Polanski's most worthwhile effort since *Knife in the Water*, although some regretted that he continued to squander his gifts on such 'non-serious' material as a suspense story about witchcraft. 'Polanski must no longer be burdened by the standards he set up for himself in *Knife in the Water,'* wrote critic Stanley Kaufmann in the *New Republic* of 15 June 1968. 'Since then, he has only been trying to entertain us and . . . he is at last succeeding . . . as a manufacturer of intelligent thrillers, clever and insubstantial.'

With the release of *Rosemary's Baby,* Polanski decided to remain in Los Angeles to work on further projects for Paramount. He liked Hollywood, he said, and he liked such enlightened production heads as Paramount's Robert Evans. 'The machinery at my disposal, and the possibilities are incomparable. And I have more freedom there than I have ever had before in other countries. So, at this stage, I think that's the best place to make films.'

But it was not just its film-making convenience that convinced Polanski that Hollywood was the place to be. The success of *Rosemary's Baby* had turned him into the darling of the West Coast film and rock-music communities. The freedom he talked about referred to the making of motion pictures, but he might just as well have meant the freedom of his many new friends' lifestyles.

The hippie-influenced drug-and-sex culture had blossomed into full flower in Hollywood. Top young stars of the film community simply weren't in unless they were 'out of it'. It was not long before just about anyone who was anyone was singing the praises of the new free life of the senses.

Hollywood was like a brand new toy store for Polanski, far more varied in its easily available merchandise than London had been before, and Paris before that. Another difference was that he now spoke English fairly well and, with the success of *Rosemary's Baby,* became an insider much more quickly. Indeed, he and Sharon were soon among the leading hosts and hostesses of Hippie Hollywood.

Sharon, according to a friend, 'managed to keep her head screwed on straight. I mean, she did drugs and all, but she didn't get terribly impressed with what was going on. Roman, on the other hand, went off the deep end. He was down on Sunset Boulevard almost every night, haunting the strip clubs and picking up girls in his car, taking them up into the hills, snorting a few pinches of cocaine and then screwing them. One of the things that kept him busy at it was that he had these friends showing up from Poland all the time, guys he'd gone to school with and such. They'd show up and he just had to take them out and show them the underbelly of Hollywood.'

While Polanski and his friends were getting to know the underbelly of Hollywood, just a few miles away another group of friends was in the process of adding a new dimension to that underbelly. In Hollywood, 'letting it all hang out' had become a convenient excuse for certain social behavior that would never have been tolerated otherwise. To be a 'freak' or to 'freak out' in public was not only amusedly accepted, it was fast becoming a fashionable mode of conduct. It was in such a freewheeling atmosphere that a man named Charles Manson was able to operate without attracting any adverse attention.

Manson was a congenital sociopath, an habitual petty criminal who had been released from a California prison on parole in March 1967 after serving six years and nine months for his most recent bungled crime. In prison he had developed a taste for the drug-rock music that was becoming the rage in California and had taken to befriending marijuana offenders, most of whom were better educated and much softer in spirit than the cons he had associated with all his life.

After his release, Manson wandered into the Haight-Ashbury district of San Francisco. His hair grown long and straggly, he quickly melded into the hippie dope-and-love community that was then rising to its zenith there. A beard and a guitar later, the thirty-two-year-old paroled convict was handing out free LSD to the young people he encountered on the street.

Acid would prove to be Manson's passport back into society. Soon he was surrounded by a following of teenage runaway girls, dropouts and car thieves. 'Charlie is in love with us and we are all in love with Charlie,' exclaimed one of Manson's female devotees. 'He writes songs for us and sings them with the voice of an angel.'

Manson's striking presence, based on, as *Time* Magazine later put it, 'the eyes of Rasputin and a mystic patter that mixed the Beatles with Scientology,' eventually gained him access to the fringes of the New Hollywood. He struck up passing acquaintances with several important people in the Los Angeles rock-music business, including Frank Zappa, Dennis Wilson of the Beach Boys, and Terry Melcher, a young record producer who was the son of Doris Day. By then Manson, at best a discordant guitar plucker, fancied himself as a potential rock star. Consequently he began to hound Melcher, who had connections with the record companies, for an audition.

Melcher, not a little fascinated by Manson, finally arranged for one. After hearing Manson sing, though, he lost his enthusiasm. Manson would not be denied, however. All his life a social outcast, he knew a brushoff when he saw one.

One day in 1968 Manson appeared at Melcher's rented house in a fashionable canyon above Beverly Hills. He pleaded for another chance to audition. Melcher dismissed him, suggesting that he had a long way to go before he would be skillful enough to call himself a musician.

Manson became livid with rage at the rejection. He retreated to the sanctuary of the Spahn Ranch, a little-used movie location that he and his followers had expropriated in the hills of northernmost Los Angeles. There he turned his and his disciples' energies to witchcraft, Jesus-freaking, sexual excess, dope-dealing, ritualistic bloodletting and mind-rattling paranoia.

It was there that the ugly fate of Sharon Tate would be sealed.

While Manson was insanely brooding at the Spahn Ranch, Roman Polanski rented a house for Sharon and himself on a ridge high above Beverly Hills. Once they were settled in, the director went to work developing new ideas for films while Sharon half-heartedly pursued further acting roles. Her pursuit was half-hearted because she was not that enthusiastic about continuing as an actress. Now married, she wanted to have a child by Polanski. He resisted the idea, recalling his own bitter childhood to her and saying, 'I would never inflict the possibility of that on another human being.'

Sharon, however, continued to pester him. 'She became a bit of a nag after a while, in fact,' says a friend. 'The more she nagged him for a child, the more Roman tried to escape. He

231

started coming home less and less, claiming that he had business meetings and such. What he was really doing was going out with other girls on the sly.'

But it was impossible to maintain on-the-sly relationships for very long in Hollywood. Although Polanski tried to maintain secrecy, word of his infidelities quickly got around and eventually reached Sharon. Although she never confronted him about it, she began to complain to friends.

One was the then-Judy Gutowski. 'This was when I really began to dislike Roman,' she says today. 'He was really treating her abominably. She would never say anything to him because she was afraid of frightening him away. But she'd cry on my shoulder, "Why must he be this way, he's humiliating me, why can't he be faithful, I've done everything he's wanted me to do?" Then I'd talk to Roman, bawl him out, and he'd pretend to be just as unhappy. "Oh, Judy," he'd say, "I can't change what I am. She knew what she was getting. If I could change, I really would." '

Sharon remained convinced that if marriage could not change her husband, a baby would. She raised the pressure on him for a child. He finally agreed. After several months of trying, she became pregnant in December of 1968.

Despite her old-fashioned values, when Sharon had lived with Jay Sebring, a heavy drug user, she had become a drug user herself. And despite these same values, when she became involved with Polanski she went along with him in some of his more bizarre sexual habits – allowing him, for instance, to videotape the two of them making love and then sitting by quietly while he screened the tapes for friends at parties.

But these were not the only tapes Polanski made. One of Sharon's closest friends recalls traveling to San Francisco with her early in 1969 to visit her family for a few days. Polanski remained behind at the Beverly Hills house. When they returned a day before having planned to, Polanski was not at the house. 'Sharon went into the bedroom to put her case away and found some tapes that she hadn't seen before. We put them on the machine, and they turned out to be of Roman making love to two or three girls on their bed. Sharon turned white, and then got madder than hell. The marriage almost ended there. It probably would have, except she had just found out she was pregnant.'

Once pregnant, Sharon gave up all drugs. But not a desire for revenge. Two months later, before her pregnancy started to show, she went to Rome to appear in an Anglo-Italian comedy film with Italian star Vittorio Gassman.

'While she was in Rome those three weeks,' the same friend recounted for me, 'she had an affair. She came back and told me about it. She was proud of herself. The man didn't mean that much to her, she said, but the fact that she had done it made her feel good about herself. She could play the same game Roman played. But she never told him, for fear of how he would react. And he never found out. One of the reasons she did it was because he wouldn't go to Rome with her. He claimed he had to be in London, but she knew that he just wanted to be away from her for a while so that he'd have the opportunity to carry on with his own sex life without her finding out about it. He still had plenty of girls waiting around for him, and she knew he was still fooling around, despite her pregnancy. So she just went off and had her affair on her own initiative. It wasn't so much to punish Roman as it was to get even. I remember her saying, "Well, now I've gotten even with him, I feel better." He didn't have to know. In fact to this day he doesn't know that Sharon was unfaithful to him in Italy.'

Just prior to her early 1969 trip to Italy, Sharon and Roman had moved into another, more sumptuous house high on a remote hillside above Benedict Canyon. The house, at 10050 Cielo Drive, was owned by movie agent Rudi Altobelli. Before the Polanski's rented it for $3000 a month, it had been the house that Terry Melcher, the rock-producing son of Doris Day and acquaintance of Charles Manson, had lived in.

The house was set on a large property at the end of a cul-de-sac off Cielo Drive and afforded a fantastic view of Los Angeles, from downtown on the east to the ocean on the west. Protected by electronic gates at the foot of the drive, it was a spacious ranch-style home surrounded by lawns, gardens and a swimming pool. Along the perimeter of the property, facing a steep drop-off into a canyon, ran a rustic post-and-rail fence. When the Polanski's moved in, they found the fence strung along its entire length with gaily colored Christmas lights that could be seen clearly at night from Sunset Boulevard, a mile below. They decided to leave the lights up as a beacon to their friends.

Their friends were becoming legion. Kirk Douglas, Warren Beatty, Steve McQueen, James Coburn, Yul Brynner, Peter Sellers, Lee Marvin, Jane Fonda, Peter Fonda – these were only a few of the celebrities who were regular visitors once Polanski and Sharon moved in.

Among friends not so well known was Vojtek Frykowski, Polanski's old schoolmate from Lodz. Polanski had helped Frykowski get out of Poland a few years before, and Frykowski had been following him ever since, from Paris to London to New York to Hollywood. In New York, Frykowski had met a wealthy American coffee heiress named Abigail Folger. They had started to live together and had moved on to Hollywood when Polanski decided to settle there after *Rosemary's Baby*. They were regular fixtures on the Polanski social scene, and Frykowski even talked of trying to make a go of it himself in American films. In the meantime, in order to support himself, he took to dealing in drugs. Along with Sharon's former boyfriend, Jay Sebring, who remained a friend of the Polanskis, he became the main supplier of drugs to the Polanski household.

Polanski continued to work on various movie projects during the spring of 1969, traveling back and forth between Los Angeles and London, while Sharon blossomed into full-scale pregnancy.

'It was like the baby growing inside her made everything else insignificant,' recalls another close friend. 'Even her troubles with Roman became secondary. She sort of accepted the way he was and decided to ignore it. She put all her emotions in the baby. She even quit all drugs. She was determined to have a healthy child. She still clung to the hope that after the baby was born, Roman would settle down.'

Polanski and Sharon spent most of the summer in London

while she did dubbing for her film with Gassman and he worked on a script that he and Gene Gutowski planned to produce under the banner of Cadre Films.

'The summer did nothing to improve their relationship,' recalls a friend who was on the scene. 'God knows Sharon tried, she tried almost too much. But he was bored with her being pregnant. He treated her like she was a piece of excess baggage. He was even pointedly cruel to her in front of others at times, calling her a dumb hag and criticizing her whenever she expressed an opinion.'

Sharon's baby was due late in August. She had planned to return to the United States in mid-July by ocean liner. Polanski had promised to accompany her, and she was hoping that a week alone together at sea would help mend their relationship.

The day before they were going to sail, Polanski informed Sharon that he would not be going, that he still had a few more days of work to complete and that she would have to make the voyage by herself.

Sharon stubbornly announced that she would wait for him. This was not what Polanski wanted to hear. 'No,' he said, 'you go on the ship now. We cannot get another ship reservation. That means you would have to fly back with me. But the airlines will not let you fly – you are too pregnant.'

Sharon argued, but to no avail. Polanski was insistent that he wanted his child to be born in the United States. 'Don't worry, you go on the ship. I will fly over in a few days. I will be there ahead of you. I'll meet you in New York.'

Sharon made the ocean crossing alone. When she arrived in New York, Polanski was not there. A phone call established that he was still not finished with his work in London. He promised to fly directly to California in the next few days. 'Maybe I beat you there.'

But he didn't. Sharon arrived back at the house on Cielo Drive to find, not her husband, but Wojtek Frykowski and Abigail Folger. Polanski had asked his friend Frykowski to move into the house and look after Sharon until he returned. Sharon was angry, disappointed by Polanski's continuing absence but even more so because she could not stand

Frykowski. She felt helpless to do anything, however. So she put on a cheerful face and sat back resignedly to await Polanski's return.

It was the beginning of August, and Polanski still remained in London. It was true that he was laboring over a script, but he was not rushing to finish the work so that he could return to California. As he told a friend, 'I can't stand seeing Sharon blown up the way she is. This pregnancy has made her such an insecure, nagging bitch. If I could, I'd wait until she gives birth. Then maybe I could go back and find Sharon the way she used to be.' He soothed his disenchantment nightly with a series of girls he picked up at various parties around London.

On Friday, 8 August Sharon woke up at nine in the morning and tried to phone Polanski in London. It was six in the evening there, and she wanted to get him before he went out for the night, as she knew he would. She had given up asking when he was going to return, but she could not stand having the over-bearing Frykowski and Abigail Folger around the house any longer. Frykowski and Folger, constantly stoned on drugs, engaged in interminable arguments. They were driving her crazy, making her tense, and she feared that her growing anxiety would have a negative effect on the baby. She wanted Polanski to order them to pack up and leave, since she didn't dare do it herself.

Unable to reach her husband, she left a message for him to call back as soon as possible. Polanski returned the call at eleven in the morning, eight p.m. London time. They argued – Polanski had thought that the urgency of her message meant that the baby had been born prematurely or something else had gone wrong. 'Never do that to me again!' he shouted at Sharon over the long-distance cable.

Polanski refused to tell Frykowski to leave. 'It is my house, and he stays there until I return.'

'When do you suppose that will be?' Sharon asked sarcastically.

'Soon.'

'Your birthday is next week. Do you think you'll be back in time for that? I was sort of planning a party for you.'

236

'Definitely.'

Polanski quickly ended the conversation and hung up. Sharon lay in bed and cried for a while.

It was a hot day in Los Angeles. Sharon got up about noon and went for a swim, relieved that Frykowski and Abigail were nowhere about. Winifred Chapman, the cleaning woman, later said that Sharon looked like she could have given birth at any moment.

At one, a couple of Sharon's friends dropped by for lunch, the actress Joanna Pettet, and Barbara Lewis. Frykowski and Folger showed up soon afterwards and, uninvited, joined them while they were eating. Sharon had wanted to unload her troubles on her two friends, but with Frykowski there she didn't dare complain about her husband. She had the feeling that he was like a secret policeman, always hovering around and checking up on her.

Sharon's friends left at three, Frykowski and Folger shortly thereafter. Sharon phoned Jay Sebring and said she had to talk to him. He was busy for the rest of the afternoon, he said, but he promised to come to the house that evening.

With nothing else to do, Sharon lay down and went to sleep for the rest of the afternoon. The housekeeper left, and a humid silence settled over the Cielo Drive property.

It had been a warm day in London, too, though nothing like Los Angeles. Now it was late at night – two a.m. Saturday morning, actually – and Polanski was just arriving at his mews house in the company of an airline stewardess he had met a few days before. It was the first time she had been to the house, and he watched in quiet amusement as she gushed over the furnishings, most of which reflected his interest in sex. He opened a bottle of champagne and invited the girl into the bedroom. He planned to sleep late in the morning. 'You don't have anywhere to go, do you, darling?'' he said to the girl as he began to remove his clothes.

She giggled. 'Nowhere.'

Polanski awoke Saturday at about nine. The girl in the bed next to him was snoring gently. He ran his hand over her slim body. She stirred. Soon they were making love again.

It was midnight in Los Angeles. At Cielo Drive, all was quiet. Friends later recalled that Wojtek Frykowski and Abigail Folger had had a furious argument earlier in the evening over money and Frykowski's excessive drug use. When Frykowski took mescaline, one friend later observed, he invariably became insulting and abusive toward Abigail.

Abigail was now in the guest bedroom at one end of the low, rambling house. Clad in a long white nightgown, she was trying to read herself to sleep after taking a heavy dose of valium. If she had glanced through the nearby window, she would have seen the glow of the Christmas lights that were strung along the fence in front of the house.

Frykowski was in the spacious, open-beamed living room in the middle of the house. Wearing a garish purple shirt, multicolored bellbottom jeans and short black boots, he lay sprawled in a drugged sleep on a sofa facing the massive stone fireplace. Over the back of the sofa was draped a large American flag.

Sharon Tate was in the master bedroom, next to the room where Abigail Folger lay reading. With her was Jay Sebring, her former boyfriend. She was sitting in the middle of her oversized bed, dressed only in panties and bra, her once svelte midsection bulging with the baby she carried.

It was an exceptionally warm night. Wearing a tissue-thin blue shirt and white duck trousers, Sebring sat on the edge of Sharon's bed, drawing on a marijuana cigarette. According to their friends, Sebring was probably listening to Sharon's complaints about Frykowski and about her husband's continuing presence in London.

Over the low hum of the swimming pool filter outside Sharon's bedroom window, the sound of a car could be heard coming up the driveway from the gates on Cielo Drive. The sound of the car's engine suddenly stopped. If Sharon and Sebring had heard the car, they next would have noticed two or three muffled popping noises, and a dog barking in the distance. A sports car buff, Sebring most likely would have attributed the noises to a faulty engine.

Outside, as Sharon and Sebring continued to talk in the

238

bedroom, four shadowy human figures darted across a pool of soft reflected light on the lawn, then stole toward the far end of the house. One was a man, the other three were girls. They huddled together for a moment, whispering, beneath the low window of an unlighted room – the dining room. One of them, the man, broke off and made a stealthy circuit of the house, his head ducking up and down as he peeked into lighted windows. He carried a coil of rope around his neck, and as he passed close to one window its light glinted off the blade of the bayonet in his hand.

When the man returned, there was more whispering. The three girls moved in crouches toward the front porch of the house. The man silently slit the window screen with the bayonet and removed the screen from its frame. He slowly raised the unlocked window and hoisted himself through the opening.

The coil of rope still around his neck and the bayonet in his fist, the man tiptoed across the dark dining room and emerged through a short hallway into the light of the living room. Dressed in tattered black clothes, he was young and athletic-looking behind his scruffy beard and long hippie-style hair. The light revealed the butt of a pistol protruding from his belt. It also revealed his eyes as they quickly surveyed the room. Dark and dilated, they glowed with manic ferocity.

The intruder's name was Charles Watson, but within the drug-, sex- and death-obsessed Los Angeles tribe ruled by Charles Manson he was known simply as Tex. Once a star football player for his hometown high school in Farmerville, Texas, he had dropped out of college in 1967 with a drug habit and drifted to California. There he faded into the burgeoning hippie culture and eventually met up with Manson. He soon became one of Manson's closest cohorts, and with his mind diffused with drugs he learned to blindly take orders from the deranged gang leader. His orders that night were to invade the house once lived in by Terry Melcher and dispatch its inhabitants to another life. The three girls he had brought with him, once also decent kids but now worshipful, doped-up Manson handmaidens, were to be his combat squad.

The first thing Watson noticed as he scanned the living room was a large steamer trunk blocking his path to the front door. Then the American flag draped over the sofa. And then a booted foot hanging over the arm of the sofa.

He glided silently across the room and gazed down at the sleeping form of Wojtek Frykowski. Hearing muffled voices in conversation at the far end of the house, he next moved to the front door and opened it. Standing on the porch, waiting for him, were the three girls – Susan Atkins, known in the Manson clan as Sadie Mae, Patricia Krenwinkle, known as Katie, and Linda Kasabian. All were about twenty, and their faces reflected the ravages of drugs, malnutrition and venereal disease.

Watson motioned the girls in. Susan Atkins and Patricia Krenwinkle darted through the door, carrying knives. Linda Kasabian melted back into the darkness of the porch, whispering that she would keep watch.

Watson, yanking the long-barreled pistol from his belt, led the two girls to the sofa. 'Wake up!' he barked at Frykowski, nudging him from behind the sofa with the gun.

The drugged Pole came half awake, stretching his arms over his head and blinking up at Watson and the girls. 'What time is it?' he said, shaking the cobwebs out of his head.

Watson leaped over the sofa and crouched in front of Frykowski, holding the gun in his face. 'Don't move a muscle!'

Frykowski smiled as if he was onto the joke. 'Who do you . . . '

'Shut up!'

' . . . But . . . '

'Shut up or you're a dead man!'

Frykowski paused and stared into the barrel of the pistol. Then he started to rise. 'Who are you?' he said.

Watson pushed him back. 'I'm the Devil, and I'm here to do the Devil's business.'

'Come on, man,' Frykowski said, his accent heavy and his eyes beginning to shine with alarm. 'This is some game of Roman's, no?'

'No fuckin' game, man. Keep your mouth shut, understand?'

Watson ordered Susan Atkins to check the bedrooms and find out how many people were there. He sent Patricia Krenwinkle to the other end of the house to make sure it was empty.

While they were gone, Frykowski realized that the scraggly man with the crazed eyes and the gun pointing at his head was no jokester. 'What do you want?' he said. 'Drugs? Money?'

'You'll see, man,' said Watson. 'Don't move!'

'Don't you know whose house this is?'

'Yup.'

'So why are you . . . ?'

'Shut up, motherfucker! I already killed one smartass tonight.'

Susan Atkins returned first. 'Three people back there,' she said. 'One of them saw me. She smiled at me. Shit, Tex, it was weird.'

Watson nodded, his earlier survey of the house confirmed. When Krenwinkle returned and reported that there was no one in the other end of the house – the kitchen area and servant quarters – he tossed his rope at the girls and ordered them to tie Frykowski up. This accomplished, he sent them back to the bedroom wing to bring out the others.

Atkins and Krenwinkle made their way to Abigail Folger's bedroom first. Abigail was the one who had seen Atkins a few moments before and smiled at her. She smiled again when Atkins and Krenwinkle entered the guest room. Atkins quickly wiped the smile off her face. She leaped onto the bed and held a knife to her throat. 'Get up and go into the living room,' Atkins said. 'Don't ask any questions. Just do as I say and you won't get hurt. Understand?'

Abigail Folger, her face suddenly a mask of fright, nodded. Patricia Krenwinkle took charge of her, prodding her toward the living room with her own knife while Atkins crossed the hall to fetch the man and woman in the big bedroom.

The door to the master bedroom was slightly ajar. When Atkins kicked it open, Sharon Tate and Jay Sebring looked over in surprise. Hiding her knife, Atkins said excitedly, 'Hurry, they need you in the living room, something terrible has happened!'

'What?' said Sharon.

'Who are you?' Sebring exclaimed.

'Never mind, never mind, just hurry, they need you!'

Sharon and Sebring fell for the ruse. Atkins, her knife still hidden, let them precede her through the door. As they hastened along the hall toward the living room, however, she held the knife at the ready in case one of them turned around. When Sharon and Sebring arrived at the living room, they encountered Charles Watson with his pistol still pointed at Frykowski and Patricia Krenwinkle holding a knife on Abigail Folger.

'What is this?' Sharon exclaimed.

'What are *you* doing here?' Sebring demanded. He recognised Watson.

'Shut up!' said Watson.

Sharon spun around to run back to the bedroom. She was blocked by Atkins, who feinted at Sharon's swollen belly with her knife. Sharon shrieked.

'Get them over to the fireplace,' Watson ordered the two girls. 'Make them lie on their stomachs.'

'You people are crazy!' exclaimed Sebring. 'Get the hell out of here.'

'Move!' shouted Watson. The girls brandished their knives at Sebring.

'For God sakes,' implored Frykowski. 'Do what he says. He will shoot me if you don't, he told me that.'

Sharon, Abigail and Sebring moved toward the fireplace. 'Lie down,' said Susan Atkins. 'On your stomachs. Hands behind your backs.'

'I can't,' Sharon protested. 'Can't you see I'm pregnant?'

'I don't give a fuck what you are,' Watson shouted from the sofa. 'Lie on your belly like she said.'

Sharon broke into tears.

'For Christ sake, man,' Sebring called to Watson, 'be reasonable. The woman'll hurt herself.' Sebring was already on his stomach next to Abigail.

Watson marched toward him. 'Don't talk to me about no Christ!' he shouted. Then he leaned over and shot Sebring in the back. The hair stylist tried to struggle to his feet, but collapsed in anguished moaning. Sharon and Abigail screamed.

'That's just to show you we mean business!' Watson said, going back to the sofa. 'Now you do what I tell you to do. And the first thing I'm telling you is cut that noise. Now!'

Jay Sebring began to twitch as he lay on the floor, blood spreading over the back of his shirt. His moans became weaker.

'Please . . . please,' cried Abigail Folger.

'Who's got money?' said Watson.

'She does!' Frykowski replied, indicating Abigail.

'Where is it?' Susan Atkins said to Abigail.

'In the bedroom . . . in my purse.'

'Get the purse,' Watson said to Atkins.

Atkins disappeared into the hallway while Krenwinkle threatened Abigail and Sharon with her knife. When Atkins returned with the bag she handed it to Abigail. The coffee heiress fished out all the bills she could find, seventy-two dollars. 'Here,' she pleaded, 'take my credit cards, take anything else, my jewelry, anything. Just leave us alone.'

Jay Sebring gave one final heave and died with a gurgling cough. Sharon, stark terror on her face, cowered on the floor. Abigail was on her hands and knees, looking beseechingly at Watson. Watson still covered Frykowski.

'Go get a towel,' the gunman said to Atkins. 'You did a shitass job of tying this motherfucker. Get a towel and tie his hands up tight. I've gotta use the rope.'

Atkins did as ordered. When Frykowski's hands were bound with the towel, Watson unraveled the rope from him. 'Watch him,' he said to Atkins. He dragged the rope over to Sebring's body. He tied a loop around Sebring's neck, then made two connecting loops around Sharon and Abigail's necks. He threw the other end of the rope over one of the ceiling beams. Then he reached up and pulled it down hard. Sharon and Abigail were forced to their feet by the nooses suddenly tightening around their throats. Watson held the tension for a moment, then relaxed it.

'What are you going to do with us?' Sharon said, gasping for breath.

'You're all going to die, pigs!' he started to taunt Sharon, shouting, 'Look at you, you look like a pig with that belly of yours, a piggie, a sow, a piggie sow . . . ' Watson worked himself up into a frenzy. He grabbed the knife from Krenwinkle and plunged it into Sebring's body three or four times. Then he held the bloody knife in front of Sharon. 'You will die like a pig!'

Sharon recoiled. Watson threw the knife back to Krenwinkle. She wiped it on her jeans. Abigail Folger wailed in terror. Wojtek Frykowski, still on the sofa, trembled with fear as he tried to work his hands loose from the towel. Watson stalked back to the sofa and saw what Frykowski was doing. Holding his pistol on the Pole, he said to Susan Atkins, 'Kill him, Sadie, kill him.'

Atkins raised her knife to plunge it into Frykowski's neck. He spun around and cried, 'No, no, not me!' Watson kicked him back onto the cushions while Atkins wound up again with her knife. Frykowski flung himself over the back of the sofa at her, his loosely bound hands grabbing her knife arm and wrestled her to the floor. They struggled furiously and the towel binding Frykowski's hands came loose. He tored at Atkin's hair and she started screaming for help. Frykowski screamed too when Atkins, her arm flailing, caught him in the side with the razor-sharp knife, then got him again in the leg.

Realizing he had been stabbed, Frykowski rolled away from Atkins and began to crawl toward the front door, howling in Polish for help. Watson, on top of him in a split second, began beating him on the head with the butt of his pistol. The gun's grip shattered. Frykowski struggled to his feet and staggered the rest of the way to the door, blood pouring down his face and darkening his shirt. 'Help!' he screamed in agony. 'Somebody help me . . . '

Watson caught him at the door and fired two shots into him. Frykowski reeled out the door and collapsed on the porch. Assuming he was dead, Watson raced back into the living room. But Frykowski was not yet dead. He managed to pick himself up, then fell again. Moaning, blood welling in his lungs, he crawled off the porch through a hedge and onto the lawn. He kept crawling – away from the house.

With the others diverted momentarily by Frykowski, Abigail Folger managed to slip from her noose. Charging back into the living room, Watson saw her edging toward the hall. 'Get her!' he shouted at Atkins and Krenwinkle. Patricia Krenwinkle lunged at Abigail, sinking her knife into the fleeing woman's back. Abigail fell at the entrance to the hallway. When Krenwinkle withdrew the knife, Abigail flopped over on her back and started screaming at her. Krenwinkle thrust again, but Abigail avoided the knife. Then Watson plunged his bayonet into her stomach. As Sharon Tate screamed in the background, Abigail got to her feet and started running down the hallway, holding her stomach. Krenwinkle pursued her, followed by the frenzied Watson. Abigail made it through the French doors in Sharon's bedroom and onto the patio leading to the swimming pool before Watson caught her. He grabbed her by the hair and again thrust his bayonet into her midsection. Krenwinkle arrived and joined in the slashing. Blood pumped out of Abigail, splashing all over Watson and Krenwinkle.

'Keep it up!' Watson exhorted Krenwinkle before running back into the house. As Abigail stumbled down the lawn past the pool, Krenwinkle followed, repeatedly stabbing her. Abigail's tortured cries had turned into muffled gurgles. Bloodsoaked, she collapsed in a heap at the bottom of the lawn near the Christmas lights. By the time she hit the ground she was dead. But Krenwinkle went on stabbing her, grunting with obscene joy.

Watson arrived back in the living room to find Sharon Tate struggling to get out of her noose and Susan Atkins shouting at her. 'Kill her!' he shrieked.

'No, no, no!' Sharon wailed. 'My baby, my baby . . . '

Atkins grabbed Sharon around the neck, throttling her cries. Sharon thrashed and fell to the floor with Atkins beneath her. 'Godamnit!' Watson cried, 'I said off the bitch pig!'

'I can't!' Atkins shouted back, fighting to hold Sharon still.

'My baby, I want to have my baby!' Sharon screamed.

'Help me, Tex!' Susan Atkins yelled.

'Shit!' Watson exclaimed. With that he fell to his knees next to Sharon Tate and drove his bayonet into her swollen belly. 'Oh noooo . . . ' Sharon moaned.

'Now you!' Watson called to Atkins. From beneath, Atkins sliced her knife into Sharon's left breast. Watson followed with another bayonet thrust in the same area. Then he leapt to his feet. As he ran to the front door, he called back, 'Finish her off!'

Atkins let Sharon, now thrusting about spasmodically, slide off her. She got on top of the actress and continued stabbing her – through the neck, through the right breast, into the stomach. Sharon remained conscious for a moment longer, gurgling incoherently. As she gazed at the blood and other fluids oozing from Sharon's abdomen, Atkins had an idea. She would cut the blond woman open, take out the baby and bring it back to Charlie Manson. She thrust her knife again into Sharon's stomach and tried frantically to rip the flesh and sinew away. The knife jammed. She yanked it out and was about to try again when Watson called to her from the door. 'Let's go!'

Atkins leaped to her feet and headed for the door, where she met Watson and Krenwinkle. Watson called out for Linda Kasabian, their lookout. When he got no response, he said, 'Move out. Back to the car.'

As the three trotted back down the lawn, Watson paused to plunge his bayonet a few more times into the dead Frykowski. Then he kicked him. 'Shit!' he exclaimed.

'What is it?' Atkins asked.

'I forgot. Charlie said to leave a message.'

'I'll do it,' Atkins said. 'Wait here.' She ran back to the house and into the living room, then stopped in her tracks, confused. What kind of message should she leave?

Immediately she thought of Tex's chant about pigs, about everyone dying like pigs. She saw the towel they had used to bind Frykowski's hands still lying on the floor by the couch. She rushed over, picked it up, and moved to the inert, blood-drenched body of Sharon Tate. Sharon was still bleeding, blood was still pumping from her. Atkins plunged her knife into her once more and the pumping stopped.

Atkins dipped the towel into one of Sharon's wounds and let

246

the blood soak up into its fabric. Then she got to her feet and scurried to the front door. With the blood-soaked towel, she wrote "PIG" in big, irregular letters across the door's white-painted panels. She wanted to add an S, make it "PIGS," but the cloth had run dry, like a fountain pen. Disgusted, she hurled the towel back into the living room. She watched in fascination as it landed on the face of the dead Jay Sebring.

That gave her another idea. 'Sadie, let's go!' came Tex Watson's call from the lawn below. She ignored it. She moved back into the living room and tightened the noose around Sharon Tate's neck. Then she dragged the actress's body a few feet away so that the rope connecting Sharon to Sebring was taut. Another message. She remembered how the two had been when she first saw them, both of them on the bed.

With that piece of work accomplished, Atkins sprinted from the house and caught up with Watson and Krenwinkle. The three disappeared into the night. *

It was almost ten in the morning in London. Polanski and the stewardess had just flopped back on the bed, exhaused from their latest sexual labors. The girl wanted to go back to sleep, but Polanski's mood suddenly changed. He had to be alone now, he said, he had work to do. He suggested that she get dressed and leave. At first she thought he was joking. He quickly made it clear that he wasn't. She teased him for a minute.

'Get out!' he said.

'I don't believe this,' she said. Polanski sighed impatiently. So she got dressed and left.

The murders at the Polanski house on Cielo Drive were not discovered until eight-thirty on Saturday morning, when Winifred Chapman reported for her housecleaning work. The police did not arrive until nearly nine-thirty, and it was not until

* This re-creation of the slaughter of Sharon Tate and her house guests is based on the grand jury testimony of Susan Atkins at the time of her arrest late in 1969, and on police reconstructions.

noon that Bill Tennant, Polanski's Hollywood agent and friend, was called to the house to identify some of the bodies. After being sick, Tennant put in a call to London.

It was ten at night in London. Polanski had spent most of Saturday lazing about his house. An hour or so before, a couple of friends had arrived. The three were sitting around sipping champagne, passing a marijuana cigarette among themselves, and discussing a movie project, when the phone rang.

Polanski, champagne glass in hand, ambled to the phone and picked it up. He could tell immediately that the call was from overseas. Covering the receiver with his hand, he announced to his friends, 'Shit, it's Sharon calling to hassle me again.'

He was therefore surprised to hear the voice of Bill Tennant when he put the receiver back to his ear.

'Roman,' Tennant's voice cried out over the wire, 'there's been a disaster in a house . . . '

Polanski couldn't imagine what Tennant was talking about. Had he heard right? The connection was full of static. 'Which house?' he said.

'Your house.' Tennant was making funny sounds. It sounded as though he was weeping.

'Bill,' said Polanski, 'What are you . . . ?'

'Roman, Sharon is dead. And Wojtek. And Gibby and Jay. There's been a slaughter . . . '

INTERLOG 9

Just before Christmas, 1977, time ran out on Roman Polanski. Judge Rittenband refused to grant him any further stays. Rittenband ordered him to surrender to Los Angeles police authorities on 19 December for processing into California's Chino prison for men, fifty miles east of Los Angeles. There he would undergo psychiatric evaluation and a pre-sentencing probation investigation that could last up to ninety days. Although Chino was a minimum security prison, it was still a prison. Polanski would be locked up.

Once Douglas Dalton realized that no further stays would be granted, he urged Polanski to get the ordeal over with as quickly as possible. He persuaded the judge to allow Polanski to report directly to Chino rather than go through the police processing routine.

Accordingly, the director reluctantly showed up at Chino with Dalton a few days before scheduled. He arrived in an outwardly cheerful mood and joked with reporters present. Confident that the state psychiatrists would clear him, and assured by Dalton that the time he spent at Chino would probably satisfy the judge as sufficient punishment for his guilty plea. Polanski had decided to while away his time at the prison by writing his life story. Well-known Hollywood literary agent Irving (Swifty) Lazar had told him that he would get at least half a million dollars for his autobiography, and Polanski had agreed to write it.

His cheerfulness vanished soon after he entered Chino. He was immediately clamped into solitary confinement and remained there through Christmas. Then went through several more days of processing. Finally he was assigned a cell in a top security section of the prison and 'confined to quarters' for the duration of his stay. He was not allowed to mingle with the regular prison population on the ground that his life was in danger. A 'child rapist' was considered by the regular prisoners as the lowest form of criminal. Numerous regular inmates would vie for the honor of being the first to kill or maim Polanski.

A graphic picture of Polanski's life inside Chino is provided by Terry Lee Koker, a twenty-four-year-old parole violator from Murietta, California, who was ensconced in a nearby cell. Koker says that by the time Polanski was released from solitary confinement and placed in the 'confined to quarters' section, where he met him, the director was in a deep depression.

'He realized what he was in for after a couple of days. They wouldn't let him out except for his psychiatry sessions or to see visitors. As time went on he got lonelier and lonelier, and more and more depressed. He was told there were guys in the regular cell blocks who were just dying to get him for being a 'baby-raper', all that kind of stuff. In our tier the group were pretty tame, so he didn't have to worry too much as long as he was isolated from the real hard-core guys.'

Koker claims that Polanski adopted him as his best friend at Chino, that the two became 'like brothers,' and that it was only to him that Polanski talked other than to the prison psychiatrists.

'He had an extra-heavy guard whenever he went to his psycho sessions or to see visitors. He had lots of visitors – his lawyer, a bunch of movie types like Jack Nicholson, even John Lennon, the ex-Beatle, came by once or twice. Roman said he knew all the Beatles and that they were all friends. And he got a lot of mail and young girls sending him their pictures. One of the girls I remember sending him letters was Linda Blair [the teenage star of *The Exorcist* who was arrested in Florida and charged with being a cog in an international cocaine-smuggling ring]. They treated Polanski better than most inmates – I mean, he had unlimited visitors' privileges.'

And what did Polanski have to say to Koker about the crime he was convicted of?

'That he got a bum rap. He said it was all the mother's fault. She used her daughter to set him up. He said the girl was willing to have sex with him and that she promised not to tell her mother. What she didn't know was that she was being used by her mother to set Polanski up. The mother was pissed at Roman because he wouldn't get her a part in a movie he was making. He told me he was originally going to give her a small part, but then he had to write the part out of the script. So he didn't have a part to give her, and she decided to get revenge.'

Koker is the father of a young daughter. Did he believe this?

'Oh, sure. Roman was a good guy – I mean he wasn't any sex criminal or anything. Jesus, he gave me an autographed picture of himself – autographed to my daughter. He wanted to put my little girl in the movies. Except for him being low at being locked up, he was no psycho case. He told me that after his wife and baby were killed, he changed. He started having sex with young people because he couldn't bear to be with regular women. Regular women wanted commitment from him, and he felt he would be betraying Sharon if he got involved with another woman. So he went after these young girls. That way there was no commitment.'

When queried on his impressions about Polanski's psychiatric examination, Koker says that the director 'went up to the doctor's office a lot of times for his formal tests, I guess you'd call them. But one of the doctors also came down to his cell almost every day to talk to him. He got special treatment from the shrinks – I mean, you'd never see another inmate being visited by the doctors every day. Every time Roman had a squawk about the food or he wasn't getting enough vitamin pills

251

or somebody on the tier was bothering him, the doctor would come running. He told me he had the shrinks sewed up. He said they were going to give him a good report and that they were going to say he wasn't a sex offender and he didn't need any rehabilitation and that he was an ordinary guy who got trapped by circumstances. Knowing how things sometimes work at Chino, I figured he might have been getting a special break. So I asked him if he was paying the docs any money. And he said, "I can't tell you that." '

Polanski was examined by two psychiastrists, and notwithstanding 'how things sometimes work at Chino,' they gave him a clean bill of mental health. One, Dr Ronald Markham, declared that Polanski did not qualify as a mentally disordered sex offender and was therefore not in need of hospitalization. In his report to Judge Rittenband, he indicated that the offense for which Polanski had been convicted was not a forceful or aggressive sexual assault of the kind usually associated with rape. Although Markham advised that Polanski would benefit from psychiatric treatment, the treatment he had in mind did not relate to a sexual problem but to Polanski's 'state of unresolved depression' stemming from 'a series of traumatic incidents in his life.'

The report of the second psychiastrist was even more considerate of Polanski. The doctor, Alvin Davis, recommended against any further incarceration of Polanski on the ground that an unusual degree of emotional stress and hardship would result.

With the question of Polanski's mental health settled, there remained only the probation investigation. Probation reports are often commissioned by judges for guidance in their deliberations on what sentences to give convicted felons when the judges have sentencing options at their disposal. Polanski's probation report, along with the reports of the psychiatrists, would spark a battle between Judge Rittenband and Douglas Dalton that has lasted to this day.

While Polanski languished in prison during late December

and early January of 1978, the state probation investigators to whom his case was assigned busied themselves interviewing all the principals involved, including the girl and her mother. Then, when they wrote their report, they practically absolved Polanski of any serious wrongdoing. The report made him appear a victim of his own celebrity and his foreigner's ignorance of American customs and laws. While acknowledging that the director 'had exercised poor judgment,' the report described his offense as spontaneous, implying that had his thirteen-year-old victim resisted in any convincing way, he probably would have halted his assault on her.

Since Polanski had had the 'furnishing-drugs-to-a-minor' charge against him dropped when he pleaded guilty to unlawful intercourse, the fact that he had given the girl alcohol and a substantial dose of Quaalude, a potent transquilizer, was not noted by the probation officers. This would become the core of Judge Rittenband's later displeasure over the report. 'How was the girl supposed to resist,' he would say in sarcasm to a reporter, 'when she was tranquilized to her eyebrows?'

Holding the girl's mother equally to blame for having allowed her daughter to be alone with Polanski, the authors of the probation report addressed themselves to the question of whether Polanski should receive a prison sentence. After rehashing the facts in the case and citing Polanski's 'remorse over the entire matter,' they wrote: 'Jail is not being recommended at the present time . . . It is believed that incalculable emotional damage could result from incarcerating the defendant, whose own life has been a seemingly unending series of punishments.'

Instead of a prison sentence, the probation report recommended, among other things, that Polanski be substantially fined and that he be placed under court order 'not to associate with children under the age of eighteen except in the presence of adults.'

A number of things in the probation report riled Judge Rittenband when he received it toward the end of January. One was what he considered to be the specious reasoning of its authors in their attempt to trivialize Polanski's guilt.

Another was a series of extracts from letters that Douglas Dalton had gotten friends and acquaintances of Polanski to write to the probation officials in praise of Polanski's character and 'contributions to mankind'. Although the solicitation of such letters was a standard procedure, Rittenband believed that the probation investigators had been overly beguiled by them.

Particularly galling was a letter from de Laurentiis, who had given testimony at the October hearing on Polanski's trip to Munich.

Among the letters was one from Hollywood producer Howard Koch, who painted Polanski as a 'man of tremendous integrity'. Koch went on: 'I'm sure the situation he finds himself in now is one of those things that could happen to any one of us. It certainly was not premeditated. I'm sure that given the chance to redeem himself he will live an exemplary life in the future.'

Mia Farrow wrote to say that Polanski was ' . . . a loyal friend important to me, a distinguished director, important to the motion picture industry, and a brave and brilliant man important to all people.'

Producer Robert Evans wrote, 'I know the suffering that has gone into [Polanski's] life, especially these last ten years, and I feel that the press has maligned him terribly. He may make for provocative headlines, but with rare exception, the press has never captured the beauty of Roman's soul . . . If ever a person is deserving of compassion, I think it is Roman. I only hope it is afforded him.'

The Polanski described in such laudatory terms in the letters was not the Polanski Rittenband had seen and perceived during the succession of court appearances. The Polanski he had perceived was in his judgment, an evil little man who, Rittenband was convinced, used his bizarre motion-picture celebrity to prey on young girls. The judge had heard of other instances in which the Pole had gotten himself into trouble, and had just learned about the sixteen-year-old Natassia Kinski.

Rittenband was now certain that the probation investigators had allowed themselves to be fooled by the letter-writing campaign, by the psychiatrists, and by Polanski's expressions of remorse. 'How can I believe this remorse stuff,' the judge told a reporter in private, 'when the son of a bitch was playing around in Europe with a sixteen-year-old at the same time he was about to go on trial here for raping a thirteen-year-old?' A man did not have to be certifiably disordered to be a chronic sex offender, Rittenband said, and Polanski's behavior proved it. There was no place in America for a man like him. He was going to see to it that the Pole was forever banished from the country.

After reading the probation report and publicly calling it a 'whitewash,' Rittenband called in Douglas Dalton and prosecutor Gunson. He was ready to sentence Polanski, he announced. He would order the director's release from Chino on Friday, 27 January after forty-two days behind bars. Sentencing would take place the following Monday, 30 January, 1978.

CHAPTER 10

' . . . THERE'S BEEN a slaughter . . . '

Polanski still wasn't sure he had heard right. What was Tennant talking about? The hills above Hollywood were notorious for mud slides and brush fires. Was that what he was saying?'

'Roman,' came Tennant's voice again, 'Sharon is dead. Can you hear me? Sharon and Wojtek and Gibby and Jay.'

This time Polanski heard. His first reaction was to laugh. There was a joke going on – it was a trick on Sharon's part to get him back to California.

But then a chill came over him. Tennant wouldn't participate in such a grisly joke. 'What are you saying?' he shouted into the phone.

'They're dead, Roman.'

'How?'

It took Tennant another minute to convince Polanski that Sharon and the others had been murdered.

'I'm coming,' Polanski said. He was trembling with shock and fear, one of the men who was with him said later.

Gene Gutowski describes the aftermath of the phone call

from Tennant in Los Angeles to Polanski in London on Saturday night, 9 August 1969. 'Roman called me to tell me what Tennant had said. I couldn't believe what I was hearing, but then I reached Bill and learned it was all true. Sharon was dead, Wojtek, the others. I rushed over to Roman's house. He was in control of himself – after all, he was not a stranger to horror. Roman was trying to make arrangements to fly to Los Angeles immediately. But it was mid-summer, the tourist season was at its height, and it was not easy to get airplane seats at such short notice. Roman asked me to go with him. I managed to get two seats on a flight the next afternoon. On the plane, Roman still refused to believe anything had happened. It was all a dream, he said, and we'd arrive to find everything okay. It was a bad joke that Sharon was playing to get him back a few days early. But when we arrived at L.A. airport Sunday night, it was clear it was no joke. The press ghouls were out in force at the airport. I had arranged with Paramount to have a car there for us and to put us up in an apartment at the studio. Roman couldn't talk to the press, so I had to become his spokesman. It was probably the most unpleasant experience I have ever had.'

The grisly murder of Sharon Tate Polanski and three friends, plus the youth who had been visiting the caretaker of the Altobelli property, was splashed all over the front pages of Los Angeles newspapers when Polanski and Gutowski arrived. Press speculation was rife about who could have committed such bestiality and why. Stories had Sharon Tate not only stabbed countless times, but her breasts cut off and her soon-to-be-born child ripped out of her belly. Her blood coated the walls of the house, and the other victims were similarly mutilated. It had all the signs of a ritual murder.

Other stories attributed the horror to drugs. Wojtek Frykowski had become a bigtime narcotics kingpin, according to authoritative sources, and the slaughter must have had something to do with that. Police would be sure to question the many movie-star friends of Polanski and Frykowski.

Everyone agreed that a group of maniacs must be loose in filmland. There was another double murder the following night that had all the earmarks of the same killers. And the day after that, William Lennon, the father of the famous Lennon Sisters singing group, was shot dead. Frank Sinatra, ex-husband of Mia Farrow, the original Hollywood flower child and one of Polanski and Sharon Tate's closest friends, hired a professional gunman to protect him. Jerry Lewis had round-the-clock bodyguards stationed at his Bel Air estate. Sonny and Cher bought a watchdog, and a number of other stars began to pack pistols.

Still other reports blamed the murders on Polanski himself. They did not suggest that he had anything directly to do with them. But they painted his lifestyle in such lurid terms that readers were encouraged to conclude nothing else than that the chickens had come home to roost.

What is generally not known is that when Polanski arrived in Los Angeles with Gene Gutowski, he immediately became an official police suspect. The fact that Sharon's ex-boyfriend, Jay Sebring, was among the victims led investigators to conclude that the murders might have been committed at Polanski's behest.

'We were working on a number of different theories,' says a veteran Los Angeles homicide detective who was one of the first on the scene. 'Who knew what a bunch of Poles might be capable of doing? We had to consider the possibility that Polanski had learned his wife was fooling around with Sebring, particularly because of the way we found them with a rope connecting the two bodies and her in nothing but underpants. While Polanski was well removed in London, he could have hired someone or several people to knock off Sebring and his wife. Maybe even people they knew. We thought it strange that there seemed to be so few signs of resistance. And that fellow Frykowski was among the victims. He was supposed to have been a pretty tough cookie, from all the information we had. We thought he must have known the killer or killers. Maybe he was even part of the plot and got knocked off so there wouldn't be anyone around to talk. Anyway, this is one theory we worked on. That Polanski had commissioned the murders, and that the killers were probably Polish.'

While the police were sifting theories, Gene Gutowski was

busy repeatedly denying to the press stories about a marital rift between Polanski and his wife.

Polanski refused to talk to the police until after Sharon Tate's funeral on Wednesday, 13 August. More than 150 people attended the rites at the Holy Cross Cemetery in Culver City, just south of Beverly Hills. Among them were Kirk Douglas, Warren Beatty, Steve McQueen, Lee Marvin, James Coburn, Yul Brynner and Peter Sellers. Polanski, wearing dark glasses, broke into tears several times during the ceremony, as did Sharon's parents and her two younger sisters, Deborah and Patricia. Polanski attended services for Jay Sebring later in the day.

When the director finally submitted to a long questioning session the following Saturday, he was not of much help. He could give detectives no idea about possible motives for the multiple murders. The police were now working on their primary theory – that the killings had something to do with drugs. Drugs in some quantity had been found in the house. Sebring was known to have been a customer of various Los Angeles drug dealers. Sharon Tate had a history of drug use. And Wojtek Frykowski, it had been learned, was trying to set himself up in business as a drug dealer just before the murders.

The theory that Polanski might have been involved in the murders was discounted the night he was grilled by the police, only to be revived the next day. On Sunday, he went to the house on Cielo Drive. With him were Peter Hurkos, the well-known psychic, and a writer and photographer from *Life* magazine.

'What the hell was he doing bringing magazine people there barely a week after it all happened, a lot of us wondered?' says the Los Angeles detective. 'It seemed like a strange thing to do unless he was trying to capitalize on the whole business. And if he was trying to capitalize on the publicity – you know, use the tragedy to thrust himself into the limelight – well, wasn't that just crazy enough so that he might have been crazy enough to have engineered the murders? Sure, he *seemed* to be suitably shocked and unknowing about the whole thing – who could have done it, motive, that sort of thing. But I've seen dozens of wifekillers in my time, and they're all the same way. We decided

259

that the only way to clear up our doubts about Polanski was to give him a polygraph [lie-detector] test.

Polanski agreed to take the test, on the condition that no one but the police know about it. Administered by Lieutenant Earl Deemer in a bleak room at downtown Los Angeles police headquarters, it cleared Polanski of any knowledge of or participation in the murders. But it shed some interesting light on his character. In a taped prelude to the actual test, Deemer conversed with Polanski in order to 'loosen him up, relax him.' During the conversation, Polanski described his relationship with his late wife.

Upon first meeting Sharon in 1966, Polanski told Deemer, 'I was really swinging. All I was interested in was to fuck a girl and move on. I had a very bad marriage, you know. Years before . . . . . my wife dumped me, so I was really feeling great because I was a success with women and I just liked fucking around. I was a swinger, eh?'

Polanski had wanted to see more of Sharon after meeting her. ' . . . I wanted to take her out, and she was being difficult, wanting to go out, not wanting to go out, so I said, "Fuck you," and hung up. Probably that was the beginning of everything, you know . . . She got intrigued by me. And I really played it cool, and it took me long dating before – and then I started seeing that she liked me.'

Sharon was not an easy mark for the swinging Polanski though. 'I remember I spent a night – I lost a key – and I spent a night in her house, in the same bed, you know. And I knew there was no question of making love with her. That's the type of girl she was. I mean, that rarely happens to me.'

'And then,' Polanski told Lieutenant Deemer, 'when we were on location shooting the [Vampire] film, I asked her, "Would you like to make love with me?" and she said, very sweetly, "Yes." And she was so sweet and lovely that I didn't believe it, you know. I'd had bad experiences and I didn't believe that people like that existed, and I was waiting a long time for her to show the true color, right? But she was beautiful . . . she was fantastic. She loved me . . . I didn't want her to come to my house. And she would say, "I don't want to smother you. I only want to be with you,'' etc. And I said ''You know how I am; I screw around.'' And she said, ''I don't want to change you.'' She was ready to do everything, just to be with me. She was an angel . . . '

Deemer asked Polanski about Jay Sebring, who Sharon had left when she first moved in with Polanski. Polanski described how nervous he had been when Sebring flew to London in 1966 to try to reclaim Sharon. Sebring's trip was in vain, but Sebring 'seemed happy to see Sharon happy.'

Polanski had remained uncomfortable during their next several encounters. 'But when I came to Los Angeles [in 1967], started living here, he came to our parties, etc. And I started liking Jay very very much . . . Oh, I knew of his hang-ups. He liked to whip-tie girls. Sharon told me about it. He tied her once to the bed. And she told me about it . . . '

'So there was no indication that Sharon went back to Sebring at any time?' Lieutenant Deemer asked Polanski.'

'Not a chance. I'm the bad one. I always screw around. That was Sharon's big hang-up, you know. But Sharon was absolutely not interested in Jay . . . There was not a chance of any other man getting close to Sharon.'

Deemer brought the session to a close by asking Polanski if he had any educated guesses about who was responsible for the murders. Could it have had anything to do with Polanski's movies? Had he received any hate mail after *Rosemary's Baby?*

The director conceded that he had, adding that 'I wouldn't be surprised if I were the target . . . It could be some type of witchcraft, you know. A maniac or something. This execution . . . indicates to me it must be some kind of nut.'

Polanski was not far off the mark, as it would later turn out. In the meantime, although the police had absolved him, the press, lacking any hard facts, began to print all sorts of bizarre rumors about the case. In the absence of a real villain, the victims themselves became the villains, and Polanski even more so. Countless articles were printed suggesting that Sharon Tate and her friends had brought their gory slayings upon themselves as a result of their freewheeling lifestyles. Others placed the blame solely on Polanski: as a notoriously compulsive dealer in

261

cinematic violence and terror, they declared, it was not surprising that real violence and terror should stalk and ultimately strike his life. Sharon Tate was painted as everything from a drug addict to a nymphomaniac, and Polanski was characterized as an evil Svengali whose fate, however tragic, deserved little public sympathy. Had Polanski made nice, inoffensive films, went the conclusion, Sharon Tate and the others would still be alive. Somehow there was a direct causative connection between the murders and Polanski's movie-making proclivities.

When Charles Manson and his followers were apprehended in December 1969 there was no evidence that they had ever seen a Polanski film or that they even knew who they were killing in the early morning hours of 9 August. What the police learned was that Manson had known Terry Melcher, the previous tenant of Polanski's rented house, as well as Rudi Altobelli, the owner. Indeed, shortly after the Polanskis had moved into the house the previous February, the scraggly Manson had arrived on the property in search of Melcher and Altobelli. Polanski was not there, but Sharon and Jay Sebring, along with some others, were. They were evidently inhospitable to Manson, and he nurtured a grudge for months against the house's new inhabitants. Thus, months later, when he sent his disciples out on their crazed killing mission, it was to 10050 Cielo Drive that he directed them.

For the first few weeks of the murder investigation, Polanski tried earnestly to make himself useful to the police. But once the police had written him off as a suspect, they became uninterested in his help. Smarting under the daily vitriolic press commentary about the murders, he returned to London after announcing a $25,000 reward for information leading to the arrest and conviction of the murderers. He continued to refuse to talk to the press.

The police were furious at Polanski. They knew the reward would bring all sorts of kooks out of the woodwork with phony tips, thus impeding their investigation. When a detective criticized him, Polanski cursed the efforts of the police. 'He said he wanted nothing more to do with Los Angeles – America, for that matter. He was going back to London and would forget he ever set foot in the United States. I think he was more upset at the things the media were saying and hinting about him and his wife than he was at the slowness of the investigation. He claimed he couldn't go anywhere without people pointing their fingers at him and making snide remarks.'

'Absolutely true,' confirms Gene Gutowski. 'Roman was shattered first by Sharon's death, but then maybe even more so by the way the press handled it. He couldn't understand the viciousness that was directed against him.'

But Polanski would find little relief outside America. 'In fact,' says an English friend, 'it was even worse for him in England and Europe. The press, particularly in Germany, made him out to be some sort of pariah. No matter where he went he couldn't get away from sensationalistic reminders of what had happened and who he was. It had to be a weird feeling always being referred to as the husband of Sharon Tate.'

Did Polanski suffer any residual guilt from the fact that he had been in London and not with his wife in Los Angeles when she was murdered. 'He thought about it,' says the same friend. 'And he talked about it. What he couldn't understand, once the police discovered who did it – a young guy and a couple of girls – was why Wojtek and Jay Sebring let it happen. That's what drove him crazy. After all, the killers only had one pistol and a couple of knives. Wojtek and Jay both could handle themselves. Why did they let the situation go as far as it did? Why didn't they make a move right away, grab the girls, something? Were they so stoned that it was all like a dream to them? So Roman wondered what would have happened if he had been there. He never felt guilty for not being there – guilt was not an emotion Roman ever allowed himself. But he did wonder a lot about what he would have done. He worked out all sorts of possible scenarios, but I never saw him weep or express remorse – either for the fact that he was not there or for the possibility that his lifestyle and movies might have triggered the murders. There was only one thing I ever heard him say that made me think he felt something. He said, "Jesus, do you realize that at the very moment Sharon was being cut up in L.A., I was getting laid in London.'' '

Between the time Charles Manson and his cohorts were caught, four months after the slayings, and the time they were convicted and sentenced more than a year later, Polanski endeavored to put the past events out of his mind by plunging back into work.

Or did he? asked a number of media commentators. The work he chose to do was a film version of Shakespeare's *Macbeth*. Ordinarily a play of murder and violence, mostly committed offstage, Polanski decided to make the carnage the central focus of his film. English writer Kenneth Tynan collaborated with Polanski on the script. One day in 1971, during the filming in Wales, Polanski, Tynan says, was preparing to shoot the scene in which Lady MacDuff's children are murdered. Buckets of simulated blood were brought to the set. 'He explained to a shy little four-year-old who was playing one of the children that she must lie down and pretend to be dead while he put "red paint" all over her face. "What's your name?" he said, daubing away. "Sharon," she unbelievably said.'

The filming of *Macbeth* was beset by endless difficulties. For the first time Polanski was producing without Gene Gutowski, who had decided to give up the movie business. Not only did he have to fight the ordinary and extraordinary director's problems, he also took on the financial agonies of a producer. Yet, says Tynan, he reveled in it all. Fighting with the actors, the technical crews and the film's financiers – it was Polanski's way of steeling himself against whatever sorrow he might have felt over Sharon Tate. 'Nobody is harder to faze . . . ' said Tynan at the time. 'He armors himself against showing anything that might be construed as vulnerable . . . '

When *Macbeth* was released late in 1971, dozens of critics became instant psychoanalysts. They attributed its most memorable if shocking sequences – its visual gore – to Polanski's deepening obsession with violence and bestiality, an obsession that went against the grain of the things that had happened in his real life. 'Sick,' 'morbid,' and 'twisted' were just a few of the adjectives applied to his cinematic vision. 'How,' asked one reviewer, 'do we account for this man who apparently has decided to make us pay for the tragic murder of his wife and friends by demonically bathing us in vomitous film horror?'

To claims that the sanguinary *Macbeth* was Polanski's way of acting out a manic vision further twisted by recent real-life events, friends scoff. One says, 'Roman is a showman and he likes to make money. He knows exactly how to manipulate the public. He had become a different kind of celebrity because of what happened to Sharon. So he decided to capitalize on it by making a real horror movie. He knew the publicity the movie would get, and he knew it would profit from the publicity. That Roman was purging himself or somehow acting out some bizarre psychotic fantasy when he made *Macbeth* is pure crap. I was with him during much of the filming, and I can tell you he was as normal as he always was. He used to joke on the set about how every pot of fake blood that was made was worth ten thousand tickets at the box office.'

Another friend contends that 'Roman set out to pull the wool over the critics' eyes and he succeeded beautifully. If he was trying to prove anything, it was that the press is capable of printing the most meretricious shit. He was mad at the press, and he knew they'd psychoanalyze *Macbeth* to death because of the Sharon thing. So he thought he'd help the press make a fool of itself. If anything, in making *Macbeth* he was mocking the press and the public. The film was almost a mockery of violence and brutality, with all its gouged eyeballs and slit necks. No one, of course, saw that. All they saw was a supposedly sick mind at work, and they had a field day with that. Roman was quite pleased with the way the critics in the press stumbled all over themselves trying to find the hidden meanings in *Macbeth.*'

Before *Macbeth* was released, Polanski gave a publicity interview to a reporter for the *New York Times.* The terror and violence of *Macbeth,* wrote the reporter in anticipation of the critical reaction, were certain to invite references to the murder of Sharon Tate. Polanski viewed the prospect with bored resignation. He insisted the film was not tied to his past, 'but if the audience wants to see it that way, so be it.'

Then why so graphically violent? 'You have to show violence

the way it is,' answered Polanski. *Macbeth* had been written by Shakespeare as a study of violent malevolence. 'If you don't show it realistically, that's immoral and harmful. If you don't upset people, that that's obscenity.'

Even in talking to the *New York Times,* though, Polanski may have been putting something over on the press. The reporter, Bernard Weinraub, wrote a probing, sober article on the director based on the interview. But according to those who know Polanski best, and in the words of one, 'Roman has never shared his true thoughts with the press. That's because he has no "true" thoughts – that is, no philosophy, no worldview. What Roman says to the press is really nothing more than words, whatever he's thinking at the time. For the press to presume that they can get to the bottom of Roman from what he says is absurd. He's very good at putting up a smokescreen of statements and ideas. But in reality he is a man who operates not on ideas or principles, but on instincts. He lives his life on instincts. He seems and does the things that his instincts tell him are worth having and doing. And he avoids the things his instincts say are not worthwhile. He cares little about consequences, except when it comes to making movies.'

The release of *Macbeth* marked an end and a beginning for Polanski. By the time the film came out in 1971, Charles Manson and his gang were in prison and the feverish public interest in the Tate murders had all but vanished. *Macbeth* revived that interest only briefly – the film was a moderate financial success. Polanski survived the critical psychoanalysis with his reputation as a quirky but potent film maker intact, and he decided to go on living and working as though nothing had happened.

Or almost nothing. 'He did change in one significant way,' says a woman friend. 'If before he was an active, enthusiastic participant in all that life had to offer, he thereafter became almost hyperactive. Maybe he felt that he was lucky to have escaped death once again when Sharon was killed, that fate was fickle and that maybe, like a cat, he had used up all his lives, survived too many times.

He used to talk a lot about that to me. In any event, he decided he had to live more strenuously than ever, to get everything he could possibly get out of life before it was too late. So he went after everything with a renewed vigor. There were more girls than ever, and they seemed to get younger and younger. And more parties. More trips to the Alps for skiing, a sport Roman became very good at. And to the South of France. He traveled like a demon, he started flying lessons, he did some automobile racing, and when he was in London he was a nightly fixture at Tramps [a private club and discoteque], always with two or three beautiful if vacuous girls.

Roman didn't like women who were both pretty and sharp-minded. He only liked the pretty but not pushy types – women he could take to bed once or twice and then foist off on friends. I remember him telling me one day about a woman he had met the night before at a party at the *Playboy Club*. She was a foreign lawyer or something – evidently quite beautiful, but also quite intelligent. I suppose out of curiosity she agreed to spend the night with him.

Well, the next day Roman wasn't too happy with her. "I've never met an intelligent woman who isn't a castrating bitch," he complained to me when he told me about her. She reinforced his prejudice, although exactly what she had done to get him so riled up he wouldn't tell me.

Roman has very simple tastes in women. He wants his women without complications. Which is why he began gravitating to the younger and younger types. And the dumber and dumber.'

Although *Macbeth* was a critical failure and only marginally successful at the box office, its cinematography was impressive. As a result, in 1973 he was invited back to Hollywood by Paramount's production chief Robert Evans to direct Jack Nicholson and Faye Dunaway in a 1930s-style private-eye thriller called *Chinatown,* written by Robert Towne.

Polanski accepted, gave himself a small role in the picture, and added a few gory flourishes to Towne's screenplay – most memorably, a scene in which he sliced Jack Nicholson's nose open with a knife. 'You've got to remember,' said Nicholson at the time, defending the presence of the controversial scene, 'The story was set in L.A. Roman was just letting everybody know how he felt about L.A. It was a place where blood always flows.'

The picture was a huge success. In the process of making it, Polanski's attraction to life in Hollywood revived. 'The nose scene in *Chinatown* helped him exorcise his anguish about Hollywood,' said Robert Evans.

Moreover, Hollywood wanted him back. Soon he was reunited with his old group of movie-star and film-executive friends who once again helped him turn Los Angeles into a pleasure dome. A friend, less well known, recalls the Polanski of 1975 after the success of *Chinatown*.

'My abiding memory of Roman will always be of a Jekyll and Hyde character. When it came to movies, he was all business, taking command, ordering people around, being by turns the tough and kindly administrator. He just took his authority and power for granted and brooked no interference. Although he was always sure to go over budget and schedule on any picture he made, it was all for a good cause and no one dared hassle him about it. That was what I would call the day time Polanski.

'Then there was the night time Roman. The night time Roman was a compulsive social creature. During the day, when he was working, he isolated himself, held himself off from people like a commander in battle. At night, he was just one of the troops out for a furlough binge. He was very sociable, extraordinarily easy to be with, and always had interesting things to say. He could talk on any subject, from the most mundane to the most esoteric. If he had any quirk of character, it was his thing about girls. He was always on the lookout, always anxious to demonstrate to his pals his facility in drawing a girl's attention to himself.

'It was as though he always needed to prove himself to other guys. He was about forty, forty-one at this time, and of course everybody knew that he could have just about anyone he wanted. So I could never figure out why he felt it so necessary to prove it all the time. As far as girls were concerned, he was a bit of a childish pain after a while. I mean you'd be sitting in a restaurant and trying to have a conversation, and he'd be looking around all the time and you just knew he wasn't listening. He was looking for a girl he could make some come-on remark to. Other than that, he was always fun to be with.'

'The girls became an all-encompassing thing with Roman,' says another film director with whom the Pole became close friends. 'When I first met him back in 1967, they were important to be sure. But by 1975, 1976, they were *all*-important. By then he was into group sex, and of course he hung out with this society where girls were easy to come by and a dime a dozen – the real jet-set. I was in London with him once and it was hard to tell the regular girls from the expensive hookers. Not that he paid for sex. But all the girls he hung out with looked like they could just as easily have been hookers. With all his macho enthusiam, Roman didn't realize it but he was beginning to degrade himself. The girl fetish was no longer amusing. He was becoming a parody of himself.'

A third friend recalls that, about 1973, 'Roman began hanging out with a lot of the rich Arabs who were flooding London and Paris. The Arabs were tough, no-nonsense businessmen during the day, but at night they liked to play. And, oh, did they play – money was no object. After gambling, sex was their main diversion. All kinds of sex. In Roman they found a kinsman, and pretty soon he was trying to outdo the Arabs. The only difference between Roman and the Arabs was that he wouldn't involve himself with boys.

'He finally grew tired of his Arab friends because he couldn't understand some of their sexual tastes. That was an odd thing about Roman. Although he had a no-holds-barred attitude to almost anything having to do with sex, the idea of homosexual coupling sort of revolted him. He became very intolerant of it.

'At the same time, he was growing more and more interested only in sex with young girls. By young girls I mean late teens, maybe middle teens – certainly not children. Several of his show-business pals in London were the same way. A famous English actor, and another fellow, an English singer who everybody knows. Their sexual habits were no big secret around London, and Roman didn't give a damn what people thought

269

of him anyway.'

'It really started as a joke,' says a former editor of the French men's magazine *Vogue Homme*. 'Roman was in Paris a lot in the mid-seventies – he made a film or two here. We knew of his fascination for young, emerging girls and we got him to do some photographs for us. He wanted to be known as a lover of young girls. He told me it was to put down older women, who couldn't be trusted and who inevitably became boring as they preoccupied themselves with women's concerns. He was half-joking, I'm sure, but he said he wanted to start a new movement for men where it would become socially acceptable for older men to have teenagers as lovers. When he mentioned that he was going to go back to Hollywood for a while, it gave us an idea.

He came into the office and we said, 'Roman, we have something we'd like you to do for us.'

' "What's that," he said.'

'When you go to California, we'd like you to do a photo essay on the young girls of L.A.'

' "How young?" he asked us.'

'As young as you can get them.'

INTERLOG 10

THE PRISON doors of Chino opened for Polanski on Friday, 27 January 1978. Waiting to drive him back to Los Angeles was Douglas Dalton. Polanski was scheduled to appear for sentencing the following Monday. Dalton had just received a copy of the probation report. Things looked good, he told his client. The report was favorable, recommending at worst a fine and urging Judge Rittenband not to return the director to prison as part of his sentence.

Polanski was grim. Stroking the beard he had grown at Chino, he had learned to swallow Dalton's constant optimism with a dose of salt. Although immensely relieved to be free, he could not shake his growing sense of foreboding. First of all, Dino de Laurentiis had just announced that he would no longer wait for Polanski and had hired another director to take over the *Hurricane* film.

Second, as the ride from Chino to Los Angeles progressed, Dalton's optimism gradually darkened. He had given Polanski the good news first. Now it was time for the bad news.

Dalton told Polanski that he had lost confidence in Judge Rittenband. He could not predict what the judge would do.

As the lawyer's anxiety communicated itself to Polanski, the director began to wonder aloud about what he should do. Sensing what he was thinking, Dalton warned Polanski not to do anything foolish. At worst, he only had a little further to go before he could put the entire unsavory business behind him.

Polanski spent the weekend at a rented house in Beverly Hills. Several friends threw a party for him on Saturday and encouraged him about the future. On Sunday, Jack Nicholson, feeling partly responsible for Polanski's plight, invited him to his house to discuss a future movie project. 'I was dead set on getting Roman back to work as soon as possible,' Nicholson says, 'particularly since de Laurentiis had abandoned him. That night at my house his attitude about the whole court case was positive. He was sure he'd get off with a slap on the wrist. His lawyer had arranged for the sentence to be postponed for a day or two, and Roman was a bit disappointed in that. He was looking forward to getting it over with.'

But a girl with whom Polanski spent Sunday night received a different impression. 'He was gloomy and nervous. He didn't talk about the case, but it was plainly on his mind. When Roman joked too much, you knew something was bothering him.'

Dalton had gotten the judge to postpone sentencing – from Monday to Wednesday – so that he could 'have more time to study the probation report.' Tuesday morning was used for a private meeting between Rittenband, Dalton and Gunson. The meeting confirmed Dalton's worst suspicions.

Rittenband informed Dalton and Gunson that he intended to sentence Polanski to additional time in prison. When Dalton angrily pointed out that the probation report clearly recommended against additional prison time, Rittenband replied, according to the lawyer, that the report was 'the worst he had ever seen and a complete whitewash of your client.' He intended to ignore the report and follow his own dictates as to the punishment Polanski should receive.

What did he have in mind? Dalton asked.

Rittenband said that he would probably return Polanski to Chino to serve the balance of the ninety days he had originally been given. Once he had spent the remaining forty-eight days behind bars, he would give Polanski the option of remaining in prison or voluntarily deporting himself from the United States, never to return.

Dalton was dumbfounded; even Gunson was surprised. Dalton fired back that such a sentence was improper. 'It is not within your jurisdiction to determine whether my client should be permitted to remain in the United States. You have no power as a state judge to order or compel deportation as punishment for a crime.'

Rittenband shrugged. Gunson silently cringed, thinking that the judge's action might provoke an appeal that would upset the case and wipe out his eleven months of work on the case.

After his meeting with Judge Rittenband, Dalton returned to his office and summoned Polanski. On his way to meet with the lawyer, the director spied copies of that afternoon's *Herald Examiner* in a newspaper vending machine. Splashed across the front page was the headline: 'Polanski To Be Given More Time in Jail, Says Prosecutor.'

Buying a paper, Polanski read the accompanying story on his way to Dalton's office. 'Although film director Roman Polanski is walking free now,' the story began, 'the prosecutor in his case thinks there's a 'strong possibility' Polanski will be back in jail after his sentencing tomorrow on an illicit sex charge.' The story described Gunson as having received his impression after a meeting with Judge Rittenband.

When Polanski reached Dalton's office, the lawyer confirmed the story. He described what had happened in his meeting with Rittenband and told Polanski that the judge was apparently determined to return him to Chino.

Polanski had little to say. Telling Dalton that he would see him in court the following morning at nine a.m. for the sentencing, he left the office.

Once on the street, he retrieved his rented car from a garage and drove straight to Los Angeles International Airport. He had his passport with him.

Still wearing the beard he had grown in prison, he went unrecognized when, after turning in his car and making a brief

273

phone call, he rushed to the British Airways counter.

He bought the last ticket available on Flight 598 for London.

At three minutes to six in the early evening of 31 January 1978, Polanski was on his way to Europe.

And to his new status as a fugitive from American justice.

When Judge Rittenband convened his court at nine the following morning to announce the sentence, Polanski was already at London's Heathrow Airport waiting for a flight to take him on to Paris. He had been advised by a lawyer in London not to remain in England but to proceed directly to France, where the possibility of extradition was much more remote.

In Los Angeles, meanwhile, Douglas Dalton stunned the court by telling Rittenband he had received an anonymous phone call at his home only an hour before, saying that Polanski had fled the country. The outraged Rittenband demanded to know where he had gone. Dalton couldn't tell him. He assured Rittenband that he had not known of Polanski's intention to flee.

Rittenband issued a bench warrant for the director's arrest and postponed sentencing in order to give Dalton time to locate him and persuade him to return. He also ordered Gunson to look into extradition proceedings should he not return immediately.

Polanski was located the next day by a reporter at his apartment in Paris. He was not going to return to the United States, he informed callers, because he would not any longer put his 'fate in the hands of a judge who was obviously prejudiced' against him.

In the days that followed, Dalton confirmed Polanski's intention not to return. Furious, Rittenband decided he would sentence Polanski in absentia. Fearing an even stiffer punishment for his client, Dalton sought to block sentencing by petitioning for Rittenband's removal from the case.

Dalton alleged behind-the-scenes improprieties and contended that the judge should not be allowed to pass sentence on

Polanski. Rittenband denied all of Dalton's accusations. But in denying them to the press, he did say 'I wanted him out of the country.' This unleashed another attack by Dalton.

The squabble climaxed when Rittenband, claiming that he was tired of the whole matter and had to get on with his other cases, voluntarily withdrew from the case. Another judge, George T. Breckenridge, took over and decided to postpone Polanski's sentencing indefinitely, or until he voluntarily returned or was compelled to return. Breckenridge made it clear that convicted felons who fled punishment did not rank high in his estimation.

Prosecutor Gunson, in the meantime, lamely reported to the court that it would be impossible to extradite Polanski from France because under that nation's laws, unlawful intercourse was not an extraditable crime. Scotland Yard had agreed to seize the fugitive director if he dared to venture back to England, but in France he remained out of harm's way. It was with some chagrin that Gunson later conceded to the press that had Polanski pleaded guilty and been convicted on the drug charges, he would not enjoy the protection he now did in France. Gunson stoutly assured the press that everything possible would be done to bring Polanski to justice anyway. Other countries in Europe were already accepting warrants for his arrest, should the director venture into them.

'We'll get him!' Gunson proclaimed. 'Sooner or later, we'll get him.'

As Gunson spoke those words at three in the afternoon in Los Angeles, it was midnight in Paris. Polanski lay naked on the living room floor of his apartment. He faced the huge window that looked out over the rooftops of the quiet still-wintry city. Next to him, on a blanket, was a girl, also naked. They each sipped champagne as Polanski explained what he was going to do with the amyl nitrate tablet he was rolling in his fingers. They were about to make love.

'By the way,' he said in French as he pulled the girl up onto the sofa. 'How old are you?'

'Fifteen,' replied the girl. 'Why?'

EPILOGUE

'WILL YOU ever go back to the United States?'

'How does Miss Kinski feel about your . . . '

'Is it true that . . . ?'

'What kind of sentence do you expect to receive if you . . . ?'

'How old is Miss Kinski – really?'

'Do you have anything to say about the stories in the American newspapers that you . . . ?'

'Are you going to marry her?'

'There's a report that no American film company can employ you while you remain a fugitive from US law. Do you contemplate . . . ?'

'Yes, Roman, what about that?'

And so the barrage of questions went. It was the start of another tumultuous Roman Polanski press conference. The time was May, 1979, a little more than a year after Polanski had fled the United States. The setting was a crowded banquet room of the elegant Carlton Hotel in Cannes, France. Polanski sat facing the throng of journalists in a soiled white blazer and a blue, open-necked shirt. There to promote his unfinished film version of *Tess of the D'Urbervilles,* he was wan and tired and angry looking under the hot klieg lights. At his side on the dais was Natassia Kinski, Polanski's now-celebrated teenaged lover and the film's star. At once virginal and poutily seductive she appeared ill at ease under the bombardment of questions.

After his flight to France the year before to escape sentencing, Polanski had become an instant cultural and political hero in much of France's left-wing press. He was portrayed as just another in a long line of tragic victims of repressive US laws. One Paris newspaper placed him in the great tradition, going back to Oscar Wilde, 'of artistic geniuses and free spirits persecuted for their sexual preferences.' Another compared his forty-two day imprisonment for psychiatric tests to the ordeal of Russian dissidents sent to Siberian mental asylums as punishment for their political convictions.

The Paris daily *Le Matin* blamed Polanski's troubles on America's 'excessively prudish petite bourgeoisie,' while *Le Quotidien* explained to its readers that Polanski had been 'compelled to plead guilty.' It went on to describe the director as a victim 'of the repressive ostracism of the laws of a supposedly liberal nation,' and concluded that the Polanski case proved 'that American liberties are perfectly illusory.'

After several days of consultation with French lawyers, who assured him that he was safe from arrest and extradition in France, Polanski began to appear again in his old Parisian haunts. Trailed by a succession of young girls and an army of papparazzi, he good-naturedly parried reporters' questions by saying that he was under lawyers' orders not to discuss the case. He would tell all, he added when he finished writing the book about his life.

But to one question, 'How does it feel to be a fugitive?' Polanski replied wearily, 'I am used to it. I have been a fugitive all my life.'

An American acquaintance, after encountering Polanski at a popular Paris discotheque with the then-sixteen-year-old Kinski, remarked wryly, 'Polanski seems to have shed all that remorse he convinced the California probation people he was beset by.'

Polanski's flight to France had killed the deal for his autobiography – the American company that had wanted to publish it now feared costly legal exposure if it printed the work of a fugitive convict. With nothing else to do, Polanski finally turned to the task of creating a movie out of Hardy's *Tess of the D'Urbervilles.*

Polanski decided to use *Tess,* as the picture would be called, to salvage his flagging career. He would make it a film of such lyric beauty and compelling emotion that the world would be forced once and for all to acknowledge his genius and excuse his conduct. By using two young and inexperienced performers in the leading roles – Natassia Kinski and English actor Jon Firth – he would have complete control of the filming and would not be distracted from his goal by the rantings of temperamental stars. The picture, he boasted to friends, based on a screenplay by Gerard Brach and himself, truly would be his *magnum opus.*

Thus, what had been conceived the year before as a quick, cheap costume movie to earn Polanski some sorely needed money, was turned by him into a major production. Indeed, its eventual cost of nearly $15 million would make it the most expensive movie ever done in France.

The first steep rise in the film's budget was caused by Polanski's legal status. Claude Berri, its chief producer, had originally intended to shoot the picture on location in England's rural Dorset, the locale of Hardy's book. But Polanski dared not set foot in England lest he be arrested and subjected to extradition to California. So the filming was switched to the Normandy countryside of France, near Cherbourg. As a result, extensive special sets had to be built to simulate the nineteenth-century English locales of the book, including the ancient Stonehenge.

After rewriting Gerard Brach's script, Polanski started filming in Normandy in July, 1978. Two months of incessant foul weather further escalated the production's costs. The weather delays were compounded by several deaths among key members of the film crew and by Natassia Kinski's inexperience. Although she had worked in three films prior to *Tess,* she was not yet up to carrying a major production. Polanski decided to halt production for a while and send her to England for intensive coaching in the true-to-life English accent he demanded for the film's heroine.

But it was the directorial methods of Polanski himself that shot the movie's costs to their ultimate astronomical heights. He had grown obsessive in his singleminded determination to turn out a masterpiece. He feared that anything less than perfection in even a single frame of the final film would destroy his chances of restoring his reputation. Laboring under less than ideal conditions, he became more punctilious and dictatorial than ever. He took days to shoot scenes that would only cover a few seconds in the completed film, wasted weeks waiting for the right combination of weather and light for other scenes, and ran his crew ragged with his spur-of-the-moment demands and sudden, costly changes of mind.

By the beginning of 1979, the film's financial backers were exasperated. They had expected Polanski to have the picture ready for showing at the Cannes Film Festival in May. By April it was clear that he was nowhere near completion – he was still painstakingly directing interior scenes at a studio in Boulogne. They angrily demanded that he make an appearance at the festival anyway, to promote the unfinished movie. They were desperate to start arranging distribution deals so that they could begin to recover some of the film's exorbitant costs.

It was these demands that had brought Polanski and Natassia Kinski to Cannes in May to face the press in the Carlton Hotel's jammed, overheated banquet room. In previous years Polanski had had some of the best times of his life at the Cannes festival and at the Carlton. But this year, as he had predicted, 'the jackals of the press were out to get me.'

Outside the Carlton, it was a typical balmy Cote D'Azur evening. Thousands of movie people from all over the world – hoi polloi as well as hangers on – were gathered in Cannes for the annual two-week conclave that is one-part international film fête and infinite parts bacchanal. The off-shore twinkled with the lights of dozens of luxurious yachts. Within at least a few of their staterooms, gorgeous starlets were at that very moment performing sexual acrobatics for the pleasure of aging movie moguls and financiers. Hotels along the Croisette, Cannes' palm-lined beach front boulevard, were spilling over with sleek, skimpily dressed women offering instant carnal satisfaction to producers and distributors, directors and actors, anyone of any nationality who appeared to be connected with the movie business.

The Croisette itself was jammed with pedestrians and creeping, honking cars. Cocktail bars and sidewalk cafes were packed enclosures of human flesh, female rubbing suggestively against male, male coarsely fondling female.

Overlooking the Croisette, the huge outdoor terrace of the Carlton – the place to see and be seen in Cannes – was roiling with a mob of celebrities and autograph seekers. And overlooking the terrace, staring down from the Carlton's facade, was a gigantic lighted poster. It showed, in the middle of a vast and bare expanse of cloudy blue, a girl's face with brown eyes, white bonnet, and strands of hair blown across her cheeks. The single word 'Tess' was written in black letters beneath it, and under the name a vidid red heart spilled three drops of blood.

The night air sizzled with erotic energy. High-pitched laughter and the beeping of horns were the dominant sounds in the exterior din.

The din inside the Carlton banquet room was of a different order, but no less frenetic. Here the dominant noise was the barely intelligible shouting of the fifty-odd reporters and even more numerous photographers and television cameramen as they continued to try to get Roman Polanski to respond to questions about his legal problems.

'I have no legal problems!' Polanski had barked earlier in response to one of the questions.

In a way he was telling the truth. But he was also deluding himself. Warrants for his arrest were outstanding in a number of countries in Europe that had extradition treaties with the United States. France had an extradition treaty with America as well. But Gallic law viewed 'unlawful intercourse,' or the rape of a minor, with considerably less dismay than the laws of other countries. France, after all, had a long and celebrated libertarian sexual tradition that acknowledged certain natural tendencies in men to, well, occasionally get 'carried away' in matters of the flesh. If a French citizen was unfortunate enough to get carried away in another, less enlightened, country, and to be caught in his indiscretion, it was *'vraiment malheureuse'*. But if he decided to return to France to avoid punishment, he would find eternal sanctuary there.

Had Polanski actually been convicted of drugging his victim prior to raping her, that would have been something else. But simple statutory rape – this was a mere trifle, hardly worth the concern of the French government.

So Polanski was safe in France, thanks to his plea-bargaining of the year before. But, in a way, he was also a prisoner. And he was certainly not without legal problems. Although he was not behind bars, he had discovered that no matter how brilliant *Tess* turned out to be, his future as a film-maker would still be in peril.

To practice his craft, the modern film director must be an internationalist. He must not only be able to move at will about the world, he must also be able to work in and through the American motion picture industry. It is the United States that serves as the source of most of the financing and international distribution of important films.

As an escaped convict, Polanski was automatically cut off from further access to the American film industry and its financial resources. No American company was likely to hire him – first, because whatever production it might employ him for would be uninsurable due to his status as a fugitive; and second, because the proceeds of any movie he directed would be tied up interminably in government lawsuits. Moreover, such a movie might be legally barred by the government from commercial distribution so long as Polanski remained a fugitive.

Polanski's status imposed similar restrictions on foreign film companies that might wish to hire him and then seek to distribute his films in America or in other countries in which arrest and extradition warrants against him were enforceable. The United States could conceivably call upon foreign governments to take action against Polanski films, freezing their earnings or barring their distribution.

Thus, although a free man in France, Polanski's future as a film-maker was hostage to the United States government.

281

Because of this, the unfinished *Tess* was facing trouble too.

Polanski was at the press conference to get publicity for the film and to interest the major international distributors in it. But despite the publicity, and despite the mammoth poster hanging from the facade of the Carlton, the picture's producers were encountering skepticism and resistance on the part of the distributors. Any distribution deals would have to wait until determinations were made by lawyers as to the distributors' legal exposure should they take the film on. Of course, when the picture was finished it could be shown in France. But even if it was a hit there, the revenues from that relatively small market would barely be enough to pay back its advertising costs. *Tess* was threatening to become one of the most expensive bombs in film history well before it was finished.

'No more questions about my so-called problems!' Polanski shouted into the lights. 'I'm here to talk about my picture. Ask me about the picture.'

But still the questions came. The reporters were clearly not interested in serving as promotional vehicles for *Tess*. Rumors were circulating in Cannes that Polanski, unable to line up any future directing jobs, was trying desperately to find a way to return to the United States without having to go back to prison.

'What about it, Roman?' a reporter called out.

The rumor was true. Back in California, Douglas Dalton had secretly attempted to negotiate a deal that would enable Polanski to return without punishment for having fled the country. Thus far the district attorney had rejected all Dalton's proposals. For the D.A. or a judge to agree to give Polanski special consideration, after what had happened, would be tantamount to committing political suicide. If there had been any residual public sympathy for Polanski after his conviction, it had vanished on the wings of his flight to France. If he returned to California, even voluntarily, he would have to take his chances. In addition to further time at Chino for his rape conviction, he faced up to three years in prison for having jumped bail.

Polanski ignored the question. Instead, fierce impatience showing in his face, he turned to Natassia Kinski and put his arm around her. Flashbulbs began to pop as she moved in close to him.

'Okay, Roman,' a reporter called out in an American accent, 'Here's a question about your film . . . '

'At last!' said Polanski.

'Tell us why you made *Tess*. It is the story of a very young girl who is sexually violated by an older man. Did you make it because of the parallels in your own life? The girl in your film kills the man who violated her. That is her justice, is it not? You approve of that . . . '

'Wait!' shouted Polanski, leaping to his feet. 'That's a stupid question! You're not asking a question, you're making a speech. Can't anybody ask an intelligent . . . ?'

' . . . It's a question.'

'No it is not. You're trying to . . . '

'My question is . . . you approve of Tess killing her seducer. So how can you complain all the time to the press here in France that you got a raw deal in the United States? Isn't a couple of months in prison a lot better than getting killed?'

Polanski was confused by the question. At a loss for words, he suddenly put on a comic face and shook his head from side to side, as if mocking the questioner, then hooted a few times in an artificially high-pitched voice. The throng of reporters burst into laughter. Polanski, thinking they were laughing with him, grinned conspiratorially. But the reporters weren't laughing with him. They were laughing at him.

It was a crucial moment for the director. In many respects he had led a charmed life, particularly with his repeated escapes from death. And for years he had been able to charm the international news media into shaping a favorable image of himself – a sexually hedonistic image that he had reveled in and enthusiastically lived up to.

But as one journalist who was at the press conference recently put it, 'Polanski had betrayed the press. We had created this picture of him as a charming satyr and lovable rogue, more to be envied than despised. Then he went and spoiled everything by jumping that young girl in California. Not only that, he compounded his crime by running away instead of standing up

283

like a man to take his punishment. The press had made Polanski. Now it was incumbent upon us to un-make him.'

The press's hostility toward him, first in California, then when he exposed himself to the army of reporters at Cannes, was a measure of its desire for revenge. It was his first appearance before the press since California, and the press was out to get itself off the hook for having created the sympathetic public image Polanski had so eagerly exploited and ultimately perverted.

Polanski had been warned by friends of this before he went to Cannes. He had even consulted a journalist friend from the French magazine *Paris Match* on how to disarm the reporters should their questioning at the press conference turn hostile and baiting.

'He was there to talk about the film,' says another friend, 'but we knew there would be a lot of stuff about his California episode first. We advised him to get it over with – to answer the questions sincerely and with a certain amount of regret for his mistakes, not to get combative or argumentative. We figured the sooner he got past all that, the sooner the press would focus on the film.'

So it was a crucial moment – not just in the press conference but in Polanski's life. How the press would treat Polanski thereafter depended in large part on how he handled the mob of reporters now. If he was able to bring some dignity to the proceeding, if he was able to neutralize the reporters' malevolence by responding to it in a chastened, repentant manner, he might deflect the press's anger and once again gain its sympathy. What's more, he might take a giant step toward salvaging his career, the future of which had begun to look dim.

But Polanski was not feeling chastened or repentant. Encouraged by the lionization he had received in the French papers during the past year, he had continued to maintain, to the occasional journalist to whom he had talked, that he had been thoroughly victimized – by the thirteen-year-old girl in California, by her mother, by the hypocritical American press, by the Los Angeles district attorney, and by Judge Rittenband. Thus he was in no mood to play-act repentance at Cannes.

284

The press's growing hostility at Cannes had fed his own. So, when the American journalist at the press conference doggedly trapped him in a web of rhetorical logic that he didn't quite understand but felt an instinctive need to wriggle out of, he reacted in the only way he knew how. The reaction of the rest of the throng at his mugging and hooting, which he mistook for sympathetic laughter, egged him on further.

Amid the laughter, another shouted question, this one in fractured French, penetrated Polanski's hearing: *'Monsieur Polanski, comment se sentez vous maintenant autour de . . . les jeunes filles?'* ('Mister Polanski, how do you feel now about young girls?')

Polanski once again put his arm around Natassia Kinski, and the move provoked another gale of laughter.

Polanski shouted over it, *'Mais je ne me suis jamais caché d'aimer les jeunes filles. Simplement, maintenant, je dirai encore que j'aime les très jeunes filles.'* (But I've never hidden the fact that I love young girls. I will say again, once and for all, I love *very* young girls.')

With that, Polanski suddenly turned to Natassia Kinski and planted an aggressive, open-mouthed kiss on her mouth. The reporters reacted with sardonic whistles and hoots.

'Christ,' muttered one of the producers of *Tess*, 'he never fails to make things more difficult for himself.'

Natassia Kinski responded to Polanski's kiss in a curiously abstract way. Taken by surprise, she wasn't sure about how to react at first. Then, as flashbulbs popped, she fastened her mouth on his. Polanski's eyes fluttered in mock rapture – he still believed he was entertaining the reporters, getting their approval. But Natassia's eyes were wide open and skewed sideways, mugging for the cameras. As she mugged, Polanski grasped his crotch, pretending to suppress an erection.

In the view of another who was there, 'Roman instantly looked ridiculous. He'd lost control of himself. He thought he was being funny and he wasn't. What was worse, here was this nubile young darling, young enough to be his daughter, who was clearly using him to get attention for herself. Roman thought he was being clever, reminding the reporters of his reputation. But he came across like a combination of a lecherous Groucho Marx and one of those seedy sad-sack old Europeans who ooze phony charm and sensuality to impress women and succeed only in boring them. No matter what he thought he was accomplishing, everyone was struck by the fact that the girl was exploiting him and helping him make a fool of himself. The legendary exploiter of women and convicted child rapist was having the tables turned on him. In public, no less. It was a bit sad, because he didn't realize the parody he had become of himself. The reporters knew it, though, and that's what had them laughing. And eventually the girl realized it, too. Maybe she hadn't meant to, but she was making fun of Roman with her cutesy little acting, making him look like a demented lecher, a pitiable old man.'

The clicking of cameras stopped and the laughter died to a few snickers. Polanski tried to sustain his kiss, but Natassia Kinski was suddenly alarmed and embarrassed. She withdrew, pushing the director away. He nuzzled his face in her neck and mimicked biting her.

'No!' she squealed, yanking him away by his hair.

Polanski, a sappy, dazed expression on his face, gazed out at the assemblage. 'Bitch!' he muttered. His expression turned to one of satisfaction as he grinned and winked into the lights. But then somebody booed, and his face turned to alarm.

It was then that Polanski realized that he had muffed his chance to recapture the press. But it was too late. Some of the reporters and photographers had begun to pack their gear.

Cut, as they say in movies, to the present. As I write, it is mid-November 1979. It is six months after Cannes, and Polanski's troubles have continued to pile up.

First, shortly after the disastrous press conference, Natassia Kinski left him. When it became apparent that her association with Polanski would not reap the dividends she expected, she went in search of another film-maker who not only could promise her stardom but who had the clout to deliver. She found him in Milos Forman, the middle-aged expatriate Czech director who was fresh from his triumphant and profitable movie version of *Hair*. Polanski and Forman had always had a lot in common, not the least of which was the fact that each had gained success in the West after leaving their neighboring east-European communist homelands.

Polanski's loss of Kinski was a trifle, though, compared to his agony over *Tess*, the picture on which he had mortgaged his future. After completing its filming in June 1979, he worked night and day for four months to cut its miles of expensive footage into the two-hour masterpiece he had envisaged.

Still without any foreign distribution prospects, the producers gave the movie a lavish premiere in Paris on 31 October. Its reception was less than enthusiastic. In fact, said a French film figure sympathetic to Polanski, 'It looks like it's going to be such a commercial failure that Roman is not likely to get another directing offer in Europe for a long time, if ever. If he has any future now, it would have to be in Hollywood. There, a loss like *Tess* they write off without any qualm.'

As of this writing, Polanski still remains unwilling to dare a return to Hollywood. Strapped for money, he has finally had to put his most prized possession – his Belgravia mews house in London – up for sale. Assuming that he sells it quickly, and that the British government does not decide to seize the proceeds at the request of the United States, he should net around $200,000. You and I could no doubt live adequately on such a sum for ten years. Polanski will be able to live comfortably on it for a considerably shorter time – two years, perhaps three. Indeed, by selling his house, he has found a way to buy himself some time.

But what will happen to Polanski ultimately? It is anyone's guess.

One close friend tells me, 'I would not be surprised to see Roman continue to live the good life he's accustomed to in Paris for another year or two. He'll live on what he gets from his house in London. When that money dries up, he will once again be forced to confront the question of whether or not to return to the US and face the music. It is my expectation, from the hints he has dropped, that he will not return. The longer he stays away from California, he knows, the longer time in prison he will have to spend if he returns. By then he will be fifty, or close to it. He will say to himself, 'Okay, I've had a terrific life up to now, but now the money has run out and it's over.' But instead of returning to California to spend time in prison, he will choose a less forbidding form of prison.

'By that I mean, he will return to Poland. There he will be greeted as a hero and will be able to work once more as a director – albeit at a pittance. But his star will rise again, you can be sure of that. The world has not heard the end of Roman Polanski.'